God's Best

FOR MY LIFE

Lloyd John OGILVIE

HARVEST HOUSE PUBLISHERS

EUGENE, OREGON

Cover by Koechel Peterson & Associates, Inc., Minneapolis, Minnesota

Cover photo © Stock.xchng

Every effort has been made to give proper credit for all stories, poems, and quotations. If for any reason proper credit has not been given, please notify the author or publisher and proper notation will be included on future printing.

GOD'S BEST FOR MY LIFE
Abridged and revised from previous editions.
Copyright © 1981, 2008 by Lloyd John Ogilvie
Published by Harvest House Publishers
Eugene, Oregon 97402
www.harvesthousepublishers.com

ISBN-13: 978-0-7369-2310-1

Ogilvie, Lloyd John.
God's best for my life / Lloyd John Ogilvie. p. cm.
1. Devotional calendars—Presbyterian Church. I. Title.
BV 4811.035 1997
242.' 2—dc21   97-7438

Printed in China

10 11 12 13 14 15 16 / RDS-SK / 10 9 8 7 6 5 4 3

To Bob Hawkins Sr.

A great Christian publisher with purpose;

A man filled with Christ's Spirit who exemplifies
His gentleness, faithfulness, and love;

A visionary leader who is creative and courageous;

A loving husband, an inspiring father,
a cheerleading grandfather.

—Lloyd John Ogilvie
January 2008

Preface

*It shall come to pass, that before they call, I will
answer; and while they are yet speaking, I will hear.*
(ISAIAH 65:24 KJV)

This awesome promise is the motivation for writing this daily devotional guide. We all want God's best for our lives. That desire is a gift from Him! He wants to be our Friend, to tell us about Himself, to communicate His unlimited love, to give us His wisdom for our decisions, and to help us live the adventure of the abundant life. He creates in us the desire to know Him and to talk with Him in prayer.

The longing in so many Christians today to discover a consistent, daily pattern for Bible reading and prayer is from the Lord Himself. He has given me the vision of how to maximize a quiet time with Him each day. The desire to share the thoughts and insights from the Scriptures for a whole year was clearly guided by Him, and was done in response to the thousands of requests I have received from across the years for a practical, applicable way to find God's best for their lives each day and to receive His power for daily needs.

The result is a daily guide that is intended to be revelational and relational. God reveals Himself in the Scriptures and inspires us in our relationship with Him, ourselves, others, and the world. We all need fresh grace each day. All the scriptures selected for the days of a full year will enable a renewal of our relationship with the Lord, a deeper acceptance of ourselves, and a contagious joy for our relationships and responsibilities.

The distinctly different quality of this particular guide is that it is rooted both in Scripture and in our deepest needs. Each day's meditation on the Word of God is meant to be profoundly personal. I have tried to listen to our urgent questions and deepest longings. Truth becomes real as we live it. The great need today is for Christians to rediscover a daily companionship with the Lord and to enjoy Him throughout the challenges and opportunities that each day brings. When J.B. Phillips translated the book of Acts into contemporary English, he said it was like rewiring a house with the current turned on! I hope for nothing less each day as we take the great texts of the Bible and spell out the implications for living the promises God gives us.

I have tried to be sensitive to the frustrations and feelings of failure that so many people have expressed about finding a workable plan for daily devotions. Many have told me of grand commitments to get up early or stay up late to spend a prolonged period with the Lord. Guilt and self-recrimination set in when the promise is broken or the length of the devotions shortens.

What most of us need is a daily time that is penetrating and personal, that has residual impact throughout the day. Each of these devotionals is meant to be like a capsule with time-release potency. My hope is that the truths we consider and the aching needs we confront will have a constant explosion of engendering, enabling power throughout the day. Take 15 minutes each day when you're freshest and most alert. It will give you freedom from uncertainty, frustration, and anxiety all through the day. Here are three five-minute steps:

1. *Take five minutes for praise and thanksgiving.* Praise God for who He is and thank Him for what He has done. Praise is the antidote to pride. Adoration opens our minds and hearts to receive. Review what has been happening to you—the delights and the difficulties. Get in touch with your real feelings. Only the real you can meet the reality of God. He loves you and wants to use what's happening to and around you for His glory and your growth. Review your life, relationships, challenges, and concerns. Ask the Lord to use this quiet time with Him as a deeply personal time of discovery and new direction.

2. *Next, take five minutes to read the Scripture text* indicated at the top of each day's devotional, plus the exposition I've written. Then ask yourself these questions:

   • What do this passage and message mean to me personally?

   • What has the Lord said to me in them about my life?

   • What can I do or say today to live the truth I've considered?

   • With whom am I called to implement what I've learned?

3. *Last, take five minutes for supplication and intercession.*

   • Write out or think through the needs, problems, and concerns you are facing this day. Spread them out before the Lord. Ask for His perspective and guidance. Then surrender them to Him. And leave them in His gracious and powerful care.

- Pray for specific people—loved ones, friends, people you love or need to learn to love, those for whom you are thankful, and those who frustrate you. Prayer for people in Jesus' name is a sure way to discover a creative attitude toward them!

Many of you will find these 15 minutes so exciting and satisfying that they will be the most creative, liberating part of your day. Some of you will find your 15 minutes extended because there is so much more to say to the Lord and receive from Him. The amazing thing you will discover is the miraculous way He will speak to you through His Word. I have asked Him to guide every word I've written. I know He has had you in mind and knew ahead of time what you would need. The Lord's timing is perfect: never ahead, never behind, but always exactly on time. Begin using this guide on the page of today's date. There's a progression that will catch you up in its flow.

This edition of this devotional guide is dedicated to Bob Hawkins Sr. He suggested the original title and has been an enthusiastic affirmer of the many editions through the years. This abridged edition provides a key scripture and thought for each day to help you live life to the fullest.

My prayer is that this will be one of the most exciting years of your life. Gathering these scriptures and reflecting on them with your needs in mind has been exactly that for me. Power to you as you experience God's best for your life!

—Lloyd John Ogilvie

The Best Year of Your Life!

Jeremiah 29:11-13

I know the plans I have for you, says the LORD, plans for
welfare and not for evil, to give you a future and a hope.
(JEREMIAH 29:11 RSV)

The sure sign that we have an authentic relationship with God is that we believe more in the future than in the past. The past can be neither a source of confidence for us nor a condemnation of us. God graciously divided our life into days and years so we could let go of our yesterdays and anticipate our tomorrows. For the past mistakes, He offers forgiveness and an ability to forget. For our tomorrows, He gives us the gift of expectation and excitement. He has plans for each of us—good plans for our growth in His grace—so that we can have a future with hope.

God divided our life into years
To free us from our past tears
He gives us a New Year's inning
To offer us a new beginning
He opens His forgiving heart
And provides a fresh start
He is always faithful and true
So joyous New Year to You!

God's best for my life begins with a
vibrant hope for the future.

A Year of Jubilee

Luke 4:16-21

*…To set at liberty those who are oppressed, to
proclaim the acceptable year of the LORD.*
(LUKE 4:18-19)

The shadow of the cross was over Jesus' heart as He read these words from Isaiah in His own synagogue in Nazareth. He knew He was to fulfill that prophecy in His own suffering and death.

The last sentence of the prophecy is easily misunderstood. "The acceptable year of the LORD" also meant the Year of Jubilee. Every 50 years, according to the ancient Hebrew custom, debts were canceled, prison terms were terminated, landholdings went back to the original owners, and people forgave the resentments held through the years.

The cross makes every year the Jubilee Year. Jesus' death cancels our sin and gives us the freedom to be forgiving. This is the acceptable year of the Lord for us.

Make a list of people who need your forgiveness. What is the Lord telling you to *say* and then *be* to them to assure them they are forgiven? But don't wait. Your Jubilee Year starts today. Tomorrow may be too late!

Today I will live as a forgiven, forgiving person.

A Nook with the Book

Psalm 1:1-6

His delight is in the law of the LORD, and in
His law he meditates day and night.
(PSALM 1:2 NKJV)

Thomas à Kempis said, "I have no rest but in a nook with the book." Communion with the Lord through meditation on the Scriptures provided profound rest and refreshment in the midst of the demands of life. The same theme song is sung by the psalmist. He meditated on God's law. We have the flowing streams of the whole Bible as the water of life to feed the tree of our life.

A quiet time enables quietness of soul in the din of life's demands. Jesus said, "Take care to live in Me, and let Me live in you. For a branch can't produce fruit when severed from the vine. Nor can you be fruitful apart from me."

Each day we put our roots down in the streams of the living water, Christ Himself. Then all through the day we are refreshed by what we received in His presence. We all need a quiet place for our 15 minutes to freedom each day. Christ will give us a thought that will reorient our thinking and flower in inspiration all through the day. Expect nothing less today!

My tree of life is planted in Christ. He will give
me all I need to live abundantly today.

Through the Valley of Fear

Psalm 23:1-6

Though I walk through the valley…thou art with me.
(Psalm 23:4 kjv)

Alexander Maclaren, a great Scots preacher of another generation, tells the story of his conquest of fear. As a young boy he took
a job in Glasgow, some miles away from his own village. He stayed
in the city during the week and returned home on Saturday eve-
nings. There was a ravine on the way to his home that superstition
supposed was filled with evil spirits. All during the first week at
work, the lad feared most that his long walk home would have to
include passing through this ravine.

Saturday night came, and there was nothing to do but muster
up his courage and start home. His heart pounded as he reached
the ravine. He paused in panic. His feet were like lead. Then suddenly he heard a voice calling out of the night, "Alex, it's your dad.
I came to walk through the ravine with ye."

All through his later life as one of Scotland's greatest preach-
ers, Maclaren never forgot the courage and strength he felt that
night when his father graciously walked through the frightful
glen with him.

*The Lord comes to meet us and walk
the glens of fearful worry with us.*

A Full Life with Purpose

Psalm 146:1-10

Praise the LORD! Praise the LORD, O my soul!
(PSALM 146:1)

A friend of mine celebrated his retirement by having new calling cards printed. On the card is his name and this declaration of new freedom: "No phone, no address, no business, no worries, no appointments, no prospects, no job."

The man gave me the card at a time of intense busyness in my own life. *Wouldn't that be wonderful!* I thought to myself. Then I reflected on what life would be like without all the challenges and opportunities. How would I handle life without a full schedule and more to do in any day than is humanly possible? But that led me to a time of deep gratitude for strength beyond my own to meet the demands.

Many of us complain about busy schedules, but it is good to live a full life. The important thing to consider is what we are accomplishing in all the activities. Justus Schifferes in *How to Live Longer* said, "Live longer so you can love longer, and conversely, the longer you love the longer you live." Can a Christian ever put "no prospects" on his calling card? We always have prospects for love and understanding and the chance to share our faith.

There's nothing wrong with being busy if we are doing
God's work in His way and by His power.

Stop Complaining—
Start Confessing!

Psalm 39:1-13

I said to myself, I'm going to quit complaining!
(PSALM 39:1 TLB)

I have a Southern friend who has a way of saying things in a pithy, pointed way. One of his favorite responses to critical people is, "When you're complainin', you ain't got no time for confessin'!" His phrasing is not very proper, but his prognosis of a deep human problem is very pointed!

Complaining and confessing are alternate approaches to the things that trouble us about ourselves and other people. Greatness in the Christian life is dependent on knowing one from the other.

Psalm 39 helps us identify with the psalmist. The progression of his thought gives us a plan for dealing with frustration. He expresses his consternation and then goes on to authentic confession. God is ready to hear honest feelings *if* they lead us to confess our need for His power, forgiveness, and a new beginning.

Think about what today would be like if you pulled out all the stops and dared to live life to the fullest. What would you do if you trusted God completely and knew you could not fail?

Today is a day to stop complaining and start confessing.

The Help of His Presence

Psalm 42:1-11

As the deer pants for the water brooks,
so pants my soul for You, O God.
(PSALM 42:1 NKJV)

The psalmist gives us an example of the difference between praying our prayers and truly praying. He really wanted a relationship with God more than anything else in the world. Many people pray without earnestly wanting intimacy with God. Note Psalm 42:2. Do you want God that much? Also consider the honesty of the psalmist. He talked to God about what he was feeling—really! That kind of honesty in prayer made way for God to heal the real needs and not just the surface whims.

Again, the psalmist leads us into deeper levels of prayer. It was the experience of the steadfast love of God that drew him back into close union with the Father. What God *has done* heightens our expectation of what He *will do*. Praise opens the heart. The more we praise God, the more ready we are to accept the next steps of His strategy for us. Let's make today a day in which we bless God all through the day for His goodness to us in all the problems and perplexities of life.

Prayer is meditating on the positive power of the Lord and
not just our perplexities. Then peace replaces our worry.

The Answer Is the Asking

Isaiah 65:24-25

It will also come to pass that before they call, I will answer; and while they are still speaking, I will hear.
(Isaiah 65:24)

This is one of the most exciting verses about praise in the Old Testament. It reminds us that prayer begins with God, seeps into our heart, and gives us the courage to ask for what God is more ready to give than we are to ask. God has more prepared for us than we are prepared to ask. We need to spend as much time seeking what God wants us to ask for as we do asking. Then our asking will be in keeping with His will.

Memorize the verse from Isaiah. Praying is not to get God's attention but focusing our attention on Him and what He has to say to us. Don't make prayer a one-way telephone conversation in which we hang up before we listen to what He has to say!

Prayer is seeking God with all our hearts. God can use our imaginations to give us a picture of His future for us, but with one qualification: that we seek Him with all our hearts. Many of us aim at nothing and hit it because we have not taken God at His Word. We all become what we envision. Prayer is the time to let God paint the mind picture of what we are to be and do.

Today I will not hang up on God!

Who Is Your Burden?

Psalm 55:1-23; Matthew 11:30; Galatians 6:2

Cast your burden on the LORD, and He shall sustain you.
(PSALM 55:22 NKJV)

Some time ago, I picked up a Boy Scout who was hitchhiking with a heavily packed knapsack on his back. He got in the car and rode with his pack still on his back. I thought this was absurd and said, "Young man, wouldn't you like to take your pack off while you ride?" "No, sir," he said, "it was so hard to get on and would be difficult to take off, so I'll just ride with my load on my back."

He was like most of us, who ride in God's grace with the burdens on our backs because we find it difficult to entrust them to Him. To forgive means to forget, and yet many of us carry the memories of our past failures on our backs. Also, we carry our worries about people as heavy burdens not just on our backs, but on our hearts.

Who's your burden? Whom do you carry emotionally, in memory, or in conscience? Who causes you difficult reactions of guilt, fear, frustration, or anger? That person belongs to God. He's carrying him or her too, you know!

*Today I will place my burdens
on the strong back of God.*

If God Knows, Why Pray?

John 14:1-14

*Whatever you ask in My name, that I will do, that the Father may
be glorified in the Son. If you ask anything in My name, I will do it.*
(John 14:13-14)

Most of us believe that prayer is initiated by us when we blunder
into God's presence with our requests and concerns. Not at all.
Long before we thought of praying, the God to whom we pray
was preparing us to pray. Our prayer is response. When a need
comes to our mind and we pray, it is because God has an answer
to give us for that concern.

We pray not so much to *change* but to *receive* the mind of God.
As we pray our prayers and listen to God, He is able and willing
to impress His mind upon us. Next, we pray because God has
ordained that there are resources of His power and love that will
not be released until we pray. He has called us to be His partners
in the world. He often withholds His blessings until we pray. He
desires that we come to Him to share our needs with Him. Lastly,
we pray because God seeks to bring us closer to one another
through prayer. It is His will to withhold much of what we want
for others until we pray for them.

*Through prayer we participate with God in
what He desires to do in our lives today!*

Ask and Abide

John 14:1-31; 15:7

Where I go you know, and the way you know.
(JOHN 14:4)

Prayer is cumulative friendship with God. The desire to pray is God's gift. Think of it! The Creator and Sovereign of the universe has created us for communion with Him. Jesus taught us that prayer is a means by which our desires can be redirected according to the will of God and made the focus for the direction of His will.

Our two biggest problems in life are solved by the two crucial prerequisites of powerful prayer given us by Christ. He taught us that God is omniscient. He has infinite knowledge, awareness, and concern about our needs. When we pray about our problems, we solve the first great need, which is the source of all our lesser problems—our need for communion with the Lord. When we abide, we are given life's greatest treasure—intimacy with our Creator. Our second greatest need is to discover what our Lord wants us to do in keeping with His plan. Abiding gives us the mind of the Lord for our problems and perplexities.

He who has learned to pray has learned the
greatest secret of a holy and happy life.
—WILLIAM LAW

Laying Hold of
God's Willingness

1 John 3:1-24; 5:14-15

*Beloved, if our heart does not condemn us, we
have confidence toward God.*

(1 JOHN 3:21)

*If we know that He hears us, whatever we ask, we know
that we have the petitions that we have asked of Him.*

(1 JOHN 5:15)

The apostle John gives us two "if's" about prayer: *If* our hearts do
not condemn us, and *if* we know that He hears us. The Lord is not
outdone, even by our failures. He says, "Come to Me just as you
are!" The assurance of the cross gives us boldness and confidence.
To get us to pray, the Lord removes the barriers, creates the desire,
gives us Himself, reveals His will, and then gives us the courage to
ask for what He is more ready to give than we are to ask.

Often, our reluctance to pray is our resistance to God. But
eventually life caves in, and we face problems too great for us. God
rushes in to help us in the hope that we will be so amazed at what
He can do with problems that we will begin to trust Him with our
potentials. The question is, How great do we want our life to be?

*Prayer is not overcoming God's reluctance;
it is laying hold of His highest willingness.*
—RICHARD CHENEVIX TRENCH

What Do You Expect?

John 5:1-15

*When Jesus saw him lying there, and knew that he
already had been in that condition a long time, He
said to him, "Do you want to be made well?"*
(JOHN 5:6)

"Well, what did you expect?" is a question we ask when someone
has faced a disappointment we feel he or she should have anticipated. We should also ask it when people are surprised by a gracious intervention of the Lord. Most of all, we should ask it of
ourselves. What do we expect? Expectation, multiplied by a Holy
Spirit–guided imagination, can equal dynamic prayer.

The account of the healing of the man by the pool of Bethesda
has a very crucial twist. Jesus asks the man if he wants to be healed.
Strange. The man had been ill for 38 years waiting for the waters of
the pool to be troubled by the angel's wings. Someone always got in
before him. Jesus discovered that the man may no longer have expected a miracle. Thus the question "Do you want to be healed?"

Our lack of expectation can stand in the way of the miracles
of God in all phases of our lives and relationships. Unbelief, discouragement, and disillusionment can stifle our expectation. We
expect little and are not surprised when little happens to us and
others. So here is an exhilarating motto for today:

I will expect great things from God and live expectantly.

Expecting Too Little

Acts 12:1-25

They said to her, "You are beside yourself!" Yet she kept insisting that it was so. So they said, "It is his angel." Now Peter continued knocking; and when they opened the door and saw him, they were astonished.
(Acts 12:15-16)

"How do you recognize answers to prayer?" I've been asked that question hundreds of times over the years. Many people have confusion over recognizing the answers to prayers once they have prayed. We should not be too hard on ourselves. We are in the good company of the early church.

The humorous passage of Scripture in Acts 12 tells how the church prayed for Peter and then did not (or would not) recognize God's answer. This gives us some comfort that these great athletes of the Spirit also had sagging prayer muscles, shortness of vision, and dimness of hope. This incident crystallizes a general prayer problem we all face: entrusting to the Lord our difficulties and waiting for His answer.

Once we really want God's answer, our eyes will be open to His answers. He will give us an assurance when the direction glorifies Him, keeps His commandments, communicates His love, and enables His best for others.

Our problem is not to get God to answer our prayers,
but to recognize the answers already given.

The Problem of Seemingly Unanswered Prayer

2 Corinthians 12:7-10

He said to me, "My grace is sufficient for you, for My strength is made perfect in weakness." Therefore most gladly I will rather boast in my infirmities, that the power of Christ may rest upon me.
(2 Corinthians 12:9)

Prayer is much more than giving God our list of needs with an "Amen" at the end. It is not a magical way of getting what we want. Prayer is to get us into the position of willingness to receive what God wants.

We suffer from impatience. We want everything yesterday. Waiting is not a part of our speed-oriented society. Prayer is not a computer: put in the question and out pops an answer! The Lord has all things ordered for our good. The apostle Paul prayed and found the only satisfactory solution to what seems to be unanswered prayer: The Lord is sufficient! Any answer without the Lord is no answer at all. His strength is made perfect in our weakness.

We have two choices: frustration or freedom. We can run ahead of God or run with Him. Settle the issue today. Give Him control of life and of the timing of answers to prayer. Our peace of mind, health, and relationships are at stake. There is no panic in heaven. Why should there be any in us?

The Lord Himself is the answer to all prayer.

God's Best Answer

1 Thessalonians 5:16-21

*Rejoice always; pray without ceasing; in everything give
thanks; for this is the will of God in Christ Jesus for you.*
(1 THESSALONIANS 5:16-18)

"If I thought," said John Baillie, "that God were going to grant me
all my prayers simply for the asking, without even passing them
under His own gracious review, without even bringing to bear
upon them His own greater wisdom, I think there would be very
few prayers that I would dare to pray."

Because God can see what we cannot see and knows dimensions we can never understand, He works out our answers according to a higher plan than we can conceive. We are to tell Him our
needs and then leave them with Him. It's only in retrospect that
we can see the narrowness of our vision, and see that His answer
was far better than what we could ever have anticipated.

James Denney said, "A refusal is the answer if it is so given that
God and the soul henceforth understand one another."

God created us in His own image; we should not return the
compliment!

*Prayer enlarges the heart until it is capable
of containing God's gift of Himself.*
—MOTHER TERESA OF CALCUTTA

Wandering Attention

Psalm 139:1-24

Where can I go from Your Spirit?
Or where can I flee from Your presence?
(PSALM 139:7)

"What do I do about wandering thoughts when I pray?" That's another question I've been asked repeatedly. A wandering attention simply tells us that our minds are on other things. Why not talk to God about what's really commanding our attention? Whatever our minds drift off to is an indication of what we really need to ask for help to solve or conquer.

But what about abhorrent thoughts or fantasies? They indicate a deeper need beneath the surface. Allow God to gently probe the cause. We are like a ball of yarn with one strand protruding. The Lord gets hold of that and begins to unravel us. Since He knows all about us, He's never surprised. Why do we think we can hide anything from Him? There is no place we can go, even into the depths of ourselves, where He's not there waiting for us.

Prayer is not an argument with God to persuade Him to move things our way, but a conversation in which we are enabled by His Spirit to move ourselves His way.

O to grace how great a debtor daily I'm constrained to be! Let
Your goodness, like a fetter, bind my wandering heart to Thee.
—ROBERT ROBINSON

The Eyes of the Heart

Psalm 32:1-11

*I will instruct you and teach you in the way which you
should go; I will counsel you with My eye upon you.*
(PSALM 32:8)

Have you ever had someone guide you with his or her eyes? The
eyes can give approval, express alarm, or communicate love. We've
all read how a person feels about us because of what's written in
his or her eyes. Think of a time when someone has guided you
to move to another part of a room or alerted you to another person who needs your attention simply by darting his or her eyes
in that direction.

The psalmist tells us that God guides in the same way. Intimate encounter with the face of God in prayer is like being guided
by His eyes. He gives us His reaction to what we have done or
are planning. Also, He directs our attention to people and situations where He wants us to move. The Lord will guide us. He
is at work in the people we love (and some we need to learn to
love); He is working His purposes out in the tangled mess of human problems. It is in prayer that the eyes of our heart meet the
guiding eye of the Lord.

*We all, with unveiled face, beholding as in a mirror the
glory of the Lord, are being transformed into the same
image from glory to glory as by the Spirit of the Lord.*
—2 CORINTHIANS 3:18 NKJV

Growth in Greatness

Romans 5:3-5

*We also glory in tribulations, knowing that tribulation produces
perseverance; and perseverance, character; and character, hope.*
(ROMANS 5:3-4)

Paul delineates the progression of growth in greatness: suffering,
endurance, character, hope, love. Actually, we have to read the
list backward to know what really happened to Paul. It was the
love of God communicated to him through Christ that gave him
hope. Paul's experience of the love of God had so deeply touched
the insecurity and loneliness of his militant life that he became
healed at the core. He discovered a truth so profound that his conception of God had been shattered by the truth of God's uncalculated, undeserved love freely given in Jesus Christ. Paul learned
that he could never be good enough to deserve it. In the place
of his Pharisaic piety and persistent perfectionism, he now based
his life on the absolute power, boundless love, and utter reliability
of God. Because of this he was able to face the disappointments,
the physical difficulties, and the rejections he endured. Suffering
produced endurance, and endurance produced character.

We have the same assurance. Whatever you are going through
right now, be sure of this: The Lord will not let you down or let
you go.

*All that happens to us
is for what the Lord wants to happen in us.*

God Can Change Our Moods

2 Corinthians 7:1-16

God, who comforts the downcast, comforted us.
(2 CORINTHIANS 7:6)

Does God care about how we feel? Does He understand our moods? Can He change them?

The answer to these questions is found in a deeper insight into how God deals with us. The cross proclaims that He loves us as we are. We cannot earn or deserve His love. He loves us utterly. If that's really the case, His love does not change with our moods. But it is also true that He can help us with them. Moods are the outer wrapping of our inner feelings. All moods have their roots in our reactions to what has happened, what we fear may happen, or what we urgently hope will happen.

God helps us with our moods by penetrating into the inner reason for our feelings. He forces us to see our resentment, self-pity, defensiveness, fear, anxiety, or insecurity for what they are in the light of His love revealed on the cross. Tell Him about your mood right now, and ask Him to help you penetrate to the real reasons you feel the way you do. He can and will heal whatever is unresolved, unfinished, or unforgiven. So thank the Lord in advance for changing bad moods and giving you a mood of blessing.

The transformation of our moods is a prayer away.

Something More Than Happiness

John 15:11; James 1:2; Hebrews 12:2;
1 Thessalonians 1:6; Romans 15:13

May the God of hope fill you with all joy
and peace in believing.
(ROMANS 15:13)

There is a real difference between happiness and joy. Happiness is that condition that is dependent upon the circumstances of our life; joy exists in spite of the circumstances around us.

Joy can exist when all else seems wrong and disturbed. *Joy* is closely related in its root to the word *grace*. Grace is defined as the unearnable, unmerited, unqualified love of God. When a person knows that God loves him just as he is, and accepts His grace in Jesus Christ, then he knows the precious experience of joy.

Open the New Testament anywhere and you hear a note of joy struck in the midst of unfortunate and discouraging circumstances. One could trace our Lord's progress through the country-side by the joy He left behind in the lives of people who dared to accept His unchanging love for them. How about you? Are you a joyous person? Or have you lost yourself in the frantic search for happiness that does not last?

Christ does more than make us happy; He gives us joy!

Back to Grace and On to Joy

Philippians 2:1-30

Let this mind be in you which was also in Christ Jesus...
(PHILIPPIANS 2:5)

The word for *mind* in today's scripture can also be translated *disposition*. "Have in you this disposition which was also in Christ" is a challenging rendering of the meaning. Think what that could do for us today if we believed it and claimed it! Our dispositions are the outward impact of what's going on in our minds and emotions. We become what we are thinking and feeling.

How's your disposition today? What's your mood? If it's anything but joy, we have the responsibility to sort out what in our minds, feelings, or body is causing this bad mood. Joy is the only option. Christ does not change, and therefore we can change our disposition and mood by getting at its root and experiencing His love, forgiveness, and strength. We are responsible. No one or no thing can depress our disposition without our permission. Christ can change us! When He is invited to live in us we receive His disposition.

Remember, joy is an outward expression of grace. What does Christ's grace need to transform in you today?

Don't wait one minute more: Get back to grace and give out joy!

Brooders

Nehemiah 9:17; Mark 11:25-26

They refused to listen, and did not remember Your wondrous deeds
which You had performed among them; so they became stubborn
and appointed a leader to return to their slavery in Egypt. But You
are a God of forgiveness, gracious and compassionate, slow to anger
and abounding in lovingkindness; and You did not forsake them.
(NEHEMIAH 9:17)

"Can God help a brooder?"

We play God when we brood over what people have said
or done to us, and we refuse to forgive and forget. The result is
that we become habitual brooders, and eventually become cold
and cautious.

God forgives and forgets. He can enable us to do the same.
If we don't, there is a fracture in our relationship with Him that
deepens until our prayers are ineffective, the joy of life drains away,
and we become negative, critical people. It is then that we need
to recover the basic truth in our two scriptures for today. Think
deeply about that. Are you willing to surrender your brooding to
God and let go of the slights and oversights, the hurts and harm
that people have done?

Brooding is missing the blessing!

A Joy-infused Temperament

Philippians 3:1-21; Nehemiah 8:10

The joy of the LORD is your strength.
(Nehemiah 8:10)

Can our temperament be changed, altered, or transformed? Our temperament is the composite characteristics of our mental and emotional peculiarities as manifested in our reactions. It is our makeup, our personality constitution. Our temperament is the result of conditioning, experience, and the influence of people in our growing years. The Latin noun for *temperament* means "a proper mixture," and the verb means "to mix in proper proportions."

Conversion to Christ—being born again—and then being filled with His Spirit changes the proportions. He remixes and transforms the things that make us what we are in our temperament.

How would you describe your temperament? What difference has Christ made in your peculiarities manifested in your reactions? Now look again at Nehemiah 8:10. That's today's refrain for our new temperament: "The joy of the LORD is your (my!) strength."

*When I came to believe in Christ...the direction of my life, desires,
became different. What was good and bad changed places.*
—Leo Tolstoy

A Mood Modifier

Philippians 4:10-20

*My God shall supply all your need according
to His riches in glory by Christ Jesus.*
(PHILIPPIANS 4:19)

The formula is eternally true: impression without expression equals depression. We are depressed in a mood until we are released to say, "Lord, this is how I feel right now. Do You care, really? What do You want me to do with the person, situation, or frustrating circumstance causing my mood?"

Now listen quietly for His answer. Along with the insight into the mood will come an inrush of His Spirit with amazing love and acceptance. Listen: *I love you and will not let you go. Your mood is caused by your self-condemnation for what you have or have not done or been. I am greater than that mood. Give it to Me! Your joyous mood will be maximized, and your bad moods transformed by My grace. Believe My promise and live today in full assurance!*

St. Richard of Chichester penned a prayer that gives us the key to unlock the Lord's mood changing power:

*Day by day, dear Lord,
Of three things, I pray:
To see Thee more clearly
Love Thee more dearly,
Follow Thee more nearly,
Day by day.*

When We Don't Feel Like It

John 5:17; Luke 2:20;
2 Thessalonians 3:10-12

*Jesus' answer to them was this: "My Father is still
at work and therefore I work as well."*
(JOHN 5:17 PHILLIPS)

The secret of life in Christ is challenging: Do the thing that love demands and you will feel the love that life requires. Glib formula? No, it works! When we get bogged down in our feelings, action is required to change our mood. When we are frustrated about some person, there is something we must do to break the tension. Act—don't react.

Feelings are like clouds which hide the sunshine. The day can seem dark and bleak. But the clouds cannot change the fact that the sun is still there. We can be fogged in by bad feelings, but Christ has not changed! His love and power are just as available as when things were sunny and bright. But is our life orbiting around Him? Or have we tried to be the center of our universe? Doing the thing that love demands will send us jetting through the clouds of feeling, up to a level of life where the *Son* is visible again. We can fly above the clouds. The feelings may still be there, but the strong winds of the Spirit will begin to blow again, and the horizon will be clear.

D.W.L.D.:
Do What Love Demands!

What Is Your Body Saying?

Matthew 11:28-29; Mark 6:31

*He said to them, "Come aside by yourselves to a deserted
place and rest a while." For there were many coming
and going, and they did not even have time to eat.*

(MARK 6:31)

Many of our difficult moods are physically induced. We feel bad
in our emotions because of physical disorders. There are times
we analyze our emotions with little release from a mood because
the cause is in our bodies. Introspection does not help; we probably need rest, a break from routine, a vacation, or a chance to
rebuild our strength.

Jesus honored the need for rest. He actually left the needs of
people to be quiet in prayer. What the Son of God found necessary should not be neglected by us. Often our most creative times
come after a time of resting our minds and bodies. There is an
ebb-and-flow rhythm to life in Christ. We should not feel guilty
for loving ourselves as loved by Him and enjoying the pleasure of
being in good physical shape. Christ gives us strength for the impossible if we have taken time to get the strength from Him.

*A tired-out, burned-out Christian
is a contradiction in terms.*

A Luxury We Cannot Afford

Romans 8:26-39

The Spirit also helps in our weaknesses.
(ROMANS 8:26)

Admit, submit, commit—these are three steps that can change our mood. Most of our moods trouble us because we do not admit to God how we really feel. We keep the mood hidden, and it festers and grows. When we *admit* we are feeling blue or bland, frustrated or fearful, down or discouraged, impatient or insecure, we have taken the first step to getting free.

The next step is to *submit* our mood to God. When we tell Him how we feel and ask for the power to be different, we experience the internal ministry of the Spirit. We are promised that when we don't know how to pray about our feelings, His Spirit enters in and helps us in our praying. The Spirit interprets our deeper trouble and sorts out the real cause of our mood. He prays on our behalf, giving us the courage to actually *commit* how we feel to God and leave it with Him. He knows what we need to break the bind and get on with more creative living.

Bad moods are a luxury no one can afford; life is too short, and people need our support too much for us to be out of commission.

The high cost of a bad mood is ineffectiveness
in our calling to care for others.

The Decision to Love—Anyhow!

1 John 4:7-12

Beloved, let us love one another, for love is of God; and
everyone who loves is born of God and knows God.
(1 JOHN 4:7)

We talked about the man's wife all afternoon. He tried to analyze the broken relationship that had grown between them over the previous weeks. His wife was acting coldly and angrily, but he could not locate how it had begun or what contributed to it.

I felt guided to ask a question. "What would you do if you could never find the cause?" "Well," he said, "I suppose I would have to love her and affirm her anyway." "Exactly!" I said. "Then why not love her in spite of your lack of insight over what has gone wrong? Is your love conditioned on insight? Do you love her only when you have things straightened out and everything analyzed carefully? Could it be that you are deadlocked in the necessity of talking things out in order to love rather than loving in order to be able to talk freely again?"

That night the man went home and acted as he would if he had clearly understood the situation. His wife responded. Communication was reestablished. To this day he does not know what was wrong. He doesn't need to know now!

Be an initiative lover today!

Failure to Allow
God to Use Failures

Acts 12:25; 13:13; 15:37-39; 1 Peter 5:4-14

"…Mark my son."
(1 PETER 5:13)

Can God use even our failures for our ultimate good? Yes! Consider Mark. He became a missionary dropout. He was not able to take the rigors of the missionary journeys with Paul. He was sent home as a failure. Later, when Barnabas wanted to take the young man on the second missionary adventure, Paul refused. A rift between Paul and Barnabas resulted over what to do with Mark. Finally Barnabas took Mark and went to Cyprus. The name Barnabas means "Son of encouragement." That's exactly what he was to Mark. He nurtured a failure back to faith. God had not given up on Mark; nor would Barnabas. Later, the rebuilding ministry was taken over by Peter. He knew what it was like to fail the Lord and be given a new beginning. Out of his own experience he was able to give courage and hope to young Mark. With Peter, Mark learned firsthand about Christ's life, message, and ministry. Then he wrote the first Gospel, recording what Christ did and said as Savior.

Failure is not sin. Faithlessness is.
—HENRIETTA MEARS

A Bloomin' Fret!

Psalm 37:1-40

Rest in the LORD and wait patiently for Him; do not fret.
(PSALM 37:7)

I overheard a cockney in London describe his boss: "'E's a bloomin' fret…the gov'ner is a worrying fretter. 'E puts on 'is walking shoes and climbs over molehills as if each one was a mountain."

I know too well what he meant. I checked the molehills I was climbing as if they were mountains. I made a list of all the frets of my life, responsibilities, and relationships. I decided to ask the Lord to help me declare war on fretting. I committed each one to Him and kept a record of what happened. Some of the frets never happened, many of them were resolved by the Lord's intervention, and others were the source of growing in patient trust. Now, years later, this week I reviewed the list. *Why in the world did I fret about that?* I asked myself.

Fretting is the misuse of the gift of imagination to picture the worst that could happen. A Christ-captivated imagination enables us to imagine with greater clarity what He wants to do with those people and situations that make us fret. In James Weldon Johnson's "Listen Lord," his prayer for the preacher is a good one for all fretters: "Lord, turpentine his imagination…"

Lord, turpentine my imagination
and set me free of fretting!

Strain and Stress

Psalm 37:10-40

The salvation of the righteous is from the LORD;
He is their strength in time of trouble.
(PSALM 37:39)

A Scots friend of mine has a **favorite saying:** "Dinna fret!" It's often followed by another: "Not to worry!" Sometimes that's easier said than done. I've found the objective power of Scripture much more helpful than being told not to fret or worry. Psalm 37 has been my constant companion in the pressures of life. The psalmist tells us not to fret but also tells us to trust in the Lord. The psalm gives us the four "P's" that help us stop fretting and start living: God's *providence, provision, protection,* and *promises.* Read the psalm again. Make a list of all the admonitions that are the opposite of fretting. The psalm is filled with key words like *trust, commit, wait, rest.*

Picture the kind of person you would be if you lived this psalm. Actually form the picture of a new you being and doing what the psalmist challenges. How would today be different? Now thank the Lord that the image you have formed will be true! The only way to stop fretting is to "get the picture" in our minds of what the Lord can and will do.

Tell the Lord you're tired of fretting and you are
ready to accept the freedom of faith in Him.

Power for Pressure

2 Corinthians 4:16-18; 11:22-28

*We do not lose heart. Even though our outward man is
perishing, yet the inward man is being renewed day by day.*
(2 CORINTHIANS 4:16)

We all live under pressure and pass pressure onto each other. How
can we live in a pressure-filled world in a relaxed and released
way? Our two texts today join together to form a central message for us.

The inner pressure of God's love is the only equalizer for the
pressure of the world. The gospel has creative pressure of its own.
When we take Jesus seriously and listen intently to His message,
look long and hard at His death, sense His impelling presence,
we know a liberating pressure. We feel the pressure to love and
forgive, bring our lives and society under His lordship, be the
sacrificial "person for others" He calls us to be. This holy pressure
presses us on to grow, share, change. Day by day, as we respond
to His gentle, persuasive pressure to reform and renew all of life,
we feel the pressure of the world less and less.

*Today I will allow the inner, creative pressure of Christ's
indwelling power to equalize the external pressures of life.*

The Pressure Habit

Ecclesiastes 3:1-8

*There is an appointed time for everything. And
there is a time for every event under heaven.*
(ECCLESIASTES 3:1)

"I don't know why, but I seem to work better under pressure." How
often we have heard people and ourselves say this! The syndrome
of pressure is constantly at work. We take on more than we can
do, put too much in one day, make more commitments than we
can possibly meet, and try to handle more responsibilities than
we can care for effectively. We do it to ourselves, however much
we blame other people. We become so accustomed to a frantic
life that we are actually ill-at-ease when there is nothing frazzling
our nerves. A habit pattern is formed.

There are several reasons for this. Some of us need an excuse
for doing things in a mediocre way. Others are afraid of quiet, un-
pressured times. Still others are troubled by deep relationships. If
we run hard enough we don't have to develop caring relationships.
And then some of us justify our existence with busyness. Behind
all this are decisions we make about the use of time. How about
you? Ever troubled by the pressure habit?

*A Christian is free to stop running
away from life in overinvolvement.*

Let Go!

Ecclesiastes 3:10-15

*I know that there is nothing better for them than
to rejoice and to do good in one's lifetime.*
(ECCLESIASTES 3:12)

Freedom in pressure is to be found in the sure knowledge that God is at work in the people and circumstances of life. When we lose that firm conviction, we become grim. If we live with the feeling that everything depends on us, that if we don't do everything it won't get done, or that the only things that are happening are what we can see and account for ourselves, we will be defeated by life's pressure.

The life Christ lived He now seeks to live in us. He gives us insight, strength, an answer, a new chance, or power—when we least expect it. He can take our limited human resources and make something creative that we could never devise. His delight is to surprise us with His innovations on human mistakes.

What a relief! The things we want most are gifts: an insight for someone we love, a healing of a relationship, an opportunity to solve a perplexing problem, the chance to make a difference. We can work hard because the results are up to Christ. We offer Him our intentionality; He provides the inspiration.

*Today I will let go and give
Christ control of my life.*

The Pressure of Religion

Galatians 5:1-15

Stand fast therefore in the liberty with which Christ has made us free, and do not be entangled again with a yoke of bondage.
(GALATIANS 5:1)

Religion is one of the most troublesome sources of destructive pressure in our lives. Religion is man's effort to reach, please, earn, and deserve God. Through rites, rituals, rules, and regulations we desperately seek to be good enough for God.

This is how it works. The spiritual resources of prayer, worship, study, church activity, and customs become goals, and we feel that we *must* do them in order to please God. These things become an end in themselves. Jesus came that we might have life—abundant life without reservations. He did not come to tie people down with more religion.

When our purpose is to know Him, then we no longer *have* to do the "required" thing, but instead we *want* to do the very things that righteousness motivates. Now the disciplines of discipleship become a delight instead of a duty. We desire to do what for most people is a duty. The pressure is off, and the motivation of love is on!

There is no limit to the good things we can do when love is the motivation.

Under Pressure,
or a Source of Pressure?

1 John 3:1-3

We shall be like Him.
(1 John 3:2)

In what ways are we contributing to the unhealthy pressure in other people's lives?

Think about our judgments that create the anxiety of never measuring up to what we demand. Consider the subtle pressure by which we communicate standards of what we want people to be, rather than affirmation of what they actually are. Have we taken time to help people discover a motive to do the things we press on them? Are we creating people in our image of them, or are we helping them to discover their true selves and potential? Is our love quietly conditioned on their performance? Are they free to fail and begin again without incrimination?

As the people in our lives come into focus in our mind's eye, we can see the times that our pressure has been transferred to them. When we drive ourselves, our drives are felt by others.

Christ's love communicated through us is the only hope for this. His love is unencumbered by adequacy standards, and it liberates a person to do his or her best with joy and creative motivation.

With Christ in us, we can inspire people to their best.

An Undeniable Purpose

Romans 12:1-2

Don't let the world around you squeeze you into its own mold.
(ROMANS 12:2 PHILLIPS)

The undeniables…what are they for you? At the core of your being, what are the undeniable values that you can insist on for your life? What do you want? Are you getting out of life what you believe is irrevocably crucial?

This causes us to ask what our essential goal in living really is. What does God want us to do with our lives? There must be an undergirding purpose that is applicable wherever we are. We often get entangled in wrestling to achieve secondary goals, and thus we miss the real reason we are alive.

Our purpose is to receive and give love. Wherever we are, there are people who desperately need enabling concern and care. When *people* become the focus of our purpose, it is less important where we live, what position we hold, what external circumstances we experience. Often we hope and plan to find life in these things. But we were created in such a way that ultimate joy can never be found until we are involved in caring for people. That's the one undeniable that reorients everything else.

Who needs your loving care today?

Under Direction or
Off in All Directions?

Psalm 48:1-14

He will be our guide for ever.
(Psalm 48:14 rsv)

There is always enough time in any one day to do the things Christ wants us to do! Many of us are trying to get His power to live out commitments that He may not have guided. If we are about to go under from pressure, it is probably because we are off in all directions without His direction. He has called us to be faithful, not frantic. We play God by trying to handle more than He has willed for us.

This leads to some penetrating questions about our lives:

How much of what we are doing is an extension of God's will for us?

What would God communicate to us about our commitments?

If you could tell God about your life, what would you say?

If this were your last year to live, what would you do with it?

What would you continue doing? What would you delete?

If you could start all over, what would you do differently?

Christ gives us the strength to do those things He has called us to do.

Living with Conflict

Philippians 1:27-30

*…Having the same conflict which you
saw in me and now hear is in me.*
(PHILIPPIANS 1:30)

Most of us find it difficult to live in conflict. It is painful for us to disagree with people whom we love. When good people disagree, what should we do?

First, don't be surprised. We stand in a heritage of conflict. In the early church there was conflict within the church and between the church and the world. Jesus brought conflict through His radical message and call to discipleship. In His own band of disciples there was conflict. Later Peter and Paul had their difficulties understanding each other. There have always been differing theologies through the ages.

Secondly, be thankful. Paul said, "In all things give thanks." In the turbulent seas of conflict, God is teaching us something we need to learn.

Thirdly, learn to listen in love. When we listen in love we are able to wait long enough for a person to say what he or she really means. An interrupted man said, "You haven't let me finish." The interrupter said, "I don't want you to finish. I want you to hear what I've got to say because you won't say what you are about to say if you hear what I've got to say."

Keep a sense of humor.

The Peace That Lasts

Philippians 4:6-7

*Be anxious for nothing, but in everything by prayer and
supplication, with thanksgiving, let your requests be made known
to God; and the peace of God, which surpasses all understanding,
will guard your hearts and minds through Christ Jesus.*
(PHILIPPIANS 4:6-7)

Repeat the above words each morning when you start the day
and each evening when you retire. They will change your life.
Note the progression. We are to rejoice! Why? The Lord is at hand.
That's the reason we can be free from worry. Each problem, challenge, or opportunity should be surrendered to the Lord in prayer,
asking for His guidance and power. Then the peace of God comes
flooding into our minds and hearts.

Paul tells us that it is a peace which surpasses understanding.
This does not mean that it cannot be experienced, but that the
total breadth and depth of it is beyond human comprehension.
We cannot produce the peace of God. It is impossible to capture it.
Nor can we earn or deserve it. Peace is a gift of God. It cost Him
Calvary and is synonymous with His indwelling Spirit. Peace is
the Spirit of God in Christ reproducing His character in us.

*Peace that cannot be contrived or totally comprehended is a gift. I
can be at peace when all the world around me is in turmoil.*

Love Lifts the Burdens

Proverbs 12:1-28

*Anxiety in a man's heart weighs it down,
but a good word makes it glad.*
(PROVERBS 12:25)

I asked a friend how he was. His response was intriguing: "Well, I'd be all right if it were not for the boulders in my shoe." "What do you mean by that?" I asked laughingly. "Well," he said with a sigh, "I've got some worries that seem big, but when I look at them they are not anything really. They are like little pebbles in my shoes that feel like boulders until I take off my shoe, shake them out, and feel amazed that such a little thing could feel so big!"

Do you have any pebbles in your shoes? Who doesn't? They feel like big problems until we examine them. They are the cause of a common human disability: burdens. Burdens are a low-grade worry. Like a low-grade fever, they are not enough to put us on our back, but they drain our energies and resiliency. A burden may be a person, an unresolved relationship, or an impossible task for which we have inadequate resources. What has the power to do that to you? What disappointment with life, people, or your-self is crushing out your peace of mind? God has a good word for us: "I will come under the burden with you and lift it today. Trust Me!"

The boulders are only pebbles. Shake them out!

A Host with Hope

Romans 12:13; Hebrews 13:2;
1 Peter 4:9; 3 John 1-8

*Beloved, you do faithfully whatever you do
for the brethren and for strangers.*
(3 John 5)

Max Beerbohm, the English critic, once said, "The world is divided into guests and hosts." The cross can make a host out of a guest.

We all know people who are guests wherever they are. They do not take the responsibility of a host for people's feelings, comfort, hospitality, needs, or concerns. They are in the world to be served, not serve. Someone else is always responsible to take care of them. When they come into a room they say, "Well, I'm here," instead of saying, "Well, look who's here. I'm glad to see you! How are you?"

That's what communicating the faith is all about. When the forgiving love of the cross has healed us at the core, our abiding concern is for the guests that God puts in our lives. If conversation, sharing of experience, inquiring into another person's need, patient listening, and liberating empathy are seen in the context of joyous listening, we will come across as a person whom others cannot resist. They will want to be with us and know our Savior.

Today I will be a host with hope.

Beyond Glibness to Greatness

Matthew 21:28-32

Which of the two did the will of his father?
(MATTHEW 21:31)

Take a piece of paper. Fold it in half. On the left side list the priorities of your life in the order of importance. What do you think is most crucial to demand your time, energy, and money? On the right side of the folded paper list these same priorities according to the amount of time, energy, and money you actually spend. Amazing difference.

This points up the great distance between what we say and what we do. Words and affirmations of convictions come all too easily for most of us Christians.

Jesus was more concerned about follow-through than about easy words of promise. His parable of the two sons makes His point. Our trouble is that most of us are a mixture of both sons. Sometimes we attempt nothing and accomplish it magnificently! Jesus' challenge for us to be perfect as our heavenly Father is perfect is to lift us out of glibness.

That's just where Jesus wanted His proud listeners to end up: "Who then can be saved?" No one...apart from God's love and forgiveness. Once we acknowledge our need for that, we will be on our way to perfection on God's terms.

In my prayers I will say what I mean and mean what I say.

Loneliness

Psalm 25:1-22

*Turn to me and be gracious to me,
for I am lonely and afflicted.*
(PSALM 25:16)

Loneliness is the anxiety of unrelatedness. It is caused by an inability to establish, develop, and nurture deep, lasting, and satisfying relationships with other people. Most of us do not lack for human contact. We usually have more encounters with other people than we can handle effectively. Our problem is not in the lack of opportunity, but in our deep sense of unrelatedness with those with whom we do have contact.

A man who had been married for 40 years put it this way: "We have had a good life together. We have worked hard. Now we are ready and capable for retirement. But we have never really gotten to know each other." The anxiety of unrelatedness. Augustine prayed, "Lord, Thou hast created us for Thyself and made our hearts restless until they rest in Thee." Our loneliness is rooted in the lack of fellowship with God for which we were created. It is in relationship with Him that we learn what it is to be loved and accepted as we are, and then love others as we have been loved.

*We will be lonely in spite of the people around us
until we experience friendship with God.*

Who Will Remember?

Ecclesiastes 2:12-17

*I said to myself, "As is the fate of the fool, it will
also befall me. Why then have I been extremely
wise?" So I said to myself, "This too is vanity."*
(ECCLESIASTES 2:15)

It was time for the funeral to begin, but no one was there except
for the lawyer, the funeral director, and me. The lawyer stepped
forward and handed me an envelope containing a check for my
services. "But this is not necessary," I said. "I didn't even know
the man." "What difference does that make?" came the tart reply.
"Apparently no one else did either!"

This man had spent his life on himself. He had never married;
he had lived alone. He had saved his money and died a wealthy man.
He never knew the joy of sharing what he had earned with others.

The auspicious arrangements showed that someone had
planned ahead. But no one really knew the man. No one was
close to him. No one confided in him, and he allowed no one
close to him as a friend.

He had not cared about people, and in the end no one really
cared about him. What are the things for which you will be remembered? Whose life is different, really enriched, because of you?

*The final results of our lives will be
written in what we did for people.*

Life's Awesome Choice

Luke 18:18-23

A certain ruler asked Him, saying, "Good Teacher,
what shall I do to inherit eternal life?"
(LUKE 18:18)

An old man was dying. He related his consistent compromise with life. In college he put off a personal decision about the Christian faith because he said he did not have all the facts. After college he became engulfed in personal advancement in business. Then, when he was married and had a family, he attended church because it was good for the family, but Christ meant little to him as a Person. Now his family was raised and he was retired. As he looked back over his life, he realized he had never done anything that would make the world different because he had lived.

Jesus loved the rich young ruler enough not to violate his freedom. He let him say "No." He did not run after him solicitously, changing his terms to meet his perception of his adequacy. He let him go. The young ruler had said "No" once too often. How about you?

Mathematician that I was, I had forgotten two magnitudes—
the shortness of time and the vastness of eternity.
—THOMAS CHALMERS

When Our Name Is Legion

Mark 5:1-20

He answered, saying, "My name is Legion; for we are many."
(MARK 5:9)

How did Legion get that way? What did life do to him, and then, because of that, what did he do to himself? What was he afraid he would do to others because of what he was doing to himself? What memories tormented this desperate man? What led him to a self-imposed separation from the people he loved? If the pain and difficulties of encountering and grappling with people in reality are too difficult or painful, or if we find repeated rejection, the syndrome of self-pity and remorse follow quickly. Legion had removed himself from the source of healing. He was a leaderless Legion, marching off in all directions.

Who is the legion of the hurt child, the frustrated, rejected teenager, the aspiring but disappointed young adult, the memory-laden failure, the demanding parent, the accusing judge, the guilt-infusing elder brother, who lives in our skin? Most of us are a bundle of conflicting inner persons jockeying for recognition. We are a bundle of the unresolved. We too are legion…we know it is so by the strange way we react, almost inadvertently, in some situations. Jesus healed Legion, and He can unify our legion of competitive drives and mixed natures.

We can be healed and whole because
we are marching to His drumbeat.

Divine Discontent

Mark 6:1-6

*He could do no mighty work there, except that He laid
His hands on a few sick people and healed them.*
(MARK 6:5)

Tell me what makes you **discontent** and I will tell you what drives
you. Show me your indignations and I will show you the impera-
tives by which you live. Tell me what stirs you up enough to want
to change things, and I will tell you whether you are living while
you are alive. This inventory can show us quickly whether we are
dealing with soul-sized issues or piddling about in the eddies of
irrelevant self-pity.

Jesus affirms a creative discontent as a major characteristic of
discipleship. He took His listeners from an abstraction about God
and brought them to the concrete evidences in them and society
that indicated they had no right to be satisfied. They were proud
of their growth, but He showed them they had hardly begun; they
were proud of their heritage, but He showed them the tremendous responsibilities they had in sharing the secret of God's love
with the world. Today a sure sign we are in touch with Christ is
that we know He loves us as we are but won't leave us that way.

*When our dissatisfactions are in harmony with Christ's, then
we know that we can depend on His power to change.*

When We Are Not Able

Mark 10:35-45

Are you able to drink the cup that I drink?
(Mark 10:38)

James and John misunderstood the real meaning of greatness. They wanted to be given places of power and dignity. Jesus responded by asking if they were able to drink the cup that He would drink and be baptized with the baptism with which He would be baptized. He implied His forthcoming cross and suffering. Still the competitive, recognition-hungry disciples did not comprehend. "We are able!" they responded. Then Jesus told them that greatness would mean being a servant. We ponder with awe His challenge: "Whoever of you desires to be first shall be slave of all. For even the Son of Man did not come to be served but to serve and to give His life as a ransom for many."

The secret of the Christian life is not that *we* are able but that *Christ* is able. Paul asserts, "He is able." But before we can comprehend this promise, we must know that we are not able without Him. More important than what we are able to do for Christ is what He is able to do through us. When we get clearly in mind what we are called to be and do as servants, then we know we can't make it alone, but with Christ nothing is impossible!

Our motto is not "We are able," but "He is able!"

Intercessory Involvement

Hebrews 7:25; Romans 7:1–8:39

He is also able to save to the uttermost those who come to God through Him, seeing He ever lives to make intercession for them.
(HEBREWS 7:25)

Christ, our High Priest, has made the ultimate, never-to-be-repeated sacrifice for our sins. He offers us the gift of salvation, but also daily power to become new in every facet of life. Once we have experienced salvation by faith in Christ's death and resurrection, we become recipients of the implications of that salvation for all of life. To be saved means to be liberated from our sins, freed from fear of death, and then given the gift of sublime companionship with the Savior. Salvation also means healing, wholeness, health, protection, and providential care. We are not in the battle alone. *He is able* is with us.

The meaning of "save to the uttermost" should be the center of our attention in this message about the victory of the cross in daily living. Romans 7 and 8 form a backdrop for the dedication of our struggles and how we can receive fresh strength for each new battle. We don't need the bootstrap psychology by which most of us live, which denies us the delight and dynamic of dependence on Christ, the High Priest who ever (constantly and consistently) makes intercession for us.

He is able!

He Knows All About It

Hebrews 2:10-18

*In that He Himself has suffered, being tempted, He
is able to aid those who are tempted.*
(HEBREWS 2:18)

Christ is able to help us when we are tempted. The greatest temptation is to be our own gods and try to run our own lives. We constantly break the First Commandment: There are other gods we are tempted to worship. They are all related to the worship of self. All other temptations flow from that. When we take charge of our own lives and try to be director of the drama of life, we become vulnerable to doing and saying those things that distort our relationship with the Lord and throw our lives into confusion.

Our confidence in temptation is that the Lord is with us. There are things we would never consider doing with the Lord there with us. If we could not do or say a thing with Him with us, it is surely wrong. But in addition to that, when we are tempted to weaken under the pressure of temptation, He actually takes charge and gives us the courage to resist. He knows what we are going through: He's faced it all. Think of it! He's constantly pulling for us.

We can win over temptation—Christ is on our side!

Christ Makes Us Stable

Romans 16:25-27

…To Him who is able to establish you.
(ROMANS 16:25)

We all long to get off the yo-yo vacillation of ups and downs. Our desire is to be the kind of people who are consistent regardless of what's happening around us.

Paul's benediction at the conclusion of Romans provides us with another "He is able" declaration. Christ is able to *establish* us. Note the key words in this dynamic promise: "Now to Him who is able to establish you according to my gospel…" The word for *able* in Greek is *dunamai,* from the word for *power.* All power in heaven and earth can be released through Christ for us.

But for what purpose? To establish us. Here the Greek word is *sterixai,* from *sterizo,* "to make stable." Christ is the Stabilizer. Paul uses the personal pronoun when he tells us the foundation of that stability. When he speaks of "my gospel," he is talking about the good news of Jesus Christ—His life, message, death, resurrection, and indwelling power. Paul was a stable person because he believed for himself that nothing could separate him from the love of Christ. Claim this great "He is able" affirmation as your promise today.

Christ makes us stable in a very unstable world.

Stability in the Storm

James 1:2-8

*Let patience have its perfect work, that you may
be perfect and complete, lacking nothing.*
(JAMES 1:4)

A stable person established in the gospel can be distinguished by patience. He or she knows that God is in charge and is working out His purposes. That was James's conviction from years of experience. He wrote to his friends to encourage them. Note that he did not say *if* but *when* we fall into trials we are to count it all joy. The reason is that trials produce patience. In the midst of difficulty we are to ask the Lord for wisdom, asking in faith, knowing that He will give us exactly what we need to stand firm. The strength of a great oak tree is in its roots. The winds that blow against it only strengthen the roots.

James gives us a frightening metaphor for an unstable person: a wave of the sea driven and tossed by the wind. But the One who is able gives us courage to match the wind.

*We must wait for God, meekly, in wind and wet, in
thunder and lightning, in cold and the dark. Wait, and He
will come. He never comes to those who do not wait.*
—FREDERICK FABER

The Stability of Our Times

Isaiah 33:5-6; Colossians 1:21-23

He will be the stability of your times.
(ISAIAH 33:6)

Isaiah gives us our **thought for today**. Memorize it; repeat it often today: *The Lord shall be the stability of your times.* Our task is not to try to be a stable person for the Lord, but to allow Him to be our stability. Our text gives us a reminder of what His stability provides: a wealth of salvation, wisdom, and knowledge—three great resources to draw upon today. The Lord has saved us through the cross. We are loved and forgiven, reconciled and regenerated because of His grace. That gives us a willingness to receive His wisdom for our decisions. The gift of knowledge is His wisdom in application to the challenges of life.

Today most passenger ships have gigantic steel shafts which protrude from the hull of the ship to make the sailing more comfortable in a stormy sea. Christ does that to our lives. The waves around us are no different, but we can move through them with an even course. With Him we have "equipoise," an equal distribution of hope, courage, and fortitude.

God has promised strength for the day,
Rest amid labors, light for the way…
Unfailing sympathy, undying love.
—ANNIE JOHNSON FLINT

A Vision for the Night

Acts 18:1-28

The Lord spoke to Paul in the night by a vision: "Do not be afraid,
but speak, and do not keep silent; for I am with you, and no one
will attack you to hurt you; for I have many people in this city."
(ACTS 18:9-10)

Paul's vision while in Corinth gives us a formula for stable, confident living. Paul was one of the most stable persons in Christ who ever lived. We are given the source of that stability in this passage. Note the condition of this great man's heart during the turbulent times of rejection and trouble. He was afraid, tempted to be silent, and in constant danger. Balance that with the confidence the Lord gave him. The Lord promised that He would be with him and that He had many people in the city who would help him.

The same vision and constant companionship with the Lord is needed by all of us for courageous Christian living. There are times when we are afraid. We all have fears of something or someone. The Lord's admonition "Do not be afraid" is always coupled with "For I am with you." The presence of the Lord is the only assurance that can dispel our fears.

God incarnate is the end of fear. And the heart that realizes that He
is in the midst, that takes heed to the assurance of His loving presence,
will be quiet in the midst of alarm. Only be patient and be quiet.
—F.B. MEYER

Fullness to Fill the Emptiness

Ephesians 4:7-16

He who descended is also the One who ascended far
above all the heavens, that He might fill all things.
(EPHESIANS 4:10)

Athanasius said, "Christ became what we are that He might make us what He is." An awesome thought! True stability is growth in Christlikeness. That's the startling message of today's Scripture reading. We have been called to "the measure of the stature of the fullness of Christ." Paul goes on to say that we are programmed to grow. All of life is used by the Lord to make us more like Himself. We are no longer like children in the faith, "tossed to and fro and carried about with every wind of doctrine," but we are to "grow into Him who is the head—Christ."

We are all in the process of becoming what we dare to envision. What is your image of yourself in the fullness of Christ? What would you be like when filled with His Spirit, transformed by His love, shaped by His will? Picture yourself! Never let go of that compelling vision. The more we get to know Christ, the more we become like Him in attitude and action, thought and character.

To become Christlike is the only thing in the world
worth caring for, the thing before which every ambition
of man is folly and all lower achievements vain.
—HENRY DRUMMOND

Exceeding Joy

Jude 1-25

Now to Him who is able to keep you from stumbling, and to present you faultless before the presence of His glory with exceeding joy.
(JUDE 24)

The theme of the little letter of Jude is found in verse 24. The key word is *keep*. Two groups of Christians are in focus: Those who have not kept the faith and those who are being kept by the power of Christ. Notice the relationship between verses 21 and 24. Jude admonishes us to keep ourselves in the love of God, "looking for the mercy of our Lord Jesus Christ to eternal life." The emphasis is on living in Christ now and forever. Christ keeps us from stumbling. He guards us from anything that would separate us from Him in this life, so we can claim assurance that we shall live with Him forever.

A Christian who is being "kept" in the grace of Christ knows that his or her destination is assured. It's a great way to live—experiencing each day as if it were the last, taking care of anything that would make us uncomfortable in seeing the Lord face-to-face!

I came from God, and I'm going back to God, and I won't have any gaps of death in the middle of life.
—GEORGE MACDONALD

Life's Most Crucial Decision

Luke 16:19-31

*Between us and you there is a great gulf fixed, so that
those who want to pass from here to you cannot, nor
can those who want to come from there pass to us.*
(LUKE 16:26)

In the parable of Dives and Lazarus Jesus tells us that death is a demarcation, that our decision about where we will spend eternity must be made in this life. We will all live forever, but the question is, Will we live in heaven with the Lord?

What if we could hear voices from the dead? What would they tell us? What difference would it make to us? Would some of us be assured and others alarmed? What if people who have died came back across the great divide to tell us what they have experienced in either the joy of heaven or the excruciating separation from the Lord in hell?

Dives, as the rich man in Jesus' parable has been called by tradition, wanted to send a message back to his five brothers. Think about what he might have said. And what do you think Lazarus would have wanted to say if He had had a chance to share the glory of eternal life with the Lord?

The parable is a shocking reminder that our eternal status will be determined on the basis of our faith in Christ, His death for our sins, and complete trust in His lordship in our lives.

We will live forever—but where?

Hope for the Hassled

Philippians 3:17-21

He is able even to subdue all things to Himself.
(PHILIPPIANS 3:21)

This "He is able" statement is like a trumpet blast. Paul had experienced the conquering power of Christ over Satan, death, physical handicaps, and his own human nature. Today we focus on the powers and forces in life that we need Christ to subdue. When we consider verse 21 as a whole, we see that the subduing ministry of Christ in and around us is to conform us into His likeness (also note Romans 8:29). Christ is constantly working to conquer anything that will debilitate us in realizing that magnificent purpose.

What has the power to hassle you? What makes it difficult for you to be faithful and obedient to Christ? Think of the situations, circumstances, people, and problems through which Satan seeks to frustrate your discipleship. Focus on that, and then focus on the "He is able" power of Christ. Be specific, and then surrender the problem to Him. Make this a day in which you trust Christ's subduing power.

Christ waits for our relinquishment of our needs before
He acts. He wants to amaze us by what He can do
with problems submitted to His subduing power.

Once and for All and Daily in All

2 Timothy 1:1-12

*I also suffer these things; nevertheless I am not ashamed, for I
know whom I have believed and am persuaded that He is able
to keep what I have committed to Him until that Day.*
(2 TIMOTHY 1:12)

Paul gives us a good description of what a committed Christian
is in this grand "He is able" assurance to Timothy. He knew in
whom he believed. He was sure of Christ. If you can say what Paul
said in verse 12, you're a committed Christian indeed!

There are two ways in which the Greek of Paul's statement
can be read. Both are correct. One is, "What I have committed
to Him"; the other is, "What He has committed to me." In verse
14 Paul reminds Timothy that he is to keep what has been committed to him.

The Lord is wholly committed to us, so we can be unreservedly committed to Him. Our commitment is to accept His love,
forgiveness, and guidance, and then surrender our will to Him.
He will *keep* what we commit. The word *keep* in Greek means
"guard." *Committed* is an ancient banking term implying a deposit.
Literally, Paul means that our deposit of ourselves and our needs
is secure in the bank of heaven. When we commit our lives to
Christ, our eternal status is set. When we commit our daily lives
to Him, abundant life begins.

I am persuaded; I am commited; I am empowered.

Supernatural Power

Ephesians 3:14-21

Now to Him who is able to do exceedingly abundantly above all
that we ask or think, according to the power that works in us.
(Ephesians 3:20)

This final "He is able!" assertion is a triumphant crescendo of all
the previous ones we have considered in the past few days. Christ
is able to do exceedingly abundantly by His power at work in us.
What is this power? His own Spirit. Within us He releases the
same power that raised Him from the dead. This "He is able!"
statement is a promise of our resurrection now. By His power, He
raises us from our old life to a new one. Resurrection and regeneration must be kept together. "The old has passed away—behold,
the new has come!"

We all need power. We need an inner energizing of our minds
and wills. We were meant to be recreated to be like Jesus. We cannot do it on our own, but He is able! The indwelling Christ, the
power at work in us, infuses our brains with a vivid picture of the
person we can become. Then He guides each decision and discernment of our wills. He shows us how we are to act and react as new
creatures. Our depleted energies are engendered with strength. We
actually have supernatural power to think, and act, courageously.

Christ works within us
to reveal what He is able to do around us.

Missing the Mark

Romans 3:1-31

All have sinned and fall short of the glory of God.
(Romans 3:23)

What is sin really? Sin is separation from God. Sins are what we do because of that separation. The human condition of estrangement, rebellion, and obsession with self is the essence of what the Bible calls sin. It is seeking to be our own gods and running our own lives. All the sins of pride, jealousy, anger, hatred, self-centeredness, and willfulness are caused by the fracture of the relationship with God for which we were created. The root of the Greek word for sin means "to miss the mark," as a misaimed arrow hits wide of the target. A sinner is one who has not fulfilled the reason that he or she was born.

God is more concerned about our *sin* than our sins. That's why He came in Jesus Christ to love and reconcile us. Spend today praising God that He did not leave us in our estrangement. On the cross Christ became our substitutionary sacrifice. We have been forgiven; we are reconciled; we are loved!

The measure of God's anger against sin is the measure of the love that is prepared to forgive the sinner and to love him in spite of his sin.
—David Martyn Lloyd-Jones

Creative Pride

Romans 11:20; 15:17;
1 Corinthians 1:14; 5:12; Philippians 1:26

…That your rejoicing for me may be more abundant
in Jesus Christ by my coming to you again.
(PHILIPPIANS 1:26)

Is it wrong to be proud? We can get to the answer of that question by a clearer translation of the Greek meaning of our text for today. What is suggested is, "In order that your pride in me may abound in Christ Jesus."

The Philippians were proud of Paul, and he made no effort to conceal his pride for them. Yet, with a gentle reminder, he brings them back to the source of their relationship in the Master and not each other. If he is able to come to them, it will be because the Lord has made it possible.

Elsewhere, in Romans 11:20, Paul gives the formula for creative pride—"Do not become proud, but stand in awe" (RSV). There is a kind of pride that comes from thinking that what we have or are is our own accomplishment, and a kind of pride that comes from an awesome realization that Christ alone is the source of our strength. Without Christ Paul could do nothing of any value. Nor can we!

When we recognize God's gifts in us or the people we love or the things we do, then there is a deep sense of gratitude that issues in creative pride.

The Mighty Mite

Mark 12:41-44

He called His disciples to Himself and said to them, "Assuredly, I say to you that this poor widow has put in more than all those who have given to the treasury; for they all put in out of their abundance, but she out of her poverty put in all that she had, her whole livelihood."

(MARK 12:43-44)

Jesus sat among the alms boxes and watched people making their contributions. Then a humble, little widow moved Him to exclamation. What He saw was authentic. Out of love and gratitude the widow gave what she had, probably the money that would have been used for her next meal. The 13 big alms receptacles looked like ear trumpets. They made loud noises when large coins were pretentiously hurled in by contributors who desired recognition.

Not for the widow. Her coins made little or no sound. She gave two of the smallest coins of all, about two cents in our money. But the slight sound drew Jesus' attention. He was profoundly moved.

Jesus has memorialized the widow's mite for eternity. No longer can we say our little gift of self or our possessions will not matter to God. The size of the gift matters not; the size of the gratitude means everything.

The attitude of gratitude gives us an aptitude for greatness.

Criticism of Greatness

Isaiah 29:17-24

Those who criticize will accept instruction.
(Isaiah 29:24)

The story is told that when **Michelangelo** had completed his sculpture of David, the governor of Florence came to look at the finished work. He was pleased with what he observed, but as he looked at it he dared to offer a criticism. "The nose...the nose is too large, is it not?" Michelangelo looked carefully at David and quietly answered, "Yes, I think it is a little too large." He picked up a chisel and mallet, and also a handful of marble dust, and mounted the scaffolding. Carefully he hammered, permitting small amounts of dust to fall to the ground with each blow. He finally stopped and asked, "Now look at the nose. Is it correct?" "Ah," responded the governor, "I like it...I like it much better. You have given it life."

Michelangelo descended, according to the old chronicle, "with great compassion for those who desire to appear to be good judges of matters whereof they know nothing." What maturity the great artist displayed in being able to take criticism! What about you? With the Lord's help we can reject negative criticism and accept creative criticism.

*When we are secure in the Lord we can listen to criticism,
learn from it, change it if need be, and move on!*

The Ultimate Miracle

Colossians 1:1-29

It pleased the Father that in Him all the fullness should dwell.
(COLOSSIANS 1:19)

Christ Himself is the greatest miracle of history. The incarnation, as the central miracle, helps us interpret the miracles done by the "I Am," Yahweh with us. These special acts of the power of God present with us in Immanuel were signs, wonders, and works of the Almighty Lord of all creation. They are not infractions of natural law, but the intervention of a higher law of love for human need. All of Jesus' miracles were part of the "people business" He came to do as God incarnate. Each mighty work was done so that some person, His followers, and all of Israel might know, "I am He!" Someone has said that the miracles of Jesus were and are the dinner bell ringing, calling us to the banquet prepared for us to enjoy with Him.

The question is, Do miracles still happen? Yes! The miracle of life, our salvation, the transformation of personality, and specific interventions of healing and blessing. A belief in miracles leads us to an "all things are possible" kind of faith for daily living and our needs, and our concerns for others. Physical, emotional, and spiritual healings are still being done daily by the Great Physician!

Jesus was Himself the one convincing and permanent miracle.
—IAN MACLAREN

The Miracle Is You!

Luke 6:17-19

The whole multitude sought to touch Him, for power went out from Him and healed them all.
(LUKE 6:19)

The second greatest miracle, next to Christ, is what happens to a person who comes to know Christ personally. When we commit our lives to Him and invite Him to live in us, our days are filled with a constant succession of surprises. He is Lord of all life, has unlimited power, and can arrange events and circumstances to bless us. Our only task is to surrender our needs to Him, and then leave the results to Him.

Christ did not use the word *miracle*. He talked about the "works of God." Wherever He went, He did "works" that defied both the expected and the anticipated. The reason was that He was the power of God, the "fullness of the Godhead bodily" (Colossians 2:9). That explains what happened in the scripture we read for today. "They were all struggling to touch Him; for power kept issuing from Him; and He healed them, every one!" We struggle with our needs, but do we struggle to get those needs to Him? It is not our task to decide what, when, or how He will deal with our need, but only to make contact with Him in prayer.

Persist! Don't give up. At all costs make your way to the Master. Tell Him your need, and then leave it with Him.

The Power of Prayer

Matthew 17:14-21

*The disciples came to Jesus privately and
said, "Why could we not cast it out?"*
(MATTHEW 17:19)

The man's son was possessed by a demon. The disciples failed
to heal him. Jesus performed the miracle. After the man had left
with His healed son, rejoicing, the disciples were eager to know
why they had failed so miserably. "What did we do wrong? Why
could we not cast out this demon?"

They asked for it! They left themselves wide open. It was a
moment for truth. Jesus was simple and direct: "This kind cannot
be driven out by anything but prayer."

What Jesus meant was, "In a life of sustained communion
with God lies the power to deal with evil. You have not paid a sufficient price of personal devotion to be able to deal with a problem
like this." The reason was in their need for prayer.

Jesus' answer would be no different today. If we were to ask
Him why we are so ineffective in healing human needs, affecting
our society, and shaping our history, He would tell us that the
answer is to be found in prayer. The complex needs of a time like
this can be met only with the power of prayer. Then our words
will be a clarion call with a ring of reality.

*We have only as much spiritual power and insight
as we can communicate to another person.*

The Gift of Joy

John 15:1-17

*These things I have spoken to you, that My joy may
remain in you, and that your joy may be full.*
(John 15:11)

The secret source of joy for us is the indwelling Spirit of Christ. In today's scripture there is a powerful progression. Christ tells us that He is the vine and we are the branches. We are to abide in Him and He in us. That means we are to draw on the living power of His Spirit to produce the fruit of joy.

John 15:11 tells us that the reason He teaches us to abide in Him is so that His joy may be in us and that our joy may be full. The joy we can't produce and the world can't take away is the joy He imputes by His Spirit. The word *abide* means "to dwell, inhabit, live, lodge, reside, and rest." It implies continuance, faithfulness, and remaining constantly without limit.

The joy we are to put out, Christ puts in. To abide in Him means that we consistently draw on the resources of His matchless grace. His abiding in us means that His characteristic joy becomes the dominant note of our disposition. We are made like Christ! Would the one word people use to describe you be joy? If not, why not?

Joy is being in His presence. Joy is the center of His will.
—Ralph Carmichael

The Courage of Commitment

Luke 9:51-53

*It came to pass, when the time had come for Him to be received
up, that He steadfastly set His face to go to Jerusalem.*
(LUKE 9:51)

What Christ has committed to us, plus our commitment to obey,
equals our Jerusalem. There is a Jerusalem for all of us for which
we were born and to which our life is leading. Jesus set His face
steadfastly to go to Jerusalem, knowing that there He would have
to face the cross and die for the sins of the world.

Our Jerusalem is whatever prayer has discerned is the Lord's
will for us. It is a symbolic city of reality rather than a wish-dream
and easy religion. It is commitment instead of comfort. But we
can set our faces to our purpose with joy and not grimness. Because Christ has gone before us, and now goes with us, we have
His victorious presence to give us raw courage. Once we have
committed our lives completely to Him, then we are able because He is able. His strength flows through us as we attempt
great things for Him and by His power. After He has control of
the nerve center of our wills, He can use us to do what otherwise
would be impossible. Just as He went to His Jerusalem believing
in God's vindication, so too we can live out our commitment
knowing that He will give us victory.

What is your Jerusalem?

The Confirmation of Closed Doors

Luke 9:54-56

They went to another village.
(Luke 9:56)

There's a profound truth in the scripture we read yesterday that warrants further thought. Note verse 53: After Jesus set His face like flint to go to Jerusalem, a Samaritan village did not receive Him. God closed other doors in affirmation of the fact that Jesus had committed Himself to go through the door of His ordained destiny. It was as if God ratified the decision to go to Jerusalem. The Master had greater works to do than ministering to one village. His task now was to save the world.

God opens and closes doors. A closed door can affirm another open door. When we commit ourselves to do the will of the Lord, He slams other distracting, lesser doors to assure us that we have made the right decision.

The task of a committed Christian is to walk through the open doors and not try to beat down the closed doors. There are times when it is clear that we should move on to the next step of God's strategy.

Find out what the Lord wants you to do, make
a commitment, and get on with it!

The Cost of Following Jesus

Luke 9:56-62

"Follow me."
(LUKE 9:59)

Jesus' mood is determined and decisive: He is on the way to Jerusalem, and He wants followers who can count the cost. The three different levels of commitment shown in people He met expose the ways many Christians relate to their discipleship today.

The first man made a grand, pious commitment that went no deeper than words. He promised to follow the Master wherever He went. Jesus challenged the man to count the cost. So often we come to Christ to receive what we want to solve problems or gain inspiration for our challenges. He gives both with abundance, but then calls us into a ministry of concern and caring. We are to do for others what He has done for us. Loving and forgiving are not always easy.

The second man had unfinished business from the past. He wanted to follow Christ, but a secondary loyalty kept him tied to the past. In substance, Christ said, "Forget the past; follow Me!"

The third person wanted to say goodbye to his family. Jesus stresses the urgency of our commitment. Our commitment must be unreserved to seek *first* His kingdom.

*Are there entangling loyalties you have brought into
the Christian life that make it difficult to give your
whole mind and heart and will to Christ?*

The Way of the Cross Leads Home

Matthew 7:13-14; John 14:1-6

*Enter by the narrow gate; for wide is the gate and broad is
the way that leads to destruction, and there are many who
go in by it. Because narrow is the gate and difficult is the
way which leads to life, and there are few who find it.*

(MATTHEW 7:13-14)

The Lord who declares that He is the way, the truth, and the life
is the one who points the way to the narrow gate to eternal life.
What does He mean? We find the answer in His cross and His
challenge that we take up our cross. The cross is the narrow gate.
It is the only way to know Him, to live forever, and to live now
in profound happiness. In the words of the old hymn, "The way
of the cross leads home." Eventually we must face the crisis of our
helplessness to save ourselves.

The cross was where our eternal life was won. And there is
no other way for us to go but through Him and what He did for
us. No one goes to the Father, to heaven, or to present joy except
through Christ. Not good works, moral achievement, or human
accomplishment. There are not many roads that lead to God;
there is one road with a narrow gate.

*When we water down the cross, we drown in our
confusion and take others down with us.*

There's No Other Place to Go

John 6:41-71

*Jesus said to the twelve, "Do you also want to go away?" But
Simon Peter answered Him, "Lord, to whom shall we go?"*
(John 6:67-68)

Jesus' words are filled with pathos: "Do you also want to go
away?" Many of Jesus' followers had turned away. They could
not take the challenge He had given. He had boldly proclaimed
that He was the Bread of Life to fill their emptiness. Then He
said that His followers must eat His flesh and drink His blood.
To the Hebrew person, that meant accepting Him completely
and taking His message and life into themselves. The words were
symbolic but not simplistic. Bread meant sustenance, and blood
meant life. Many people followed Jesus for the signs and wonders
He did, and not for the message He proclaimed.

Many of us have the same problem. We want our Lord for
answers to our needs, but when it comes to absolute faithfulness and obedience, we too are tempted to turn away. But we all
know a hunger that no one else can fill. And so we say with Peter,
"Lord, to whom shall we go? You have the words of eternal life."
Tell the Lord that!

Today is the day to rejoin Christ in mind, heart, and action.

Self-pity

Matthew 20:29-34

Jesus, deeply moved with pity, touched their eyes.
(MATTHEW 20:34 PHILLIPS)

The cross is the antidote to self-pity. We are moved to love others regardless of what they say or do. Jesus' prayer, "Father, forgive them, for they know not what they do," is the prayer to pray for release of self-pity. Most people do what they do because of what they are. They cannot change what they do until they change what they are. Self-pity is usually related to what other people have done or said to us. It is an alarm signal that there is something wrong in our relationship with them. Rejection and hostility are caused by something in another person that needs to be healed.

The cross liberates us from the necessity of "rising to the bait" and being hooked on a hurt feeling. We are freed to care more for reconciliation than being "right." The love of the cross alerts us to the need in the offender of our pride and focuses a new opportunity for ministry to them. That's the costly love of the cross!

What's troubling you? Tell Christ about it, ask for His perspective on the situation, confess your part of the difficulty, and surrender the hurt to Him.

Christ's pity overcomes the need for self-pity.

A Calvary Within Calvary

Galatians 2:1-21

*I have been crucified with Christ; it is no longer I who live, but
Christ lives in me; and the life which I now live in the flesh I live by
faith in the Son of God, who loved me and gave Himself for me.*

(GALATIANS 2:20)

We all have a tiny calvary within Christ's Calvary.

Paul said, "I have been crucified with Christ; it is no longer I
who live, but Christ lives in me." The Christian life begins with
crucifixion—our own. Becoming a Christian means a deathlike
surrender of our life to Christ. We die to our own rights, control
of our life, and plans for our future. We will to be willing to receive,
do, go, stay, speak, and serve as He wills. Christ then comes to live
within us to express His loving mercy for others through us.

The cross becomes the basis of our relationships. Our time,
energy, resources, and skill are put at Christ's disposal for others.
We forgive because we have been forgiven. People do not need
to measure up any more than we had to measure up in order for
Christ to love us. We take on the troubles, frustrations, and problems of others as Christ took the cross. We find our new purpose
in discovering ways of communicating the power of Christ to
solve their problems. Because we have died to self, we have nothing to lose and everything to give.

The cross is the meaning and motivation of great living.

Today's Cross

Luke 9:23-27

*Whoever desires to save his life will lose it, but
whoever loses his life for My sake will save it.*
(LUKE 9:24)

Our commitment to follow the Master is once and for all, but also
daily in all. We are challenged to love Christ with obedience. Luther said, "He who believes obeys; He who obeys believes." The
Christian life is not conservation of self-interest but abandonment—adventure, not acquisitiveness. That demand is so challenging that it has to be acted on daily in every relationship and
responsibility. Then we are free to give ourselves away to our Lord,
to people, and to situations of need.

There will be a cross in every relationship and responsibility
we encounter today. At the heart of each situation is a point of
surrender to seek first the Lord's will. There will be people to be
loved and forgiven. Most of all, there will be a constant flow of
opportunities to care for them as if caring for our Lord. Samuel
Rutherford said, "If you take your cross and carry it lovingly, it
will become to you like wings to a bird and sails to a ship."

The only question is, "Lord, what do You want me to do?"

A Daily Cross of Forgiveness

Nehemiah 9:17; Matthew 10:38-40; 27:32;
Luke 9:23

*He said to them all, "If anyone desires to come after Me, let him
deny himself, and take up his cross daily, and follow Me."*
(LUKE 9:23)

The cross was an ignominious symbol of punishment and execution. Jesus knew His life would end on a cross. And yet He told
His disciples that they also would have to take up their crosses.
Often the meaning of the admonition is diluted into general discipleship or into some disability we must bear or problem we must
endure. But remember, the Lord said "daily." We can understand
and accept *our* cross only if we accept the essential meaning of *His*
cross. In His cross He suffered for the sins of the whole world so
that humankind might be forgiven. Our cross, then, is forgiving
and forgetting what people have been and done.

Our cross is not simply some physical, emotional, or circumstantial burden we must carry. Our cross is *people*—persons who
need our forgiveness. To be a follower of Jesus may mean a mar-
tyr's death, but right now it means taking up a cross of forgiveness.
That must be spelled out in words and reconciling action, regardless of the cost to our pride or what we think are our rights.

My cross is to forgive as Christ has forgiven me.

We Can Never Say It All

John 21:24-25

*There are also many other things that Jesus did, which if they
were written one by one, I suppose that even the world itself
could not contain the books that would be written. Amen.*
(JOHN 21:25)

Whatever we say, there is still something we have left out. No insight, theory, theological viewpoint, isolated scripture, or idea captures all the dimensions of the magnificent truth revealed in the cross. It is like a diamond held aloft. As you turn it, light flashes from its many facets. That is what we must do with the cross: turn it over in our minds and hearts and allow the many-sided truth to penetrate our thinking and character. No single doctrine of the cross is sufficient to hold all the truth.

Paul felt the wonder: "God forbid that I should glory, save in the cross" (KJV). We glory in the cross when we grapple with what it means to us—our needs, our failures, our hopes, our dreams. What difference does it make to you that Christ was crucified?

How would you put into words what the cross means to you? Write out a brief paragraph saying what you think and feel is the meaning of the cross. Then consider how you would express that to someone who needs Christ.

*Whatever we say about the cross, our words can
never express all that there is to say.*

Where Are the Figs?

Mark 11:12-14

Jesus said to it, "Let no one eat fruit from you ever again."
(MARK 11:14)

Why the great consternation over a fig tree that has no figs? Two things must be kept in mind. Mark says that Jesus found nothing but leaves on the fig tree. Leaves on a fig tree never precede the fruitage of figs. They sometimes accompany, but usually follow the fruit. Jesus, seeing the leaves, would expect to find figs. The other unusual circumstance was that the time of the year for figs was late in May or early June. Passover week was sometime between the last of March and the middle of April. It was most unusual for this fig tree to be in the leaf stage at the time of Passover.

The issue for Jesus was that the tree had leaves, but no fruit. All the life of the tree had run to the leaf. That's the reason for the consternation: The leafy tree represented pretentious people who were religious but did not really know God. It happens. It is possible for a person, a church, to be all outward leaf but have no fruit. What would you say are the figs of fruitfulness Christ expects from you and me today? Make a list and see how you did by the end of the day!

The Lord has blessed us so we could
be a part of His blessing of others.

Unbinding People

John 11:28-57

Jesus said to them, "Loose him, and let him go."
(John 11:44)

This passage is filled with liberating truth. Christ raised Lazarus from the dead as His greatest physical miracle. It was a prelude to the time in which He, as resurrected Lord, would raise the dead among the living—people like you and me, those who are alive but dead to what life was meant to be. Put your name in the verse: "_____, come forth." Come alive and live forever!

But there is another miracle here in this passage. Jesus commanded the people to unbind Lazarus and let him go. He was out of the tomb but bound by graveclothes. Again, like so many of us and our friends, we are out of the tomb through belief in Christ, but are not yet see free to live life to the fullest. Note that Jesus did not unwind the graveclothes. He commanded the people to do that. The same is true today. We are to be the people who unbind others from the graveclothes of fear, sick memories, caution, and reservation. How can we do that? By showing them what it means to be free ourselves and then enabling them by listening, loving, and praying for and with them.

The ministry of every Christian is to unbind people in Christ's name.

The Password to Power

Mark 11:1-10

If anyone says to you, "Why are you doing this?" say, "The Lord has need of it," and immediately he will send it here.
(MARK 11:3)

When the disciples were sent into Bethany to get a donkey, the password was "The Lord has need of it." That's all they needed to say. There obviously had been advance planning. A colt had been arranged for and placed at a strategic spot, and a password had been worked out in case of difficulty. The owners of the colt refused to let it go until the magic words were spoken. The underground network of Jesus' followers knew the password.

What a tremendous password of power this should be for us today! As we prepare for Palm Sunday and Easter, Christians should be ready to release anything they have or are when this password is given. "The Lord has need of it" is all we should need to know as we minister to each other in the church and together in the world.

Listen for the password today, and give Jesus Christ control of everything.

The password for Christians is "The Lord has need of it." That should be all we need to know in our lives and giving.

Nothing to Lose and
Everything to Give

John 13:3-11

*After that, He poured water into a basin and
began to wash the disciples' feet.*
(John 13:5)

Someone was missing. When the disciples entered the upper room to celebrate the Passover Feast with Jesus, they whispered to each other, "Where is the servant? Who will wash our feet?"

Tradition has it that the Passover meal was observed by Jesus and the disciples in the home of the mother of Mark. Why had he overlooked this expression of hospitality? The disciples felt uncomfortable all through the first portion of the meal. Should one of them offer to wash the others' feet? The thought was dismissed as beneath them. No wonder they were shocked when the Master got up from the meal, took a towel and wash basin, and began to wash their feet! How can this be? They should be washing His feet!

Then Jesus underlined the lesson: "If I then, your Lord and teacher, have washed your feet, you also ought to wash one another's feet." That means more than water and a towel. Serving one another means really caring, lifting burdens, standing with each other in difficulties, and doing the forgiving, reconciling things regardless of cost to us.

Whose feet do you need to wash today?

Save Now!

Mark 11:9-10; John 5:1-18

*Blessed is the Kingdom of our father David that comes
in the name of the Lord! Hosanna in the highest!*
(MARK 11:10)

Hosanna! This is a very interesting word. It is a word of exclaimed supplication. It really means "Save now!" It was used by Jesus' followers and the crowds of pilgrims as a prayer to God to accomplish the expected salvation through the Messiah. For them this meant release from Rome and power for Israel among the nations. But God had a deeper salvation in mind than the release from political bondage or protection in battle. God would answer their "Hosannas," but in His own way: with the cross.

The salvation God provided would meet our deepest need. The death of Jesus on the cross was for the forgiveness of the sins of the whole world. Sin means separation, missing the mark. On the cross, the love expressed in both judgment and forgiveness was exposed. God did not change His mind about man's sin on the cross, He revealed what His mind had been all along. There was a cross in the mind of God long before there was a cross on Calvary. And there is forgiveness and salvation in that cross for you and me today.

Help always is just a Hosanna away.

When God Cried

Luke 19:28-44

As He drew near, He saw the city and wept over it.
(LUKE 19:41)

What a mixture of emotions there was on the day of the triumphal entry of Jesus into Jerusalem! The Passover crowds viewed Jesus as a conquering Messiah.

No wonder Jesus wept. The people had the wrong idea of the Messiah. Had they not heard all that He had said about who He was and what He had come to do? "Save now!" Yes, He would save, but in a much more ultimate sense. The people misunderstood Him because they had not listened; the leaders of Israel were plotting His demise as the parade passed by because they had heard all too well.

When we empathize with what was going on inside Jesus as He rode in that parade observing the crowd—the mixed motives, the expectations, the hatred—we can understand why His heart broke open with sobs of anguish. But remember who He was…and is! He was none other than God with us. It was God who cried that day. What He said as He sobbed tells us why. The people did not know the things that belonged to their true peace. They were missing the time of God's visitation.

What in my life makes God cry?

You Bet Your Life

John 12:20-26

Most assuredly, I say to you, unless a grain of wheat falls into the ground and dies, it remains alone; but if it dies, it produces much grain.
(JOHN 12:24)

In my early years at college, I worked as a part-time radio announcer to earn money to stay in school. The engineer who worked with me, named Lee, was an old radio man who had a saying that he used in response to most anything. Regardless of what you said, his response was, "You bet your life!"

During that time in my life I was seriously considering the Christian faith. A couple of friends who were winsome witnesses to Christ's love and forgiveness really had caught my attention. I began listening to what they had to say. One of my new Christian friends said, "Lloyd, you've got to bet your life. It's the only gamble in which you always win." I will never forget the night I did just that. I got down on my knees and surrendered my life to Christ. I have been collecting the abundant life ever since.

One of the first people I wanted to tell was Lee. "You know, Lee, how you always say, 'You bet your life'? I don't know what you mean when you say that, but let me tell you what it now means to me. Last night I bet my life on Christ!"

He was a gambler, too, my Christ. He took His life and threw it for a world redeemed.
—G.A. STUDDERT KENNEDY

Rejoice Greatly!

Zechariah 9:1-10; 12:1-10

*Rejoice greatly, O daughter of Zion! Shout in triumph, O
daughter of Jerusalem! Behold, your king is coming to
you; He is just and endowed with salvation, humble, and
mounted on a donkey, even on a colt, the foal of a donkey.*
(ZECHARIAH 9:9)

No prophet is more specific about the coming of the Messiah
than Zechariah.

The passages we read capture the meaning of Palm Sunday:
joyous celebration of the triumphal entry, but also the shadow of
the cross. Jesus entered Jerusalem with the shouts of Zechariah's
prediction of a king riding on a donkey's foal, but He knew what
was coming. He had also read Zechariah 12:10. We wonder how
He felt as He knew He would be the One who would be pierced,
and for whom His people would mourn.

Reading Zechariah helps us to grasp what our salvation cost
God. There was no other way. His gracious, forgiving love required it. He could not condone sin, and yet He had to break
its power over us. That's why Christ came and why the cross was
necessary. Only a cosmic atonement would do…for all people of
all time. For you and me!

We rejoice greatly because we are loved graciously.

The Scrutiny of Jesus

Mark 11:11

*Jesus went into Jerusalem and into the temple. So when He
had looked around at all things, as the hour was already
late, He went out to Bethany with the twelve.*
(MARK 11:11)

"And He looked around at everything." Jesus moved about the city
observing everything. He saw the Temple with its money chang-
ers, empty rites, and rituals. He saw the Roman legions tramp-
ing through the streets. He saw the placards of Roman emperor
worship. But most of all, He saw people: the expectant pilgrims,
the needy masses, the faithless multitudes. He cared most about
the people.

How would you like to have Jesus look around in the city
where you live? What would He see? Would He be pleased?
Would He say, "Now there is a city of God!"? What would He
think of your life? How would you like to have Him look around
your house, listen in on every conversation, be in on decisions of
what you do and spend? How would He get along in your church?
What would please Him? What would distress Him? There is
nothing hidden from those eyes! He sees everything and hears all.
Can we stand His scrutiny?

What would Christ drive out of our lives? Our churches? Our cities?

Paint Yourself into Calvary

Luke 23:44-49

*All His acquaintances, and the women who followed Him
from Galilee, stood at a distance, watching these things.*
(LUKE 23:49)

Careful observation of the crowd in Rembrandt's painting of the crucifixion reveals a dynamic discovery: The faces of the people are filled with pathos and wonderment. One of them is Rembrandt himself! He painted himself into the crucifixion.

Any meditation on the meaning of the cross requires that we take our place at the foot of the cross. When we get inside the skin of those who stood by watching while Jesus was crucified, we begin to capture what the cross meant. But we look at the cross through the lens of the open tomb and Pentecost. We know so much more than those who saw the anguish on Calvary. Now the living Christ comes to us to help us realize that what He did that day He does today for each of us. The same forgiving, reconciling love revealed on the historic cross is reproduced in each of us. By a special gift of faith given to each of us, we know that He died for us, that we are forgiven, that His death defeated our fear of death, and that because He lives we can live—now and forever.

Beneath the cross of Jesus I gladly take my stand.
—ELIZABETH C. CLEPHANE

Oh God, That Was My Cross

Matthew 27:15-26

Pilate said to them, "What then shall I do with Jesus who is called Christ?" They all said to him, "Let Him be crucified!"
(MATTHEW 27:22)

I have often wondered what happened to Barabbas after his release. What did he do while Jesus was being crucified? How did he feel? As an insurrectionist, he had been condemned to be crucified. Pilate's equivocation, and the manipulation of the crowds by the chief priests and the elders, had won him his freedom and Jesus' crucifixion.

Did Barabbas ever meet Jesus? We do not know. There are some who suggest that Jesus was incarcerated with him while Pilate pondered what to do to extricate himself from the dilemma the leaders of Israel had dealt him.

In my mind's eye I can see the panic on Barabbas's face when the earthquakes shook Jerusalem and rent the veil of the Temple. Did he stagger to Golgotha to see? If he did, he had to look in the Savior's face. I can hear him cry out the anguished confession, "Oh, God, that was my cross! And He took it for me!"

The cross was a substitutionary sacrifice. Christ died for our sins, in our place, taking our rap upon Himself. But instead of remorse like Barabbas's, we are filled with gratitude, praise, and love.

The Paradox of Power

Mark 15:25-32

The chief priests also, mocking among themselves with the
scribes, said, "He saved others; Himself He cannot save."
(MARK 15:31)

Little did the chief priests know that they declared the central paradox of spiritual power. They thought they had exposed Jesus. Instead, they expressed Jesus' deepest conviction about life. Of course, Jesus could have saved Himself. But He had come to save the world. He gave His life as a ransom for a sin-captivated, suffering world.

A paradox is two seemingly contradictory facts that must be kept together as inseparable parts of a basic truth. The chief priest's statement of paradox presented two aspects of the life that Christ lived and calls us to live. We are to spend ourselves on others and trust ourselves to Him.

This paradox of power is the secret of freedom. It is because the Lord has saved us that we don't have to try to save ourselves. We can become part of the Lord's strategy of saving others. We are released from the necessity of hoarding ourselves, our time, and our privacy. We have been blessed beyond measure in order to be a blessing. Our purpose is to give ourselves away in gracious caring and sharing.

We don't need to save ourselves. Christ already has done that!

Unqualified Love

Luke 23:32-37

Father, forgive them, for they do not know what they do.
(LUKE 23:34)

For whom did Jesus pray? Who was on His heart? Surely the soldiers who performed the execution of Christ on the cross did not know what they were doing.

What of Pilate and the Jewish leaders? Did they know what they were doing? Pilate suspected…his wife seemed to know and was afraid. Could ignorance be an excuse for the leaders of Israel? If they believed that Jesus was truly the Son of God, what would they have done? Ah, there's the rub! They would have had to renounce their pride and follow Him.

Was the prayer for the disciples and His followers? Some of them had fled. Judas betrayed Him; Peter denied Him. The others stood by helplessly in excruciating grief.

Jesus' prayer also was for you and me. We have no excuse. We know who He is and what He has done for us, and yet crucify Him anew many times each day. He prays that prayer for forgiveness anew in each situation, even when we know perfectly well what we are doing. The knowledge of His forgiveness before we ask frees us of the necessity of doing the very things for which we will need forgiveness.

Amazing love! We are forgiven before we ask. Knowing that, we will want to sin less and praise Christ more.

Paradise Is Now!

Luke 23:39-43

*Jesus said to him, "Assuredly, I say to you, today
you will be with Me in paradise."*
(LUKE 23:43)

The second word from the cross focuses on an old question, "What about deathbed conversion?"

It's never too late—neither in a crisis nor at the close of our life. It is not *when* but *whether* we believe that makes all the difference. We can say with Demas, who was crucified next to the Savior, "Jesus, remember me!"

It is never earned! This conversion account shows us that Demas did nothing to deserve or qualify for salvation. Those of us who still cherish the belief that our lives can be good enough to earn God's sanction and salvation need to ponder this event. "The just shall live by faith *alone!*"

It's now! If a person can know God's love at the midnight hour, and if this is the wondrous experience for which we were born, why wait? Why do we put off beginning life as it was meant to be? The other thief had said "No" for so long that he now could not say "Yes."

Paradise is for now! Heaven can begin now and physical death can have no power over us. "Whether I live or die, I am the Lord's."

Yes! Yes, Lord, yes!

A Gift to Each Other

John 19:25-27

He said to His mother, "Woman, behold your son!" Then
He said to the disciple, "Behold your mother!"
(JOHN 19:26-27)

When Jesus looked down from the cross, He saw His mother, Mary, and His cherished friend and follower, John. In a gesture of sublime love, He gave them to each other for mutual love and care. They were to be bound together in the divine bonds of love that would be the essence of the church. They were to care for each other as He had cared for each of them.

Note the differences in age, sex, personality, traits, and focus of interest. These were now superseded in a new quality of relationship. The things that naturally divide people—even culture, education, background, interests—need have little effect on Christian friendship.

Today Jesus gives us the people in our lives. Once we give them to Him in a releasing commitment, and let go of our self-willed control, He gives them back to us to be cared for and nurtured in His love. Who's at the foot of the cross with you? They are a gift. If you want to know Christ, you will find Him by serving them in His name.

Today I will "behold" each person in my life
as a trust from the crucified Lord.

The Depth of Love

Matthew 27:45-56

*About the ninth hour Jesus cried out with a loud
voice, saying, "Eli, Eli, lama sabachthani?" That is, "My
God, My God, why have You forsaken Me?"*
(MATTHEW 27:46)

The fourth word from the cross reveals the powerful truth that
Jesus really suffered. This was not a sham on the cross. Jesus died
there for the sins of the world as Son of Man for mankind. The
mystery of the incarnation can never be oversimplified by rejecting either Christ's divinity or His humanity. This word from the
cross stresses that, though divine, He plunged into the depths of
human suffering. Like all of us, He knew a time when He too
cried out for assurance in the midst of suffering.

Jesus was praying Psalm 22 (read the psalm as part of today
and tomorrow's devotion). He was reliving the anguish of the
psalmist, and He identified with the pain. But did He not also go
on to finish the triumphant note of that psalm? We are sure He
did. The subsequent words from the cross indicate that.

What does all this mean to us today? Just this: Jesus knows
what we go through in times of despair and loneliness. We can
pray to Him knowing that He will empathize and lead us out of
the valley to triumph.

*Christ has gone through the valley of death so He
can comfort us in our times of grief.*

To Quench Our Deepest Thirst

John 19:28

After this, Jesus, knowing that all things were now accomplished, that the Scripture might be fulfilled, said, "I thirst!"
(JOHN 19:28 NKJV)

This is a human, physical cry. Jesus was still repeating Psalm 22. This brought to mind His own burning thirst: "My tongue clings to My jaws." He knew deep physical pain and anguish. His thirst is indicative that the horrid stretching of the tissues of His body under the heat of the merciless Middle East sun was having its full effect. His cry of thirst was a cry for some physical relief in the midst of the suffering.

Jesus thirsted physically, not only to share our lot, but so that we might thirst much more profoundly. He had said that true joy would be found only by those who thirsted, expressed a dominant desire, for righteousness. Jesus alone can satisfy the spiritual thirst within us. Only fellowship with Him can quench our deep, inner needs for security, love, and purpose. On the cross Jesus thirsted for our thirst, yearned for our yearnings, and wanted us to want Him more than anything else.

Jesus thirsted so we may have our spiritual thirst quenched.

The Finish of the Beginning

John 19:30; 17:4-13; 6:38

*When Jesus had received the sour wine, He said, "It is
finished!" And bowing His head, He gave up His spirit.*
(JOHN 19:30)

What is finished? Jesus did not say "I am finished" but "It is finished." The work He had come to do was now complete, climaxed
in the cross. He had come to reveal God's love, to communicate
grace, to usher in the reality of the kingdom, and to set people
free from the power of sin and death. His work was done, and
yet it had only begun.

God had the final word. He took the finished work of Christ
as the basis of our salvation forever. When His incarnate work was
done, His eternal work continued. The resurrection was the next
episode in the drama of revelation of His purpose and plan.

Christ's work is not finished. It is to be done in and through
you and me today. When we finish to the best of our capacities
what God has given us to do, the resurrection of our frail efforts
is close at hand. He will take our human fumblings and use them
for His glory, making something glorious out of what we toiled
to make great.

When we feel finished, Christ has just begun.

Unreserved Trust

Luke 23:46; Psalm 31:5; 1 John 3:16;
1 Thessalonians 5:10

When Jesus had cried out with a loud voice, He
said, "Father, into Your hands I commit My spirit."
(LUKE 23:46)

The final word from the cross is a quotation from Psalm 31:5. It was as familiar to every Hebrew child in Jesus' time as the child's prayer "Now I lay me down to sleep" is in our time. At the final moment, Jesus remembers and prays this prayer of deep trust and relinquishment. His great sacrifice for the sin of the world was completed in unreserved trust.

However old we grow or wise we become, the heart of the dynamic life is in this prayer. Jesus' life had exemplified it at every turn. His times away for prayer and strength, His trust in God for each moment's decision, and His relinquishment in the Garden of Gethsemane were all expressions of the essence of this prayer. As He lived, so now He died. Jesus was not afraid; with childlike trust He affirmed the embrace of the everlasting arms of the Father.

This final prayer could mean the difference between frustration and victorious living for us today. If we could pray it without reservation, it would take the strain out of the duties, tasks, relationships, and worries we must go through today. God is in control. He is working His purposes out! Do you believe that for today?

Father, into Your hands I commit my life!

Putting Our Life on the Line

Mark 15:42-47

*Joseph of Arimathea, a prominent council member, who himself
was waiting for the kingdom of God, coming and taking
courage, went in to Pilate and asked for the body of Jesus.*
(MARK 15:43)

We admire Joseph of Arimathea's courage. He came forward
with costly courage and asked for the body of Jesus. His request
of Pilate clearly identified him as a follower and supporter of
Rome's executed criminal.

This man of position and power knew how to use influence
for the glory of God. Pilate could not take lightly this respected
member of the council of Jewish leaders. He had to listen and
comply with his request. The lovely thing that Joseph did will be
remembered forever, and his name will be spoken with respect
because of his love for Jesus.

Joseph challenges us to question how we use for the glory of
God the positive influence we have within our circle of friends
and the respect and honor that we have developed through the
years. These put us in crucial places where we can influence others for Christ. The world listens and cannot deny our authentic
witness. Joseph is conspicuous on the pages of history for the way
in which he used his position. How about you?

What influence do you have? How have you used your influence?

A Realistic Easter

1 Corinthians 15:1-19

*If Christ is not risen, your faith is futile; you are still in your sins! Then
also those who have fallen asleep in Christ have perished. If in this
life only we have hope in Christ, we are of all men the most pitiable.*
(1 CORINTHIANS 15:17-19)

Joyous Easter! Christ is risen! He can meet all our deepest needs
so that we can deal with our wants. We need to overcome our fear
of death so we can live life to the fullest. Without the resurrection,
faith would be empty, for Christ would have been defeated! The
cross would not be our assurance of forgiveness, and our hope of
eternal life would be lost.

Every need we have is met because Christ rose. A realistic
Easter is one in which we not only reflect on Jesus' resurrection,
but one in which we realize our own. Christ lived and died to
redeem us. He rose from the dead in defeat of death and to offer
us a deathless life. A personal relationship with Him offers us a
profound regeneration so that we can live a new life now as well
as forever. For resurrection living there is resurrection power and,
oh, the joy of living in each hour. All of life's an Eastertide for
those who in the living Christ abide!

*Because Christ defeated the power of death, all that our
physical death can do to us is release us to a fuller realization
of heaven that we have begun to experience now!*

Don't Be Afraid

1 Corinthians 15:21-49

The last enemy that will be destroyed is death.
(1 Corinthians 15:26)

On the cross, Jesus defeated the power of death to separate us from God. Fear of death is past.

Why then is death feared so much by Christians? Death is a transition in eternal life, not a tragedy of termination. How can we look at death as unanswered prayer? When we pray for a person's healing, and he or she dies, we feel that the worst has happened and that God did not hear our prayers.

We can't really live until we have faced our own death. Once that is behind us, we can live triumphantly. To die is gain, because we shall know the wonder of heaven, complete union with our Lord, and the fellowship of the saints. When we have come to grips with our death, then we can say, "Lord, I want to live however long You've planned, and when death comes, I'll not fear it any more than I fear going to sleep. And when I awake! Oh, that will be heaven!"

The resurrection that awaits us beyond physical death will be but the glorious consummation of the risen life which we already have in Christ.
—D.T. Niles

Making It Out Alive

1 Corinthians 15:50-58

*The sting of death is sin, and the strength of sin is the law. But thanks
be to God, who gives us the victory through our Lord Jesus Christ.*
(1 Corinthians 15:56-57)

The words printed boldly on a billboard advertising a new movie
invaded the privacy of the inner soul. They tore the carefully woven
fabric of repression separating conscious fears from deeper
anxiety. The words were: "Imagine your worst fear a reality."

Into each of our minds marches a fiendish procession of fears.
What is it for you—sickness, failure, loneliness, a loss of love or
a loved one? Whatever comes to mind, it is a manifestation of a
deeper fear, the one great fear—the fear of death and dying. And
yet, we can't really live until we face our own death. Mark Twain
said, "Don't take life so seriously; you'll never make it out alive."
Poor advice. We will make it out alive. We will all live beyond
death. The concern is where!

Death for Christians is the beginning of the next phase of our
eternal life begun here through a personal relationship with Jesus
Christ. Multiply the joy of knowing Christ now a billion times,
and we have some idea of what is ahead for us. The sting of death
has been removed. We are alive forever!

*Death is the last note of the overture to the opera
of life to be played out in heaven.*

A Transition in Living

Philippians 1:19-26

To me, to live is Christ, and to die is gain.
(PHILIPPIANS 1:21)

Most of us could say with Paul, "To me, to live is Christ," but many of us would find it difficult to say, "To die is gain." The words stick like a bone in our throats. This part of eternity, our life here, has become so important to us that we can't imagine dying being a gain. That's because we clutch living here so tightly and because we don't understand what is promised us in eternity.

I have discovered that people who live the abundant life fully now are those who are sure of heaven. When our destination is set, we are free from worry over the little disturbances of life now. Daily pressures and the frustration over things in this portion of eternal life fade into proper perspective when we know that we are on our way to heaven. God is more concerned about quality than quantity. It is not the length of our days but the depth of our lives that counts. The grave has no power over a Christian. Death is graduation.

When we look forward to heaven, life now becomes a heaven.

Between the Lightning and the Thunder

Mark 16:9-13

They went and told it to the rest,
but they did not believe them either.
(MARK 16:13)

What a different mood pervaded the upper room! Four nights earlier the disciples had gathered for the Passover feast with Jesus. Now they were back in the upper room again. But this time they had to face the cruel realities without Him. They had been through the tragedy of the crucifixion. Life had fallen apart for them. Then followed the loneliness of that dark Saturday while Jesus was in the tomb. Easter morning had brought the triumphant good news of the resurrection. But their emotions were ragged. They did not dare to believe it. Even the witness of some of their members, "We have seen the Lord!" didn't assure them. The reality of the resurrection was not yet the experience of their lives.

That's how we are until the resurrection becomes the central fact of life for us. We are afraid of life, what people do and say, and what the future will bring. We close the doors to opportunity because of fear and unbelief. That's just where many of us find ourselves. Christ is risen and He stands at the door knocking, waiting for us to invite Him into our lives.

Christ's victory can be ours!

Peace Be with You

Luke 24:36-39

Jesus himself stood in the midst of them, and
saith to them, "Peace be with you."
(LUKE 24:36 KJV)

The disciples had heard the greeting thousands of times before. They had used it themselves all through their lives. It was a normal, everyday greeting. But on that Easter night it was as if they had never heard it before. Now it was like a trumpet blast of hope and victory because of who said it and what it meant because of Him. Jesus entered the upper room and invaded the mood of gloom with the traditional, but now triumphant, "Peace be with you."

Jesus offered peace to replace their fear. He alone could bring peace to their troubled hearts. It is interesting to note that these first words spoken to His assembled disciples summarized what He had lived and died to make possible—peace.

What dominates your feelings—peace or fear? Has the peace of Christ, through forgiveness and love, invaded us to the point that the great fears of our life can be faced and healed? What makes us afraid? Christ stands beside you right now as you read this devotional. Do you dare to believe that? Can you hear Him speaking His words of greeting to you? Listen—"Peace be with you!"

I accept the gift of peace. Thank You, Lord!

An Open Door

2 Corinthians 2:12; Colossians 4:3; Acts 14:21;
John 20:26; Revelation 3:7-8

*Eight days later, his disciples were again in the house, and
Thomas was with them. The doors were shut, but Jesus came
and stood among them and said, "Peace be with you."*
(JOHN 20:26 RSV)

The doors were still shut. John keeps stressing this each time he
records a postresurrection encounter of Jesus with the disciples.
He comes to them, but they are behind tightly barred doors, still
afraid for their safety.

Their "closed-door" policy was symbolic of the condition of
their lives. They were not yet open to the challenges Christ had
given them and the power He would provide to help them respond courageously to the opportunity to join Him in changing
the world.

Christ has entrusted the keys for the opening of human lives
to His people. Just as He told Peter that the keys of the kingdom
were his, so too He tells us that these keys are ours to open the
doors of faith in the lives of unbelievers. The keys of listening in
love, sharing with honesty, bearing burdens without reservation,
communicating the gospel with clarity, and helping people begin
a life of faith—all these are entrusted keys in our hands. An awesome power has been given to us!

I open the door to Christ today.

Power to Match the Potential

John 20:19-23

Jesus said to them again, "Peace be with you. As
the Father has sent Me, even so I send you."
(JOHN 20:21 RSV)

Jesus deals with depression by giving a Great Commission. He took the discouraged disciples from frenzied fear to fearless courage.

It is an awesome challenge: "As the Father has sent Me, even so send I you." That means we are to be extensions of the incarnation, continuing the ministry He began as Jesus of Nazareth. The things He did, we are to do; the power He exposed, we are to experience; the victory He had over evil, we are to live victoriously.

The Great Commission was followed by the promise of an amazing power. Jesus said, "Receive the Holy Spirit." That's the answer to the riddle of our inadequacy. The Spirit is the inner driving power of love from within us. Jesus does not give us tasks to do greater than the power to do them that He provides in the Holy Spirit.

This is our source of courage. We do not need to apologize or equivocate. We have a purpose now. He sends us into our homes, places of work, the community, as His people—extensions of His love and power.

I will greet this day with purpose and power!

Are You Surprisable?

John 20:19-20

Jesus came and stood among them, and said
to them, "Peace be with you."
(JOHN 20:19 RSV)

Surprisability. That's a great word to describe what life can be for the Christian. Jesus surprised the disciples in the upper room. Their conception of the future was locked in the tight compartments of their own preconceptions. They had figured things from a human point of view. They had not imagined that at any moment Christ would invade their gloom with hope. Then He came and the disciples were surprised. Why? He had told them He would come to them. He had promised He would be with them to show the way. They had not really believed it to be true. The scripture used for today captures their revived surprisability: "They were glad when they saw the Lord." Indeed!

To see the Lord! That's our great need, isn't it? Not in visions of grandeur or magnificent manifestations to see or touch, but in the power of His Spirit. He comes to us in people who incarnate His love for us, in amazing, unanticipated circumstances, in answers to questions that haunt us, in resolutions of problems that were declared unsolvable.

He comes! And we are surprised—and very glad!

Lord, keep me surprisable with Your innovating power.

Honest Doubt

John 11:1-16; 20:24-29

He said to Thomas, "Reach your finger here, and look at
My hands; and reach your hand here, and put it into My
side. Do not be unbelieving, but believing." And Thomas
answered and said to Him, "My Lord and my God!"

(JOHN 20:27-28)

The Thomas in me reaches out to the Thomas in you. Here he honestly faces the reality of what will surely happen to Jesus if He goes to Jerusalem. But Thomas was faithful. When he saw the Master could not be dissuaded, he was ready to go and die with Him. But at the time of the crucifixion, Thomas was not as courageous as his words had been. He fled. When the news reached him that Jesus had been raised, the discouraged man would not accept it. Christ had to come to the upper room just for Thomas. Then he knew it was true! Discouragement was turned to delight and determination by the power of the resurrected Lord.

Thomas was an honest man. He could not pretend. Christ can help that kind of honesty. Whenever we tell Him about what's going on inside us, the answer is perfectly timed. He honors realism and integrity. However far we've come in our faith, if we confess and ask Him to help us grow, He will increase our faith, deepen our wisdom for our intellectual uncertainties, and give us a vision for how He is working out His plan in our lives.

Christ has come to you now to overcome your doubt.

The Thomas Test

John 20:24-29

Unless I see in His hands the print of the nails, and put my finger into the print of the nails, and put my hand into His side, I will not believe.
(JOHN 20:25)

The account of Thomas reveals more than the struggle of a doubter to believe. It shows the persistence of Christ to penetrate the resistance barrier of human nature. In the story we are confronted with the amazing love of Christ. It's one thing to accept and love a person on your own standards; it's something altogether different to be willing to love on the person's demands. Thomas set up the rules. He would believe only if he was satisfied according to his own presuppositions.

Our first reaction would have been to say, "Listen, Thomas, who do you think you are, making a demand like that?" But not Jesus. He leaves Thomas alone for eight days—days of anguished doubt and question. When He returned He loved the depressed disciple enough to offer Himself unreservedly to him so that he might believe. He was deeply concerned about Thomas. If touching His nail-wounded hands and side would help him, He was ready and willing.

Thomas was overcome! He knew how much Jesus loved him. His response was one of overwhelming love and loyalty, and he cried out, "My Lord and my God!"

Not even our doubts can make Christ stop loving us!

Is It a Sin to Doubt?

James 1:1-8

*Let Him ask in faith, with no doubting, for he who doubts
is like a wave of the sea driven and tossed by the wind.*
(James 1:6)

Why is it so wrong to doubt? There are two kinds of doubt—one
that is a fixed position, and the other that is a creative sign of
growth. An atheist says that there is no God and is closed to any
possibility. A deist says that God exists but has no contact with
the world He has created. An agnostic says that he simply does
not know. In all three there is a solidified stance. That's the kind of
person James is talking about. They have refused the gift of faith.
His apt description fits millions of people today.

God wants to give us the gift of faith to know Him and the
gift of wisdom to understand His ways. As we grow in both gifts,
there will be constant questions. We can accept those doubts as
growing pains and ask God for His wisdom to move beyond our
present stage of intellectual growth. He is faithful to answer!

Doubt is sin when we refuse to be open to new discoveries.
God wants us to be intellectual adventurers. However much we
have grown, it's only a beginning. There's so much beyond our
own theories and rationality.

Give God your doubts. He will overcome them one by one.

When Doubt Turns to Negativism

Matthew 13:53-58

He did not do many mighty works there because of their unbelief.
(MATTHEW 13:58)

Doubt can be lack of trust. It can be a protective mechanism to cover our lack of faith, and it results in a negativism about ourselves and other people. Often we feel sorry for ourselves and blame the Lord for what has happened to us. Actually, our lives are the result of the values and ideas we have held about life. People have lived up to our worst picture of them. We doubt whether they will ever be different.

Actually, we are doubting that the Lord will make them different. This destructive doubt debilitates our ability to trust to Him the people and situations of our life, to expect and receive what He is able to do in His timing and according to His plan. Our doubts become a contagious virus of frustration to the people around us. The Lord can and will change that today if we are willing to let Him.

*Debilitating doubt results in negativism, but trust
in the Lord makes us positive people.*

The Soul's Invincible Surmise

Ephesians 4:17-24

*Put on the new man which was created according
to God, in righteousness and true holiness.*
(EPHESIANS 4:24)

Does everyone, even a mature Christian, have some doubts? Of course. If we think of doubts as the condition of a mind on the edge of discovery, then who hasn't some doubt? The key word that described the response of the disciples and the crowds to Jesus was *astonishment.* It means "to be driven outside oneself." A mature Christian is constantly astonished by how great the Lord is and how shallow our own understanding and experience.

Our perspective is crucial. If we but dare to believe that the indwelling Christ is pressing us on to new discoveries, then we can befriend that attitude of doubt. We can say, "I am truly alive and on the move!" We will have what George Santayana called the trust of the soul's invincible surmise.

*The test of a mature Christian is that he can look back
and see how effectively Christ has moved her or him from
uncertainty to growing assurance and conviction.*

How to Handle Failure

Mark 14:66-72

*A second time the rooster crowed. Then Peter called to mind the
word that Jesus said to him, "Before the rooster crows twice, you will
deny Me three times." And when he thought about it, he wept.*
(MARK 14:72)

It is interesting to note the different ways in which Judas and Peter
dealt with failure. They both denied their Lord and betrayed Him
before others. Judas sold Him to the priests; Peter refused to acknowledge that he knew Him when asked in the courtyard while
Jesus was being tried. Defection was in both of them.

But how differently they dealt with it! Judas could not handle
his failure and hung himself; Peter broke down and wept. Judas
took his punishment into his own hands; Peter eventually trusted
Christ to forgive. One man ended his life, the other came to the
end of an old life and began a new life.

How do you deal with failure? Self-condemnation? Many
people hang themselves inch by inch with self-remorse that grows
into self-hatred. "Why did I do that!" "How could I have ever said
that!" We judge ourselves as ineffective and useless. Others, however, are finding what Peter found. Our failures are only a prelude
to deeper realization of Christ's love and enabling power. Forgiveness and change are but a prayer away from any of us!

Christ is listening right now. What do you need to tell Him?

Easter People All Through the Year

John 21:1-14

This is now the third time Jesus showed Himself to His disciples after He was raised from the dead.
(JOHN 21:14)

It is fascinating to reflect on why Jesus had instructed His disciples to go back to Galilee, where He promised He would meet them. He knew they would have to experience the reality of the resurrection in familiar surroundings to know it was true. Just above the place where Jesus met His disciples for breakfast on the seashore is the Mount of Beatitude, where He gave the Sermon on the Mount. What Jesus taught there and lived out with His disciples during His ministry, they would now be called to live in the future. They needed to be as sure of His resurrected presence as their Master.

What the risen Lord put Peter through is what we all must go through in order to be Easter people all through the year. Peter needed forgiveness for betrayal, restitution to the reality of a loving relationship with the risen Lord, and an experience of total dependence on the power of the indwelling Spirit of Christ. For that, Christ had to reintroduce Peter to himself, his loyalty and love, and give him a reorienting commission He could do only by the power of the resurrection.

Christ introduces us to our real selves longing to love, serve, and follow Him.

A New Beginning

John 21:15-19

*Jesus said to Simon Peter, "Simon, son of Jonah, do you love
Me more than these?" He said to Him, "Yes, Lord; You know
that I love You." He said to him, "Feed my lambs."*
(JOHN 21:15)

Peter was ambitious. As the leading disciple, he had shifted the
focus of his achievement-oriented nature. But he persistently denied his inner person, and eventually denied his Lord. His denial
of the Lord was really a denial of the new person being formed in
him. It was that true inward person whom Christ came back to
Galilee to reclaim. He wanted the do-er to become a be-er.

Peter's problem was allowing the Lord to love him profoundly
so he could reclaim the essential fact that Christ and His love for
him were most important to him. That is why Christ asked him
three times "Do you love Me?"—so that Peter could be sure. He
needed to know once and for all that it was not what he did or
failed to do that was important, but rather that he was loved, forgiven, and cherished.

The experience of Peter's spiritual resurrection took place that
morning beside the sea he loved so much. Now he knew he loved
Christ most of all and was ready to enact resurrection living by
feeding Christ's sheep. We will spell out further tomorrow what
this means for our resurrection living.

Christ will never let us go!

Debilitating Comparisons

John 21:20-23

Peter, seeing Him, said to Jesus, "But Lord, what about this man?"
(JOHN 21:21)

We blush with embarrassment. How like most of us Peter was. He wanted to evaluate John's assignment before he accepted his own. Would John be given a higher position, a better title, greater opportunities? How often we miss the sublime, unique calling that Christ gives to each of us by comparisons with others. How often the cultural standards of value in positions, power, salaries, size of office or home, and material possessions beguile us, and we are blinded, unable to see what has been entrusted to us.

Comparisons lead us to competition; competition leads to consternation. We muddle and then meddle with others and their lives. And the Master says, "Claim what I've given to you; assume the calling I've given you, and get moving. Never mind what I'm giving to or doing with others. You follow Me!" That will keep us so busy that there will be little time for evaluating how other people are following the Lord.

Comparisons are a denial of the once, never-
to-be-repeated miracle each of us is!

The Fellowship of the Flaming Heart

Luke 24:13-35

*Did not our heart burn within us while He talked with us
on the road, and while He opened the Scriptures to us?*
(LUKE 24:32)

Life has a way of dampening the fires of excitement and enthusiasm for living. We burn down as our energies are sapped, our reserves are depleted, and our hopes smolder. People pressures get us down; problems pile up; worries and anxieties pour cold water on the previously blazing coals. And yet, as Christians we are meant to be part of what Calvin called the "fellowship of the burning heart."

When Jesus came to the men on the road to Emmaus, He taught them from the Scriptures who He was. We can imagine how exciting it must have been to be led in a Bible study by the Lord Himself! He showed the discouraged disciples that He was the sacrificial lamb, the scapegoat, the atonement for sins. Then He guided them through the prophets, underlining for emphasis all the references to Him. It was then that the cross and Christ's resurrection became real. Later, when He broke bread in their home, they knew it was the Lord. He set a fire burning in their hearts. What happened to these men can happen to you and me today.

*Christ billows the red ember in the white ash
in our hearts and sets us aflame.*

In the Palm of His Power

Revelation 2:1

*To the angel of the church of Ephesus write, "These things
says He who holds the seven stars in His right hand, who
walks in the midst of the seven golden lampstands."*
(REVELATION 2:1)

"He's got the whole world in His hand." The spiritual goes on enumerating the situations and people that Christ has in His hand.

This is the picture of the Living Christ that John presents in our scripture. The seven candlesticks represent the seven churches to which the letters of revelation are being sent. The Greek verb "to hold" is *kratein,* which is usually followed by a genitive of what is held. It normally means that we take hold of a part of an object. When, however, the verb takes an accusative, as in this verse, it means to hold the whole of an object within one's hand.

Christ will not let us go; He is with us; He holds all of our situations and problems in the palm of His concern. He will give us the power and insight we need for today. If we ask Him, He will give us His *perspective* on our needs and His *partnership* in facing and conquering our problems, however impossible they may appear. Trust yourself and all of your cares and concerns to Christ's strong, capable hands.

I have a great need for Christ. I have a great Christ for my need.
—CHARLES H. SPURGEON

Christ Sees Beneath the Surface

Revelation 2:2

*I know your works, your labor, your patience, and that you
cannot bear those who are evil. And you have tested those who
say they are apostles and are not, and have found them liars.*
(Revelation 2:2)

Jesus Christ knows! That is both a comfort and a challenge. We are
comforted that He knows everything beneath the highly polished
surface of our lives that we show to others. He understands the
true motives and purposes that guide our lives. He sympathizes
with the limiting difficulties within us that hinder and debilitate.
He knows what we have been through. What others cannot appreciate, He knows and appreciates. This is a comfort when we
are misunderstood or unappreciated by those around us. But this
is also a challenge. There is no place to hide! Jesus' X-ray vision of
us penetrates and sees beneath our external front.

Jesus could see the patient endurance of the Ephesians, their
faithful exposure of heresies, and their unwearying work for the
cause of right. But He could also see they had lost the joy of
their relationship with Him and were trying to live by their own
resources. Let's begin anew with Him today and allow Him to
change our inner motives and values, which will produce a fresh
and vital exterior for others to see.

*Jesus Christ sees beneath the surface of our lives
and changes us from the inside out.*

The Need to Fall in Love Again

Revelation 2:4-5

Nevertheless I have this against you, that you have left your first love.
(REVELATION 2:4)

Do you remember your first love? **Do you remember the joy, the excitement, the thrill, the fulfillment, the sheer fun of being in love?**

Jesus uses this delightful human experience to help the Ephesians remember what it was like when they first knew of His love for them. When they learned of the grace and forgiveness, the plan and purpose, the power and strength, the hope and the victory of Jesus Christ, they had come alive with a new joy and excitement.

But something had happened. They had become dutiful and drab as the years had gone by. They had lost the wonder of knowing and loving Jesus. Now they were so busy living out the Christian life that they had lost that personal relationship with Him that makes the life of a Christian powerful and exciting. They had taken Christ for granted and had failed to have time with Him; they had worked *for* Him and not *with* Him, and now they were anxious and strained. Jesus asks them to remember and rediscover the joy of when He first loved them and they responded. He wants the same for us today.

Loving Christ is the passion and purpose of our lives.

Turn Around!

Revelation 2:5-6

*Remember therefore from where you have fallen; repent and
do the first works, or else I will come to you quickly and
remove your lampstand from its place—unless you repent.*
(Revelation 2:5)

The Christian life is dynamic, not static. Unless we continue to
grow in Christ, we will stagnate in immature piety. The painful truth of our scripture today is that the privilege can be taken
from us if we do not use it for God's glory, concern for people,
and service in society.

What can we do? Jesus prescribes repentance. This word conjures up many false images of tears and emotional remorse. For
the prophets and for Jesus, it meant turning around and beginning again in a new direction. If the drift of our life has been
increasingly away from Him and costly obedience to Him, then
today is the day to turn around, and we will find Him there waiting with forgiveness and a new chance. He will refresh us with
His love and send us on a new life of faithfulness to Him where
we live and work.

*Remember today what it was like when you first knew that Christ
loved you and had a plan and purpose for your life! Then turn
around and go back to Him. He is waiting with outstretched arms.*

Fruit from the Tree of Life

Genesis 2:16-17; Revelation 2:7;
Romans 8:18-24

*He who has an ear, let him hear what the Spirit says to the
churches. To him who overcomes I will give to eat of the tree
of life, which is in the midst of the Paradise of God.*
(REVELATION 2:7)

The rabbis taught that there would be a tree of life in the middle of
heaven. It was a tree symbolizing immortality and all the fruit of
eternal life with God. Unencumbered by the limitation of physical life, the joys and delights of fellowship with God would be
given without limit.

Jesus tells the Ephesians that this will be their reward if they
endure and conquer. All the trial and tragedy of their present life
would be rewarded if they remained faithful. This promise is for
us too. We are alive in eternity now. Death is not an ending, but
a triumphant transition. If we know, love, and serve the Lord now,
we will be given a taste of heaven now in friendship and fellowship with Him today and forever. Whatever trials we have faced,
whatever difficulties we are going through, they are "not worthy
to be compared with the glory which shall be revealed."

Christ is with me in any trial that may come today.

All or Not at All

Revelation 2:8-9

*To the angel of the church in Smyrna write, "These things says
the First and the Last, who was dead, and came to life."*
(REVELATION 2:8-9)

Smyrna was a city of syncretism. Here in this beautiful city of
Roman glory a person could exist with whatever private belief
he wished. All the Christians had to do was to burn a pinch of
incense, say "Caesar is Lord," receive their certificate, and go off
to worship as they pleased. In Smyrna there seemed to be no
alternative. In AD 26 the Romans erected a temple to Tiberius,
but the Christians would not conform. They refused to worship
Caesar as lord. And so history records some of the most terrible
persecution of the early church at Smyrna. Nowhere was it more
dangerous to be a Christian.

How easy it is for us to worship more than one Lord! The di-
minutive gods of materialism, professionalism, popularity, safety,
another person, our heritage, or our potential future are some of
the gods we call "Lord." Who—or what—is a competing lord of
your life? Anyone who says, "Jesus Christ is Lord" must eventually allow Him to be Lord of *all* of life.

*Christ is all or not at all! He is the One on whom we
depend, the One from whom we receive power, and
the One who requires our ultimate allegiance.*

Beyond the Breaking Point

Revelation 2:9; John 16:33

I know your works, tribulation,
and poverty (but you are rich).
(Revelation 2:9)

"In the world you will have **tribulation.**" Jesus never fools us about that. He has told us plainly. The Greek word for *tribulation* means "pressure" or "rubbing raw." We know what He means. The pressures of material circumstances, opposition, antagonism, and persecution are known by anyone who dares to be sensitive and to stand for anything worthwhile. Sometimes, though, life is too much and we cannot stand the strain. But we were never meant to take the pressure alone.

Note the parenthesis of power in today's scripture. Jesus tells the troubled, persecuted Christians that He knows their tribulation and poverty. Then in the parentheses are the words that make all the difference. They were indeed rich! They were rich beyond human standards and values. Their riches were in Him, in His love and power, and in their calling, election, and status with God as His beloved people. And so are we!

When Christ lives in us we need not break.

In Christ we can pass the breaking point and not break.

Praise and Not Presumption

Revelation 2:10

Be faithful until death, and I will give you the crown of life.
(Revelation 2:10)

The life, message, and martyrdom of Polycarp, the bishop of Smyrna, helps us to focus the meaning of Jesus' message to the church there. He would not join the Caesar worship, and he instructed the Christians to be faithful to Jesus Christ as Lord. Finally his witness cost him his life. On an excited, festal day the frenzied mobs were in an inflammable state. They gave Polycarp a choice: worship Caesar as a god or die.

Polycarp's answer has become immortal: "Eighty-six years have I served Christ, and He has never done me wrong. How can I blaspheme my King who saved me?" The people were enraged and gathered the fuel for the fire to burn him at the stake. As the flames devoured his body, he prayed a great prayer: "I thank Thee that Thou hast graciously thought me worthy of this day and of this hour, that I may receive a portion in the number of the martyrs, in the cup of Thy Christ." And so, Jesus praised the faithfulness of His people at Smyrna.

We are the recipients of a great heritage. The faith we often take for granted has been defended at great cost. We are fortunate to have freedom of worship in which we can openly follow Christ.

We dare not take our faith for granted. It should spur us
on to faithfulness and obedience to Christ today.

The Alpha and Omega

Revelation 1:9-20

I am the Alpha and the Omega, the First and the Last.
(REVELATION 1:11)

In the context of what we have learned about the difficulties of being a Christian at Smyrna, we can see why Jesus used the self-description "the First and the Last, who died and came to life."

Only One who was Lord of history could help the Christians at Smyrna. The One who was the Source and End of all could give perspective to their troubled lives. His message and life were living power for conflict.

The most triumphant, fear-dispelling fact about Him for the Christians at Smyrna was that He was the One who died and came to life. The resurrection was not just an event in history; it was the answer to the riddle of history: "Because I live, you will live also." This gave them hope for every day, and the last day in death.

Be very clear about who Jesus Christ is for you! Is He the living, resurrected Lord? If so, He is a present Lord who offers us resurrected life for today as well as the hope of eternal life.

*The One who chose and called us, who sustains and strengthens
us, is the One who is utterly reliable for life's problems.*

Given Away to Serve

2 Timothy 1:3-7

*…When I call to remembrance the unfeigned faith that is in
you, which dwelt first in your grandmother Lois and your
mother Eunice, and I am persuaded is in you also.*
(2 Timothy 1:5)

About this time in May each year we celebrate Mother's Day. Some
years ago I had an experience I will never forget. I had just finished
preaching in the church where I began my ministry. It was a time
for memories and reflection.

Suddenly I was face-to-face with a gracious, radiant woman
in her early seventies. She had tears of joy in her eyes, and some-
how a handshake was not enough for us. She embraced me and
drew me close. Then she kissed me and whispered in my ear, "Pay
no attention to me. You belong to these people tonight." She was
Kathryn Ogilvie, my mother!

She had come to attend the service from a nearby community
that had been my hometown. The memory of the visit has lin-
gered pleasantly, but her words to me in the crowd have persisted
for deep thought and reflection. The true meaning of Christian
motherhood was affirmed. She proclaimed the true essence of
Jesus' message about the special calling of mothers to prepare their
children for service, and then give them away to follow Him.

No man is poor who has had a godly mother.
—Abraham Lincoln

Never to Die

Revelation 2:11; Romans 6:1-5;
Romans 8:38-39

He who overcomes shall not be hurt by the second death.
(Revelation 2:11)

A Christian is one who lives each day with the knowledge that there is nothing that can separate him or her from the love of God.

Christians are twice-born men and women. They have had both physical and spiritual birth. Fellowship with Christ ushers us into a dimension of life that is life abundant. Nothing can destroy this spiritual vitality that lives within our frail physical bodies. Just as surely as Christ was raised from the dead, so too will we be raised up for eternal fellowship in heaven.

The term *second death* was a rabbinical Hebraism often used at that time. It meant the total extinction of the wicked. Christ turns a negative condemnation into a positive confirmation. His promise is that there is no second death for those who are twice born. We die to ourselves when we turn our lives over to Him and He comes to live in us. Only those who do not know Christ die, never to live again. For a Christian, fear of death is past.

A Christian is a twice-born miracle.

The Four "C's" of Communicating with the Lord

Revelation 2:12-17

These things says He who has the sharp two-edged sword.
(REVELATION 2:12 NKJV)

The letters to the churches in Asia Minor show us the way Christ deals with individuals and churches. There is a *confirmation* of an aspect of His nature that specifically meets our particular need. This is followed by *commendation* for our strengths and progress. This gives us an assurance of His love and affirmation of our efforts to be faithful and obedient in our discipleship. With that, we are ready to hear any creative *confrontation* of things in our lives that need to be changed. After that, we desperately need His *comfort*. He tells us what He will do to help us change what He has exposed.

Look at how this is exemplified in the letter to the church at Pergamos, the capital city of the Roman province of Asia. Christ had to condemn the fact that some in the church had blended their belief in Him with the sins of idolatry and immorality.

Christ calls us to impeccable moral integrity as an outward expression of an inner experience of His love. The comfort He offers us is a "hidden manna," which, as during the exodus of the Israelites in the wilderness, will give us daily strength from His Spirit.

The world longs to see Christians with moral integrity.

The Dearest Idol

1 John 5:19-21

Little children, keep yourselves from idols. Amen.
(1 John 5:21)

This final sentence in John's epistle was written to Christians. The apostle's admonition carries the same impact as Jesus' word to the Christians at Pergamos. They were tempted to worship all kinds of idols.

How about us today? What are the idols that beguile us in our society? What purpose, passion, person, position, place, or possession could have the power to demand our attention and adoration? Can we sing these words with William Cowper? "The dearest idol I have known, whate'er that idol be, help me to tear it from Thy throne, and worship only Thee." Our heart is a throne. Who or what reigns there? It is possible to say we believe in Christ and have something or someone else on the throne of our hearts.

The most exciting thing I see happening today among Christians is that a growing number are discovering the freedom and joy of committing the throne of their hearts to Christ. Many have been in the church for years, but suddenly realize their purpose and passion has been some idol that they have subtly syncretized with Christ. An unconditional commitment to Christ opens the floodgates for His power and love to flow into the emptiness. What about you?

An idol is any thing or person that pre-empts Christ's place in our hearts.

Follow As They Follow Christ

Revelation 2:18-20

Nevertheless I have a few things against you.
(REVELATION 2:20)

In the letter to Thyatira the name "Jezebel" stands out. The term had tragic connotations for the Christians. They knew that Jezebel had been the daughter of the king of Sidon and the wife of King Ahab of Israel. Her sin was that she had brought her own gods and goddesses, such as Baal and Astarte, and had introduced them into Israel's worship. Eventually she forced pagan rituals on Ahab's kingdom. Her name was synonymous with an evil that had plagued God's people through the years.

Jesus clearly identified one of the leading women in the church of Thyatira as a Jezebel. She had preached Christ but had led the church into the pagan guilds, where idols were worshiped and where despicable, immoral acts were condoned and encouraged. She was a prophetess who had nearly destroyed the church.

How easily the church can drift from its sole purpose and end up resisting Christ rather than preaching Christ! When we read Christian history we can see the Jezebels of both sexes who have led the church into compromise with evil. Look at the Middle Ages, or at Hitler's Germany, or at some churches in our own time.

Judgment begins with the household of God.
—1 PETER 4:17

Creative and Destructive Compromise

Revelation 2:25-27

Hold fast what you have till I come.
(REVELATION 2:25)

One of the most persistent problems of living the Christian life is compromise. The heart of the problem is to discover the difference between creative and destructive compromise. In one sense, we are free to compromise to achieve authentic unity. But the Christian is also freed from destructive compromise. He is able to seek what Christ's will is and be strong in his convictions.

In order to subsist, the Christians at Thyatira had to join the trade guilds that dealt in the wool and dyeing industry for which Thyatira was famous. But the guilds required participation in pagan religion. Their meetings began and ended in sacrifices, and in between they were filled with sexual immorality. Could a Christian participate? Many had done so, and this is the content of the challenge Jesus addressed to them. The Christians had gone too far. Their compromise was destructive to their relationship with Christ.

Consider your opportunities today: in which does Christ call you to compromise, and in which does He offer you power not to compromise?

Christ will be with you all day along the way,
to guide what you do and say.

How Churches Die

Revelation 3:1

You have a name that you are alive, and yet you are dead.
(REVELATION 3:1)

There are few criticisms of a church that would be more cutting than to say it had the reputation for being alive but was actually dead. Yet this is exactly what Christ has to say to the Sardis church. It was known for its life, but He said that it was dead. Though it had prosperity, it was dead in what really mattered. Materially there was life, but spiritually it was dead. What did He mean? When is a church dead?

First, when it worships the past. Memories are comforting and reassuring, but not always stimulating. The Sardis church was resting on its reputation. Also, a church is dead when it loves success more than Christ. The church is to be light, salt, and leaven in the world. It must do what Christ demands, not what society decides. The church at Sardis tolerated Sardis; it did not transform it. Further, a church is dead when its members are dead. A church is raised from the dead when religious people who do not know Christ trust themselves completely to Him and receive His living Spirit.

Jesus challenged the church at Sardis to wake up and strengthen what was on the point of death. A lethargic church is never acceptable to Christ.

What would Christ say about your church?

As Strong as the Weakest Point

Revelation 3:2-3

Be watchful, and strengthen the things which remain.
(REVELATION 3:2)

Sardis had been regarded as impregnable. Behind her was Mount Truolus. There was a narrow ridge of rock that went out from that mountain like a pier, and it was on that ridge that the citadel of Sardis was built. It defied assault. When Cyrus wished to capture Sardis, he offered a special reward to the man who could work out a method of scaling the unscalable cliff so the fortress could be taken.

A Mardian soldier named Hyeroeades saw a Lydian soldier pick his way down the cliff to recover his helmet, which he had dropped, and then climb back. Hyeroeades marked the way the soldier had taken. Later at night, he led a picked band of men up the cliff, and when they reached the top, they found the defenders completely unprepared, and they took the city. The warning "Watch! Stay awake!" was particularly significant to Sardis.

Churches, like people, have weak points from which the evil powers can divide and conquer. Fear of change, traditionalism, formalism, worship of leaders, indifference, self-satisfying safety, materialism—all these make easy points of entry for the enemy.

Watch!

The Need of Having No Need

Revelation 3:4-6

He who has an ear, let him hear what the Spirit says to the churches.
(REVELATION 3:6)

The church at Sardis thought it had no need. It was adequate, successful, and prosperous. The Christians were satisfied and pleased with themselves and their church. They had worked hard to build it up. There had been little resistance and no conflict. Now they settled back to enjoy being the church with their own select few whom they loved and who loved them. How delightful…and dangerous!

Strange, isn't it: We work hard to plan and provide for a comfortable life. We use our energies and skills to get life to a place where it is controllable and tolerable. We want to be responsible for ourselves and those we love. But in so doing we engineer ourselves out of a place of receiving grace. The result of our own careful management is often that we take control and no longer think we need Christ!

If we arrive at where we are headed, where will we be?
If we achieve our goals, what will we have?
If we accomplish our purpose, will it be God's best for our lives?

Opportunities Unlimited

Revelation 3:8

See, I have set before you an open door.
(Revelation 3:8)

Philadelphia had one of the most strategic sites in the world. It stood at the place where the borders of three countries, Mysia, Lydia, and Phrygia, met. The border was the gateway to the East, and it commanded one of the greatest highways in the world, which led from Europe to the East. Its position awarded it the responsibility of becoming a pivotal city for the spread of Greek culture, language, and way of life.

The very crucial site of Philadelphia made the church there strategic. The church had opportunities to spread not Greek culture but the gospel. For this reason Jesus challenged the church with a reminder that He had given them an open door that no man could shut. The self-descriptive words He used reminded the Christians that He had the keys to open these doors for them. As the One who was Himself the doorway to God, now He opened the doorway to spreading His love. The door of missionary opportunity was there before them.

"Behold, I have set before you an open door!" That's the good news for today's living. What door of opportunity has He set before you? Your family, your office, your shop, your friends, your neighbors?

All are open doors!

The Command to Persevere

1 Peter 3:20; Colossians 1:11; 1 Timothy 1:16;
2 Timothy 4:2; Revelation 3:9-10

*Because you have kept My command to persevere, I also
will keep you from the hour of trial which shall come upon
all the world, to test those who dwell on the earth.*

(Revelation 3:10)

Will right ultimately triumph?

Have you ever asked that question while reading the daily news? Of course; we all have. But the question becomes poignant and personal when something we know is right is being ignored or defamed, or when we are being judged and criticized for a stand we know is true and just.

Jesus tells the Philadelphian Christians that He is still in control of history. There will be the constant rise and fall of evil empires and the ebb and flow of the tides of godless people. The very nature of the Christian faith is that it will always be in conflict with powers and causes that are against God.

Patient endurance. That's what we need, isn't it? Patience is seeing things from Christ's point of view and by His timing. Endurance results as the strength of our lives. The sense that Christ is still at work gives us courage to get to work wherever He would deploy us in His battle with evil.

Patient endurance is the Lord's gift for living in a sick and evil world.

The Rewards of Faithfulness

Revelation 3:11-13

*Behold, I come quickly! Hold fast what you
have, that no one take your crown.*
(REVELATION 3:11)

Those who bear the cross wear the crown. The Greek word *stephanos* was used for a crown of victory given to an athlete who won in a game or race. It was also used as a word for the crown given at festive occasions to someone who had been faithful in municipal service. Both meanings are implied here. The Christian was to run the race of life, and he was also to serve faithfully in obedience to Christ.

Another promise made by Jesus to the Philadelphian Christians was that they would be made pillars in the temple of God. It was the custom in Philadelphia to honor one who served well with an inscription on a pillar in the temple of some god. But we are pillars in God's temple of heaven.

The phrase "he shall go out no more" also meant something special to the Philadelphians. At the time of an earthquake, the people would vacate the entire city, including the temple. But now there is a temple of the Lord, His eternal kingdom, from which we need not flee.

*We have been crowned by Christ. We are pillars in His
temple established in heaven. We are safe for eternity!*

When Culture Captures the Church

Revelation 3:14-19

*You say, "I am rich, have become wealthy, and have
need of nothing"—and do not know that you are
wretched, miserable, poor, blind, and naked.*

(REVELATION 3:17)

Laodicaea was a city of **commanding geographical location on the**
River Lycus. Because of this position, it was a city of commercial
prosperity. It became a very wealthy city through the cloth and
clothing industry. Added to this, it was a center of healing. A famous ear ointment made of nard and an eye powder were used
in Laodicaea. *Men,* the god of healing, had a shrine in the city.
The people developed great confidence in material prosperity and
physical health.

The church had become part of the wealth-oriented city.
It said that it was able to cope with the vicissitudes of life by
what it could buy and possess. Jesus tried to tell them that in the
things that really count, they were poor. The preoccupation with
clothing is not new today. This garment center took pride in its
products. Jesus wanted the garments of righteousness to clothe
their spiritual nakedness. Lastly, Laodicaea was arrogant about
its health center. Jesus offered them a spiritual salve to heal the
blindness of their souls.

Only Christ can make us spiritually rich, clothe us in righteousness, and give us spiritual vision.

Live today as a spiritually wealthy person.

Christ at the Door

Revelation 3:20

*Look! I have been standing at the door, and I am constantly
knocking. If anyone hears me calling him and opens the door, I
will come in and fellowship with him and he with me.*
(REVELATION 3:20 TLB)

Right at this moment, as you read this, Christ is at the door knocking. He always makes the first move. He comes to us in a new
way each day. The latchstring to open the door is on the inside.
We are given the choice to open the door of our lives or leave it
shut in the Master's face.

The invitation to open the door comes to us at the time we
are introduced to Christ. We learn of His unconditional love, His
unqualified forgiveness, and His willingness to make His home in
us. But He also knocks each day and at times of special need or
opportunity. I am constantly amazed at the number of Christians
who believe in Christ as Savior but do not daily open the door of
their lives to Him as Lord of all.

I lived as a self-propelled and self-justifying Christian for
eight years before I discovered what I now call "the second half
of the blessing": Christ in us, the hope of glory! William Law, one
of John Wesley's teachers, said, "A Christ not in us is a Christ not
ours." The abundant life really began for me when I opened the
door and invited Christ to live in me. How about you?

Christ is at your door knocking. The latch to open it is inside!

The Victorious Life

Revelation 3:21-22; 1 Corinthians 15:54-57;
1 John 5:4

*To him who overcomes I will grant to sit with Me on My throne, as
I also overcame and sat down with My Father on His throne.*
(REVELATION 3:21)

The victory that Jesus offered the Laodiceans was the victory of
coronation. He offered them, and now us, the privilege of sitting
with Him on His throne. This is colorful language, but it is also
powerful. Jesus is offering us the same victory He knew with the
same result in authority and power.

But what is Christ's victory? How does He overcome the
world? His victory is over the forces of evil. When Christ lives in
us, He continues to battle for us and through us the same beset-
ting forces of evil He met as Jesus of Nazareth. His victory is over
death. When we live in Him, we live in a fellowship that death
has no power to end. As He lives, we will live also. And His victory is final and ultimate. Though defeat is all around us, we need
to remember the cross and acknowledge that God can take over
failure and weakness and create His own glory. Christ always has
the last word. That's our victory!

*True faith is not white-knuckled, teeth-gritting determination to
survive in trouble. It is rooted in the confidence that the Lord will
invade the trouble at just the right time with His unlimited resources.*

Learning to Wait

Acts 1:1-4

Wait for the Promise of the Father.
(Acts 1:4 nkjv)

In the next days we will focus on the meaning of Pentecost. The period between the resurrection and the outpouring of the Holy Spirit at Pentecost is marked by waiting: expectant, excited, excruciating waiting.

The disciples had to learn to wait. They lived in an impetuous age. Jesus told them again and again that His kingdom was not of the kind that people yearned to establish. They persistently wanted proof of the power of His kingdom. "My kingdom is not of this world," He cautioned, and they had to learn the most difficult lesson of following the Master: They had to wait for His timing. They could not accomplish the Lord's purposes without His timing and power. They were called to be the foundation of the church, people who had learned how to wait...on Him. They dared not run ahead of Him or go off in unguided directions. They had to learn to allow Him to accomplish His mission through them. It is no different for you and me today.

Psalm 27:14 becomes our motto today: "Wait for the LORD; be strong and let your heart take courage; yes, wait for the LORD!"

Wait for the Power

Acts 1:4-8

*He said to them, "It is not for you to know times or seasons
which the Father has put in His own authority."*
(ACTS 1:7)

What was the Lord waiting for? Why didn't He give the power of
the Holy Spirit to the disciples immediately?

They were not ready! They still had the impatience of human verve. They wanted to do things for Christ in their own
strength.

It is during these periods of waiting that the Lord does His
work *in* us before He does His work *through* us. He gets us ready
to receive answers to prayers He has guided us to pray.

When we are quiet we realize our impotency to follow Christ.
We feel the inadequacy of our love at the very time we catch a
vision of the world's need for His love. It is at that moment that
preparation for Pentecost is taking place. The tremendous infilling
of power to love that the disciples received at Pentecost is exactly
the same power we are being prepared to receive today.

*Pentecost is Christ's gift for those who see the need for love in the
world but also long for the power to express it unreservedly.*

Jesus took a known, John's baptism, to teach and prepare, for an unknown (the Holy Spirit).

The Baptism of the Holy Spirit

Acts 1:5

*John truly baptized with water, but you shall be baptized
with the Holy Spirit not many days from now.*

(ACTS 1:5)

What is the baptism of the Holy Spirit that Jesus promised His disciples? Can it be experienced today? What does it mean?

Jesus took a known to teach and prepare for an unknown. He reminded them of the baptism by John.

Some of the same elements would be present in the baptism of the Holy Spirit: a sense of need, a willingness to be totally committed to God's plan and purpose, and a realization of sin and inadequacy were necessary preparation. But the great difference was that the person would be immersed not in water but in the power of the Spirit. The Spirit would come within a person as a new driving power to participate in the continuing ministry of love.

The baptism of John was a baptism of repentance; the baptism of the Holy Spirit would be the baptism of regeneration, of new life, new power, new gifts for ministry beyond human talent. The same is available to us if we will pray, "I need the Holy Spirit; I want the Holy Spirit; I am open to a fresh infilling of the Holy Spirit today."

*Before Christ sent the church into the world, He sent the Spirit
into the church. The same order must be observed today.*
—JOHN R. W. STOTT

The Threefold Test

Matthew 3:11-12

I indeed baptize you with water unto repentance, but He who is coming after me is mightier than I, whose sandals I am not worthy to carry. He will baptize you with the Holy Spirit and fire.
(MATTHEW 3:11)

John the Baptist predicted that those who believed in Jesus would be baptized with the Holy Spirit and fire. There is an identifiable fire burning in people who have received the Holy Spirit. The image is an exciting one.

First, fire means illumination. The Holy Spirit interprets the deep things of God to the believer. We have insight and discernment. We see both what is and what we can be.

The second aspect is purification. The Holy Spirit burns out the dross. To receive the Holy Spirit means a purging of old ways of thinking and feeling.

Thirdly, the Holy Spirit's fire brings the warmth of love. He kindles the emotions with love for God and other people. There is a warmth about a Holy Spirit–filled person: new affection and tenderness toward people.

There is nothing our cold world needs more than the fire of the Holy Spirit! God's frozen people in the church need to be melted and poured out in service.

Spirit of the Living God, fall afresh on me.

The Greatest Counselor in the World

John 14:16-24

I will ask the Father, and he will give you another counselor to be with you forever—the Spirit of truth…He lives with you and will be in you.
(JOHN 14:16-17 NIV)

Who is the Holy Spirit? He is the greatest counselor in the world. *Counselor* may not be the first word that comes to your mind when you think of the Holy Spirit. And yet, this is the name Jesus used to declare what the Spirit would be in the lives of His disciples after Pentecost. The Greek word *parakletos* was associated with the courts of law and signified one who was the counsel for the defense, one who pleads on behalf of another. In a broader sense, it identified one who stands by a person's side or one who was ready to aid a soldier in battle as the armor bearer.

In our lives, the counselor is the Spirit of Truth, who enables us to know the truth about ourselves and the truth of Christ. He brings to our remembrance all that Christ did for us. He convicts us of sin and judgment and then assures us of righteousness through Christ's atonement. He guides us and enables us in holiness, the awesome miracle of remaking us in Christ's likeness. Now we can see why the Holy Spirit is qualified to be our counselor in the problems, decisions, people-pressures, disappointments, struggles, and loneliness we experience in the asphalt jungle of today's modern world.

The Holy Spirit allows us to talk, listens and understands, and then guides and provides.

The Inner Special

Acts 2:1-4

They were all filled with the Holy Spirit.
(ACTS 2:4)

If you had to choose between Christmas, Good Friday, Easter, Ascension Sunday, and Pentecost, which would you say is most important? Few of us would say Pentecost. We think of it as a mysterious addendum to the gospel. And yet we would not celebrate the crucial events of the incarnation of Christ if it had not been culminated in Pentecost.

The reason Christ came, lived, taught, suffered, was resurrected, and ascended was so that He could prepare a people in whom He could live. Calvary's atonement and Easter's victory are penultimate to the ultimate gift of the Holy Spirit to live in His reconciled and expectant people. Now the Holy Spirit came within Christ's willing disciples to give them the power to live the life He had exemplified and called them to live.

The outward manifestations of Pentecost were signs of the inner. Wind represented the Breath and Spirit of God. Fire meant both purging and purification. It also signified a dynamic inclusive warmth in Jesus' followers. John had predicted that Jesus would baptize with the Holy Spirit and fire. The result was unfettered praise. Don't miss Pentecost!

*The abundant life is life as Christ lived it, life as we
live it in Him, and life as He lives it in us.*

Pentecost Is Every Day

Acts 2:5-13

*They were all amazed and perplexed, saying to one
another, "Whatever could this mean?"*
(ACTS 2:12)

Something very special happened at Pentecost. Can it be our experience today? I believe it can. How can we be prepared?

There are two questions to be answered: 1) Have we responded to the gospel of Jesus Christ, turned our life completely over to Him, and responded to His call to be totally His person? 2) Has life, in all its problems and potentials, brought us to the realization of our own inadequacy to live the Christian life on our own strength? If we can answer both of these questions with a "Yes!" Pentecost can happen to us today. It can be our personal baptism into power as the Spirit indwells our whole nature, and it can be the church's corporate rebirth to a new stage of effectiveness in our communities and our world. Here is a prayer for power:

*Holy Spirit of God, we pray for Pentecost to happen to us
and to our local churches today. We long for an outpouring
of Your power to enable us in Christ's ministry of love and
suffering for the world. We cannot do or be what You have
called us to perform in the world or exemplify to others without Your life within us. Amen.*

Pentecost can and will happen in us today!

A Spirit-filled Life

Acts 2:14-39

Repent, and let every one of you be baptized in the name of Jesus Christ for the remission of sins; and you shall receive the gift of the Holy Spirit.
(ACTS 2:38)

Yesterday's meditation was meant to be like a time-release capsule. It has residual impact as the conviction explodes within us. Peter's sermon on Pentecost gives us an intellectual framework for realizing the total sweep of God's action to prepare a people to receive and communicate His power. It outlines what God has done in the incarnation, what His people did in refusing the gift of His love in Christ, and then what He did in spite of that rejection. The sermon ends with a challenge of what we can do because of what He has done.

We say with the crowd that heard Peter's sermon, "What shall we do?" The three steps are undeniably given: *repent, believe, receive.* To *repent* means to acknowledge what we have been and done; to *believe* means to trust Christ completely for forgiveness and acceptance; to *receive* means to invite Him to live in us as absolute Lord and motivating power. The result will be that we are Spirit-filled Christians living with unlimited resources.

Beginning today I will be a riverbed for the flow of the Spirit.

Occupied by a Through Passenger

Acts 2:1-4; 4:8; 13:9; 1 Corinthians 3:16-17;
6:19; 2 Corinthians 6:16

You are the temple of the living God.
(2 Corinthians 6:16)

I have a friend who has a fascinating sign on his desk. The bold letters spell out "Occupied by a Through Passenger." He told me it was a duplicate of an occupied-seat sign he had seen on a commercial airplane flight. He used it for a conversation starter to talk about his faith: "That's what I am—an occupied, through passenger. I'm only passing through. Heaven's my destination!"

A Christian is occupied territory on his way to a sublime destination. But when Christ makes His home in us, the joy of the destination has begun already. Christ occupies our minds to think His thoughts, our emotions to express His love, and our bodies to radiate His power. We are the temple of the living Christ!

We often speak as a person being "filled" with an emotion. We say he is filled with self-pity, anger, concern, or anxiety; or we say he is filled with life, joy, peace, or excitement. Whether we are a delight or a drag to those around us depends on what is filling our thoughts and emotions.

Being occupied by Christ keeps our attention
occupied on Him and caring for others.

A Benchmark for a Great Church

Acts 2:40-47

*Those who gladly received his word were baptized; and that
day about three thousand souls were added to them.*

(ACTS 2:41)

Here is a picture of the church as it was meant to be.

It was Christ-centered. The people had responded to the straightforward preaching of Christ—crucified, resurrected, indwelling. The living Christ was their Savior, Lord, and intimate Friend.

It was a praying church. A praying church becomes a supernatural church. So many churches today are attempting only those things they can do on human strength. What is your church daring in Christ's name that only His Spirit could accomplish?

It was a caring and sharing church. They were not only committed to Christ, but also to one another and their life together in the church.

It was a healing church. The same power to heal the psychological, physical, and spiritual needs of people that had been revealed in Jesus of Nazareth was now unloosed in the church.

It was a growing church. But note that it was the *Lord* who added to the church daily. He had created a magnetic church, where people loved Him and one another.

Lord, revive my church beginning with me!

The Most Joyful People Alive

John 13:1-35

If you know these things, blessed are you if you do them.
(John 13:17)

The church is the servant society. Christians are called to be servants. The Greek word for *servant* is also used for *minister*. All Christians are called into ministry. To be in Christ is to be in the ministry. Once we turn our lives over to Christ, then people and their needs become our agenda. Our calling is to care about people—helping them to know the Savior, grow in grace, and face life's challenges. Our happiness is inseparably related to pouring ourselves out for people. That means giving up our privacy, schedules, and judgments. The Lord puts people in our lives so we can be to them what He has been to us. In every situation, our only question should be, "Lord, what am I to do as Your servant?"

A man said, "Until I changed my self-image to being a servant, I always felt put upon, drained dry by people's demands. Then I realized Christ's calling to be a servant. Now I look for opportunities to serve in Christ's name. I want to be a boost and not a burden, a lift and not a load. It has changed my life!"

Could you say what this man said? Can you say it just for today? Try it—it could change all the days of your future.

Look at Us!

Acts 3:1-10

Fixing his eyes on him, with John, Peter said, "Look at us."
(ACTS 3:4)

We live in a crippled world. Daily the crippled world cries out as surely as the lame man on the step of the Beautiful Gate of the Temple. What can we say to a sick and troubled world? Can we say, "Look at us"? "Look at the quality of new life in our faith we have discovered"? Can we say we have the answer? Peter and John unashamedly asked the lame beggar to look at them. They did have an answer.

The man fixed his gaze on them, expecting to receive *something* from them. This is the story of a man wanting *something* when what he needed was *someone.* He was the eloquent spokesman of materialism for all ages. He expected something. The disciples had nothing to offer, but they had Someone. Yes, they had Someone who had changed their lives and had given them purpose and power, healing and holiness, wisdom and will. They had no answer; they had *the* answer. The world yearns for something; we offer Someone—Christ Himself.

The discovery of God is not, then, the discovery of something in a corner of our experience. It is the discovery of Someone whose presence gathers the whole of our experience into the comprehensiveness of His being and gives it a new unity.
—H. WHEELER ROBINSON

What Do You Know for Sure?

Romans 15:22-33

I know that when I come to you, I shall come in the
fullness of the blessing of the gospel of Christ.
(ROMANS 15:29)

When I was a boy, my father would often ask, "Well, lad, what
do you know for sure?"

I am thankful I can say with Paul what he said to the Christians at Rome. He eagerly anticipated his visit to Rome, the strategic center of political and military might.

He would come to the struggling church there with an overflowing cornucopia of superabundant power. He would come
with Christ, the gospel, the blessing, and the fullness. Christ was
everything to Paul. He was the Author, Mediator, Redeemer, Vic-
tor, Essence of Indwelling Power, and Crown of Life for the apostle.
When he arrived in Rome he taught, preached, lived, and shared
Christ. While there, he wrote the Philippians, "To me, to live is
Christ." Paul's gospel was Christ. In Him all the blessings of God
had been lavishly poured out in fullness. Nothing was left out.
Christ's fullness alone can fill our emptiness!

I commit my whole life to Christ and will seek to be His faithful
disciple in all my relationships and responsibilites. For me, to live
is Christ! I am truly alive now and forever. Hallelujah and Amen.

Yes!

Matthew 12:31-32

*I say to you, every sin and blasphemy will be forgiven men, but
the blasphemy against the Spirit will not be forgiven men.*
(MATTHEW 12:31)

Is there any sin that cannot be forgiven? Yes. The sin against the
Holy Spirit.

It is to say "No!" to His overtures of grace. That sin is unforgivable in that we can say "No" only so long and after that we can
no longer say "Yes." That tells us a frightening thing about human nature. God is always ready to forgive, but He has given us
free wills to choose to let Him love us. And if we say "No"? The
unforgivable sin is to refuse to be forgiven…to resist the ministry
of the Holy Spirit! Bishop Fulton J. Sheen said, "The really unforgivable sin is the denial of sin, because, by its nature, there is
now nothing to be forgiven."

The Pharisees and scribes in today's passage refused to believe
it was God's Spirit who was at work in Jesus. But the real problem
was that to accept Christ as the Messiah would have meant listening to what He said and responding to His diagnosis of their sin
and need for forgiveness. They had stonewalled the impact of the
Spirit. The same can happen in religious people today. The danger
is saying "No!" once too often.

Our response? "Yes! Yes! Yes!"

The Crucial Question

Acts 8:1-40

As yet He had fallen upon none of them. They had only been baptized in the name of the Lord Jesus.
(ACTS 8:16)

Notice that there were two steps in the Samaritans' experience of the gospel. Philip preached the good news of Christ's death and resurrection. The people believed, and there was great joy in the city. Then Peter and John came and prayed that they might receive the Holy Spirit. Why was it necessary for the two apostles to follow up on Philip's preaching? Perhaps it was because the Samaritans needed power to live their new life. They needed the indwelling power of the same Holy Spirit who had given them the gift of faith to believe.

The great need in the lives of most of us contemporary Christians is for the Holy Spirit to infuse our human impotence with power to live the adventure of the Christian life. Would you say that your life is most like the Samaritans' before Philip preached, after they believed but had no power, or after Peter and John prayed for the gift of the indwelling Spirit? That's probably one of the most important questions you will ever answer! How you answer determines the difference between living for Christ on your power or fulfilling Christ's plans by the Holy Spirit's power.

Holy Spirit, I'm Yours. I want to keep on being filled with You all through this day.

An Engine Without Fuel

Acts 19:1-7

*He [Paul] said to them, "Did you receive the Holy Spirit
when you believed?" So they said to him, "We have not
so much as heard whether there is a Holy Spirit."*

Christians are twice-born people. We have been born into physical life in our natural birth, but we have also been born again. We started life all over…we were born again.

The great need today is for traditional, believing, struggling Christians in the church to receive the baptism of power. In Acts, Luke uses a vivid phrase to describe this: "They were *filled* with the Holy Spirit." We were created to contain and transmit the Holy Spirit. Our Christian life is not fulfilled until we have had an infilling of power. All the things we try to be and do as faithful believers in Christ are impossible until we receive the Holy Spirit's power.

We are like the men along the road whom Paul met. They knew about Jesus and about what God had done for the salvation of the world in Him. But they lacked power. Paul asked them the crucial question: "Did you receive the Holy Spirit when you believed?" They confessed they had not heard of the Holy Spirit. Then Paul prayed for them, and they received the Spirit.

How would you have answered Paul's question?

Put It in His Hands!

John 4:43-54; Matthew 17:20

Jesus said to him, "Go your way; your son lives." So the man believed the word that Jesus spoke to him, and he went his way.
(John 4:50)

Distance is no detriment to the power of prayer. Jesus did not have to travel the distance to physically touch the fevered son to heal him. This is a magnificent promise of what we can know today. We do not have to be physically present with the person for whom we pray. The same Lord who motivates our prayer is also there with the person for whom we pray.

Geography makes no difference for the prayer of faith, nor is psychological distance of any consequence. Often we are separated in various ways from people for whom we pray; some live far away from us, and others with whom we are present can be so distant in their defensiveness that it is difficult to break through their barriers. But we can pray and know that God is at work. We can participate with Him in the release of His amazing resources in their lives. If we pray His power is being released. Our job is to pray in faith; God's job is to intervene. If we do our job, He will do His!

I will live today in the liberating assurance that God has heard my prayers and is active in answering in a way that is best. I will "go my way," leaving the matter in His hands.

A Recognition of Need

Matthew 5:3; Luke 6:20,24; Ephesians 3:7-13

Blessed are the poor in spirit, for theirs is the kingdom of heaven.
(MATTHEW 5:3)

How can a person who is poor in spirit be blessed—joyous? The
Greek word used to translate Jesus' Aramaic word is *ptochos,* which
means "absolute and complete poverty." What did Jesus mean?

The answer is found in an observable spiritual law: the closer
you grow to Jesus Christ, the greater your sense of need for Him.
We know we are distant when we begin to feel self-sufficient. Self-
complacency is a sure sign of spiritual paralysis. To know one's
absolute dependence on Christ for life, love, hope, power, insight,
discernment, wisdom, courage, and strategy is to know creative
spiritual poverty. This is poverty of spirit.

The keynote of this first beatitude is realization. Joyous are
those who realize their need. To depend on God in a world that
has taught us self-reliance is difficult. Often we must be taught
by painful experience. We discover in sickness, loss of a loved one,
circumstantial failure, or interpersonal conflict that we are not as
capable as we thought. The joyous are those who recognize their
helplessness apart from God and quickly put their trust in Him.

Helplessness is unquestionably the first and surest
indication of a praying heart. Prayer and helplessness are
inseparable. Only he who is helpless can truly pray.
—OLE HALLESBY

The Poverty That Leads to Richness

Luke 18:9-14

God, be merciful to me a sinner!
(Luke 18:13)

The poor in spirit know their need and can cry out, "God be merciful to me, a poor sinner." Jesus exalts the tax collector in the parable because he could accept his need for God's mercy. The Pharisee, comparing himself with others and not with God's standard of righteousness, was thankful that he was not as other people. He was filled with pride, self-satisfaction, and self-assurance. He could not receive what Jesus offered.

Many of us do not realize our poverty of spirit, because we are not living an adventurous enough life. We aren't living courageously enough to have no other invisible means of support than Christ. Once we get involved with people and their needs, and really care about them, we will soon find that we do not have adequate patience or persistence. People try, test, and trouble us if we dare to care. Whenever we try to change social conditions, we meet obstacles of closed minds and resistant wills. Then we realize how poor in wisdom we are. We do not realize our poverty of spirit until we accept the potential challenge in which we are to live out our faith.

Once we see our potential in Christ, we realize how much we need Him to live life to the fullest.

To Be Truly Sorry

2 Corinthians 1:3-11; Matthew 5:4

Blessed are those who mourn, for they shall be comforted.
(MATTHEW 5:4)

How could it be blessed to mourn? True blessedness is being in touch with the heart of God, to feel what He feels, to delight in what He delights, and also to be disturbed by what disturbs Him. He loves us so much that anything that separates us from Him or others is of grave concern to Him. He mourns when we hurt ourselves or others. The cross is a constant reminder of how deeply He loves us and how profoundly He cares. Golgotha is the mourning of God. Our sin breaks God's heart.

When we mourn, we feel the pulse beat of that loving, forgiving heart. It encompasses deep sorrow for our sins. Jesus knew that if we ever caught a glimpse of what our sin does to God, we would mourn with Him. That would lead to confession, forgiveness, and the joy of reconciliation. There is no happiness, no joyous blessedness, quite like knowing we are accepted and loved. When we know that, we want everyone else to experience it. We mourn over what people do to us and themselves, and then we become channels of the flow of God's heart.

Allow your heart to be broken by the
things that break the heart of God.

Grief That Leads to Grace

2 Corinthians 1:3-7

*Blessed be the God and Father of our Lord Jesus Christ,
the Father of mercies and God of all comfort.*
(2 CORINTHIANS 1:3)

There is a joy to be experienced when we care deeply about people
and their needs. This joy comes when we let our hearts mourn
over the things that bring grief to the heart of God. When we are
involved with God in caring for people, we are also recipients of
God's comfort.

The more we know of the person's potential, the more we
mourn over his or her failure in squandering life. When we know
what life was meant to be, we ache for people to experience it to
the hilt.

We also mourn over what people do to one another. Our
hearts ache when we read or hear the daily news and observe the
grotesque ways people hurt and destroy one another. We dare to
get involved with the people in our lives and feel with them the
pain of what other people have done. It enables us to see what is
going on in our world and to feel the anguish of it. Comfort is
God's gift to those who share life this deeply with Him. Joy grows
out of the realization that God is at work in people's lives and calls
us to communicate His love to them in spite of everything.

Those who truly care receive the comfort of God.

Under the Reins

Ephesians 4:1-25; Matthew 5:5

*…With all lowliness and gentleness, with longsuffering,
bearing with one another in love.*
(Ephesians 4:2)

Blessed are the meek, for they shall inherit the earth.
(Matthew 5:5)

One of the uses of the Greek word for meekness, *praus*, is "domesticated." It is the word that describes a wild animal that has been brought under control. The animal now has been trained and can follow commands in accomplishing tasks. It has learned to respond to reins. Picture a wild horse that has been broken and trained and now can respond to the direction of its master.

A meek person is a God-controlled person. He or she is someone who can respond to the reins of God's direction, and he is free within the guidance of God's command. Paul speaks of himself as a prisoner of the Lord. He had a turbulent, unruly spirit until captured and guided by the love of Christ. He speaks of Jesus leading a host of captives. That has always been the vivid image of the church: a fellowship of men and women under the control and power of Jesus Christ. The meek people of the Master are sensitive to listen and obediently follow the commands of their Lord.

*The meek are not weak. They are humble
and open to the Lord's leading.*

True Comfort

Luke 6:21; Isaiah 61:1-2; 2 Thessalonians 2:16;
Acts 9:31

Blessed are you who hunger now, for you shall be filled.
Blessed are you who weep now, for you shall laugh.
(LUKE 6:21)

The motto of famous newspaperman Joseph Pulitzer owes much to
Jesus: "Comfort the afflicted and afflict the comfortable." Jesus does
just that! He comforts those who mourn over their own, others', and
the world's separation, suffering, and selfishness. The Greek word
means "to call to the side of." Christ stands by our side when we become sensitive to the need of the world and our part in it. When we
become comfortable in any other security than Him, He unsettles us
with His disturbing exposure of what life was meant to be.

Only Christ knows when we need to be comforted and when
we need to be challenged. He knows when to assure and when
to alarm.

The wonderful good news is that He stands beside us. He
comforts us by helping us to get perspective on what we face, to
see what He is teaching us in it, to learn what He can do with a
life surrendered to Him, and to experience the power of His sus-
taining Spirit. That's comfort!

The longing to know God better is His gift. It is a sure
sign that we are cherished, chosen, and called.

Flexibility

Isaiah 45:9-10; Romans 9:19-33

Will the clay say to the potter, "What are you doing?"
(Isaiah 45:9)

We are to be like clay in the potter's hand. The clay does not determine the shape of the object fashioned, nor does it argue with the wisdom or skill of the potter. The image is vivid. Think of clay rolling off the potter's wheel and saying, "Now look here, Potter, I have an idea or two about how I want to be shaped and how I want to end up. I have my rights too, you know!" How absurd! But how like our relationship with God, our Potter!

Clay responds to the potter's hand when it is warm and supple. We are to be this way in God's hand. He knows best about what we are to do and become. Meekness is the willingness to trust God with the molding of our lives. He can mold us beyond our fondest expectation. He is able to shape our lives in magnificent dimensions we could never imagine. We are to be willing, open, free. God does the rest. The meek are moldable.

> *So take and use Thy work*
> *Amend what flaws may lurk*
> *What strain o' the stuff*
> *What warping past the aim!*
> *My times are in Thy hands*
> *Perfect the cup as planned*
> —Robert Browning, from "Rabbi ben Ezra"

Moldable Meekness

1 Corinthians 2:1-16; James 3:13-18

The wisdom from above is first pure, then peaceable, gentle, open to reason, full of mercy and good fruits, without uncertainty or insincerity.
(James 3:17 rsv)

Wisdom is the special gift of the Holy Spirit. Note how wisdom, the Holy Spirit, and the mind of Christ are used almost synonymously in 1 Corinthians 2. They are all part of one experience. We can be empowered to comprehend the deep things of God's nature, purpose, and plan. Guidance, insight, and discernment are ours because the Holy Spirit dwells in us. We are not alone. The Spirit infuses our brains to think His thoughts, fills our emotions with His love, and frees our wills to know and do His will. Spirit-filled Christians are free to be channels of the living God!

Meekness is moldability. It is a dynamic freedom rooted in God's graciousness, which overflows in love for one's self in spite of our shortcomings and then love for others just as they are. Meekness is a kind of abandonment to God as the Potter of life, asking for His guiding, shaping hand to develop our life.

Have Thine own way, Lord!
Have Thine own way!
Thou art the Potter, I am the clay.
Mold me and make me after Thy will,
While I am waiting, yielded and still.
—Adelaide Pollard

Hunger and Thirst

Matthew 5:6

*Blessed are those who hunger and thirst for
righteousness, for they shall be filled.*
(MATTHEW 5:6)

This is the most difficult beatitude for us to understand, not because it is complex, but because there is so little in our experience that would give us a sense of the meaning. Few of us have ever hungered or thirsted. Food is plentiful, and a turn of the water tap brings water without limit. The hunger of which Jesus speaks is not famishment before mealtime; the thirst is more than a parched need for a refreshing drink. It is the hunger of a person who is starving and thirst of a person who will die without a drink. We have experienced nothing like that!

What are the dominant desires of our life? What do we truly long for? What demands our loyalty and allegiance? Most of us would have to be honest to say that we do not long for righteousness! Robert Louis Stevenson spoke of "the malady of not wanting." This is our malady. We do not want God enough to pray, study, worship, or serve. We retreat when following becomes difficult.

We are to hunger and thirst for righteousness as a starving person for food and a perishing, parched person for water.

I will make righteousness the dominant desire of my life.

A Family Likeness

John 17:20-26

…That they all may be one, as You, Father, are in Me, and I in You; that they also may be one in Us, that the world may believe that You have sent Me. And the glory which You gave Me I have given them, that they may be one just as We are one.
(John 17:21-22)

I was in a world of my own as I flew home. I had just finished a very emotional talk with my sisters and brother. We had prepared the old family home in Kenosha, Wisconsin, for sale. All the furnishings had to be cleared out and keepsakes divided among us. My sister, Elaine, had put in a box all the personal things left to me by my father: pictures, his diary of the First World War, some Ogilvie tartans, and his pocket watch. I had rushed to meet my flight, and then, in the anonymity of hours to myself on the flight, I opened the box and sorted through the precious gifts of memory. The pictures of my father, taken through the years, made me laugh and cry—the family portraits, the pictures of fishing trips and never-to-be-forgotten times together. I relived a portion of my life and was thankful for a dad who had loved me and believed in me.

About this time in June each year, we set aside a day to honor our fathers. It's a time for memories and gratitude, a time to say to our fathers still with us, or those with the Lord, "Dad, I love you!"

Today is a special day to claim one of Jesus' most awesome promises. We can be like our heavenly Father.

Truly Satisfied

Psalm 17:1-15

*As for me, I shall behold Your face in righteousness; I
will be satisfied with Your likeness when I awake.*
(PSALM 17:15)

Satisfied! When are we ever satisfied? When can we say in honesty that we are satisfied with what we have done or given or finished? We deal constantly with the incomplete, imperfect, and fragmented. How shall we be satisfied?

The fourth beatitude promises that those who seek righteousness will be filled. Some translations say, "Be satisfied." Our emptiness can be filled. The deepest longing of our minds and hearts can be met. What does this mean?

Just this: Our created purpose to know God, love Him, and do His will can be fulfilled. All other hungers will reoccur and persist. Only our hunger for God can be satisfied. This is a tremendous promise. We can experience the love and power of God! We shall be satisfied!

There is an assurance that comes to a Christian that drives out fear and frustration. He knows he still needs to grow and there is much that he still must discover, but he knows he is called, appointed, set apart, loved, forgiven, and elected by God to be His person. This is not arrogance; it is joyous realization of God's gift.

There is no greater satisfaction than in knowing we belong to God.

How to Be "Right" All the Time!

Romans 3:21; 4:5; 5:17; 6:13

*Now the righteousness of God apart from the law is
revealed, being witnessed by the Law and the Prophets.*
(ROMANS 3:21)

We all want to be right. But more than our desire to have our
facts right is the desire to "be right," to be in harmony with other
people. We desire open, loving relationships with everyone and
are disturbed when misunderstandings, hostilities, or resentments
occur. Something within us abhors a broken relationship as nature abhors a vacuum. We are propelled to justify ourselves to be
sure we were right and not the cause of the separation.

The same thing is more profoundly true of our relationship
with God. Because of rebellion and the desire to run our own
lives, we are separated from fellowship with God. Sin is separation. But there is also the desire to be right with God. We try to
make ourselves right by being good enough to desire His love. We
never can be, because there is in us the ambivalence of desiring
and rejecting Him at the same time.

God knew our inability to make ourselves right with Him.
Therefore He came in Jesus to reveal a righteousness that would
be given as a gift. The cross was the tangible, historical event in
which God reconciled—that is, forgave and accepted—humankind
to Himself.

Righteousness is "right-ness" with God.

Steadfast Love

Matthew 5:7; Psalm 103:1-22;
Lamentations 3:19-26

Blessed are the merciful, for they shall obtain mercy.
(MATTHEW 5:7)

This beatitude gives us another quality of family likeness we can have with God. He is merciful and wants to reproduce that crucial aspect of His nature in us. We are truly happy—blessed—when we are receiving His mercy and are communicating it to others. When we have felt God's mercy in our failures and needs, we become merciful to others in their inadequacies and mistakes. Christ is God's mercy incarnate. As He lives His life in us, our minds are captured by His amazing grace, our emotions are infused by tender love, and our wills are liberated to do whatever people need to feel loved and forgiven by us.

Mercy is profound identification. The Hebrew word implies living in another person's skin; to feel, know, and experience what he or she is going through; empathy; sensitivity. The outer manifestation of our inner experience of God's mercy is a graciousness that offers understanding, gives others another chance, and freely forgives. The qualification for receiving the continuous flow of God's mercy is to give out what He has put in.

Mercy is your pain in my heart.

To Will One Thing

Matthew 21:28-32; Matthew 5:8.

Blessed are the pure in heart, for they shall see God.
(MATTHEW 5:8)

What does it mean to have a pure heart? The sixth beatitude challenges us! *Heart* in Hebrew thought meant the whole personality. Purity in the New Testament is usually interpreted not just as cleanness but as singleness of nature. Jesus abhorred the double-mindedness of the Pharisees. Duplicity caused confusion and moral sickness. Hypocrisy is to go double. Jesus wanted people who willed one thing: to know God and do His will.

A truly joyous, blessed person is one who has finally discovered he or she has no other purpose than to be faithful and obedient to God. He has a basis of deciding the value, priority, and purpose of all he or she does and lives to glorify and enjoy Him.

The word *pure* means "unmixed, unadulterated, unalloyed." Purity of heart is freedom from mixed motives. Our basic loyalty is to God, above and beyond all other people and groups.

Purity of heart is a constant struggle. Every day, every situation, every choice presents a renewed opportunity to seek first God's purpose and plan.

Purity of heart is to will one thing—to be faithful.

The Tools of Our Trade

Romans 14:19

*Let us pursue the things which make for peace and
the things by which one may edify another.*
(ROMANS 14:19)

Paul challenges us to pursue what makes for peace. What are the
elements that contribute to peace?

Basic to all ingredients of peace is love. "Perfect love casts out
fear." Fear of each other and fear between groups rob us of peace.
Peace is usually closely combined with grace in the greetings and
benedictions of the New Testament letters. Grace is free, unreserved love. There can be no lasting peace without a gracious spirit
that accepts the inadequacies, failures, and weaknesses of others.
There is no negative judgment in grace. People can live in peace
with us because they are accepted and released.

Honesty and openness are crucial to peace. Hostility grows
from unexpressed and repressed anger or resentment. Peace can
be maintained only if we say what we think when we think it and
allow no day to end with inner feelings burning within.

Forgiveness makes for peace. We forgive because we have
been forgiven by God. Our task as Christians is to be as forgiving
as the Lord has been to us.

*"Blessed are the peacemakers for they shall be called the sons
of God." It's time to go into the Father's business!*

Healing the Wounds

2 Corinthians 5:11-21

We are ambassadors for Christ, as though God were pleading through us: we implore you in Christ's behalf, be reconciled to God.
(2 CORINTHIANS 5:20)

Peacemaking is an active task! It is a vital ministry of reconciliation that is never finished. Paul gives us the motive, perspective, example, message, and commission for our peacemaking task.

The love of Christ is our motive. There can be no peace apart from a right relationship with Christ in our mind and emotions. As long as we are unsettled with guilt, frustrated by ambivalence, or confused of purpose, we cannot be at peace or discover peace in our relationships or situations. Controlled by the love of Christ, we seek to communicate His peace. We no longer see people from a competitive point of view. We affirm what Christ has given others to use as the gifts of life. We can become a new person altogether when we are "in Christ." The war between self and Christ can come to an end, and a new person emerges.

We are challenged to share what we have found. We are to actively seek to bring reconciliation.

Here is a prayer for today:

Lord Christ, we want our lives today to be as beautiful as they were in Your mind when You first thought of us. Amen.

The Peace of a Deathless Life

Colossians 1:1-29

*...By Him to reconcile all things to Himself, by Him,
whether things on earth or things in heaven, having
made peace through the blood of His cross.*

(COLOSSIANS 1:20)

In a world like this, we are called to be peacemakers. But how can
we share peace if we have no peace? Peace must become a reality
in each of our lives before we can be involved in bringing peace
in our relationships, in groups, between nations, and in the world.
There can be no peace until we are different.

Paul spoke of Jesus as our Peace, the One who brings the
hostility to an end. Paul found a peace which enabled him to be
a peacemaker. Jesus Christ had broken down the dividing wall of
hostility between Him and others. The peace of Christ is to be
ours through what Christ has done and is doing. His death and
resurrection is the basis of our peace.

There is latent within most of us a fear of death. Our uncertainties of the future are all rooted in the question of our future
existence. Christ is our Peace because we know that in Him we
have a deathless life. We can now expend our energies bringing
His peace to others, because we have been liberated from frustrating fear. We are alive in eternity; heaven has begun.

Christ Himself is our peace.

The Zest of the World

Mark 9:50; Luke 14:34-35; Matthew 5:13

*You are the salt of the earth; but if the salt loses its flavor,
how shall it be seasoned? It is then good for nothing but
to be thrown out and trampled underfoot by men.*
(MATTHEW 5:13)

We are to be zest for the world. This is what Jesus meant when
He told His disciples they were to be the salt of the earth. Salt is
so common and inexpensive to us that we do not value the full
intent of what Jesus was saying. Salt was extremely expensive in
Jesus' day: A man's life was valued at about as much as a bag of salt.
Salt was cherished and used carefully. To be called the salt of the
earth indicated value and worth. But for what purpose? To bring
tang back into the bland, tasteless experience most people had
made of living! Christians are to be salt in a tasteless world.

Also, we are to be the source of vitality in the world. So often
our style of life is just the opposite. Piety has often equaled caution, restriction, and negation. The Christian life has been defined
by what a believer should not do! Not so with Jesus! He called His
disciples to outlive, out-love, and out-serve the whole world. He
wanted the pagan world to stop with a start and say, "Why, that's
living!" The joy of the Christian is his or her saltiness.

*We are alive with a tremendous vitality because we have
been loved, forgiven, cherished, and empowered.*

Sheer Sparkle

Psalm 150:1-6

Let everything that has breath praise the LORD. Praise the LORD!
(PSALM 150:6)

"I have been to church today, and I am not depressed." These words by Robert Louis Stevenson were recorded as if what happened was an extraordinary phenomenon.

What can be said of our worship today? It may not depress, but does it *impress* by its vitality and power?

William Barclay said, "There should be a sheer sparkle about the Christian life; and too often the Christian dresses like a mourner at a funeral, and talks like a spectre at a feast." How about us? Are we alive with joy?

Ibsen's Emperor Julian makes a cutting comment about Christians: "Have you looked at the Christians closely? Hollow-eyed, pale-cheeked, flat-breasted all; they brood their lives away, unspurred by ambition; the sun shines for them, but they do not see it; the earth offers them its fullness, but they do not deserve it; all their desire is to renounce and suffer that they may come to die." Grim criticism, that!

Samuel Chadwick said, "God is love; God is fire. The two are one. The Holy Spirit baptizes with fire. Spirit-filled souls are ablaze with God. They have a love which glows."

How would people define what it means to
be a Christian from our lives?

A Light in the Darkness

Matthew 5:14-16; 1 John 1:1-10; Ephesians 5:8

You are the light of the world. A city that
is set on a hill cannot be hidden.
(MATTHEW 5:14)

I remember seeing the city set on a hill to which Jesus supposedly referred. It was late at night. I was traveling by car along the winding road to the Sea of Galilee. The lights of the city vividly twinkled against the dark sky. It was daylight when I passed that way again. Even in the daytime, I could not miss the city. It could not be hidden.

A Christian is to be like that. The purpose of his or her life is to be a commanding witness for Jesus Christ in a dark world. What we believe, what Christ means to us, and what He has done in our character cannot be hidden.

A creative witness earns the right to be heard by living a dynamic life in the light. You can't miss a living Christian any more than I could miss that city. Our challenge is to keep our minds filled with the truth of Christ and our emotions fired with the warmth of Christ, so that we will attract the people around us with His quality of life. There is no such thing as secret discipleship. That is a contradiction of terms. Disciples cannot be hidden.

An authentic Christian cannot be overlooked.

A Hand, Not a Chip, on Our Shoulder

John 9:1-17

As long as I am in the world, I am the light of the world.
(John 9:5)

When Jesus said, "You are the light of the world," He identified His disciples with Himself. He said, "I am the light of the world." This was one of the greatest compliments He could have paid His disciples. They were to understand His ministry and do what He had done.

How were they to do this? Jesus Christ's light would illuminate them. We all admire radiant people. There is something about the sparkle of their eyes, the vitality of their countenance, and the excitement of their expression. The disciples became radiant men after the Resurrection when, at Pentecost, Jesus Christ made His postresurrection home in their minds, emotions, and words.

E. Stanley Jones gave us good advice on how to be light in darkness today:

In the pure, strong hours of the morning, when the soul of the day is at its best, lean upon the windowsill of the Lord and look into His face, and get orders for the day. Then go out into the world with a sense of a Hand upon your shoulder and not a chip.

By All Means Witness

1 Corinthians 1:22-23

Jews request a sign, and Greeks seek after wisdom; but we preach Christ crucified, to the Jews a stumbling block and to the Greeks foolishness.
(1 Corinthians 1:22-23)

"How can I become a witness?" a man asked me the other day.

"You are already," I said. "The question is, what kind?" He was startled, and so I went on to explain that we are all witnessing all the time about what Christ has or has not done in us. The way we live, how we react, and what we say or fail to say about what Christ means to us is a telling witness.

What kind of witness would you say you are on that basis? Paul presses us beyond that. He tells how the love of Christ in his heart prompted him to practice what I have called the four "I's" of authentic witness: *identification, involvement, intercession,* and *incisiveness.* Becoming "all things to all people" does not mean compromising our beliefs. Rather, it implies that we should use all our previous experience to identify with people who need Christ. Often, the things we've been through, learned, achieved, or attained by the Lord's grace give us a point of contact. Christ will use everything we've been through in both successes and failures.

With Christ, nothing is wasted.

What an Example!

Philippians 3:17; Acts 26:24-29

*Brethren, join in following my example, and note
those who so walk, as you have us for a pattern.*
(PHILIPPIANS 3:17)

"How can we communicate the faith with all our hang-ups?" many people ask.

If we don't believe that what's happened to us in our relationship to Christ ought to happen to everyone, then probably too little has happened to us. But Paul goes even deeper than this. With alarming audacity he says, "Keep on imitating me." Now I believe that's a great test of the Christian life. If we are not so excited about what we have found that we want everyone to experience it, then we have not found very much.

When Paul appeared before Agrippa, he proclaimed the winsome power of his life in Christ. Agrippa responded, knowing full well that Paul was seeking to have him find the faith the apostle had experienced, "In this short time, you think you will make me a Christian?" To this Paul said, "Whether a short time or a long time, my prayer to God is that you and all the rest of you who are listening to me today might become what I am." Here again, the same confidence: Imitate me! Can you say that—at home, at work, with your friends? If not, why not?

*Every day, people are deciding about Christ
by what they see of Him in us.*

A Full Set of Keys

Matthew 16:13-20; Revelation 1:18

*I will give you the keys of the kingdom of heaven, and
whatever you bind on earth will be bound in heaven, and
whatever you loose on earth will be loosed in heaven.*

(MATTHEW 16:19)

If we only trusted ourselves as much as Jesus does. What an amazing confidence He has in us!

He has given us the keys of the kingdom. This means we can admit or block others from the kingdom, depending upon whether we will share what we have found.

Many of us find it difficult to talk about our faith. This self-consciousness is an expensive luxury. Jesus tells us that it could result in someone never knowing the joy and peace that is available in fellowship with Him. When we refuse to share, we lock the door for someone else He desires to reach through us.

Note that there are keys. There is the key of listening, the key of caring, the key of discussion, the key of witness, the key of prayer for another, the key of unchanging love. He has given us a full key ring, so that we may unlock the varied, different doors of each kind of person we meet. We have been given power to forgive in His name and to assure people of His love. What a trust! What an opportunity!

Today I will be ready to use the full set of keys to unlock people.

Dependence Day

2 Chronicles 7:11-22

If…My people who are called by My name humble themselves and pray and seek My face and turn from their wicked ways, then I will hear from heaven, will forgive their sin and will heal their land.
(2 Chronicles 7:14)

Patriotism has not gone out of style. Independence Day is really dependence day for us. It is a day to reaffirm God's vision for America, the dream He gave to our founding forefathers, and the unique place our nation has in His strategy for history. The Fourth of July is more than a day for picnics, firecrackers, and parades. It is a day for prayer for our nation, our leaders, and God's blessing on us.

Our scripture today holds out a grand promise with a great "if." It is a pledge by God to His people. If we humble ourselves, turn from the things that contradict His vision for our nation, and earnestly pray, He will forgive and heal our ills. "One nation under God" in our Pledge of Allegiance is a commitment to work for His righteousness and justice in every part of society.

The hope of America is not in her military might or natural resources, but in God's people, you and me, as our prayers become a channel through which He can bless our land. Goodness and greatness are inseparable. America's supernatural resource for greatness is humble prayer on "Dependence Day."

God, please continue to bless America!

An Influential Person

Ephesians 6:10-20

*Take up the whole armor of God, that you may be able to
withstand in the evil day, and having done all, to stand.*
(EPHESIANS 6:13)

You are an influential person! Do you believe in your awesome
power? Christ does. Every day, in hundreds of ways, you and I
are influencing people about what it means (or does not mean!)
to live the abundant life in Christ. If the people of our lives had
to write a definition of Christianity from what they see and hear
from us, what would they write? Our influence is either positive
or negative. People are reading the signals all the time. What kind
of salt and light have we been?

People and their needs are our agenda. Our faith is to pack
a wallop for others. Everything Jesus gives us is for our influence
on others. When we settle that, life becomes blessed indeed! We
were meant to have impact, influence, and inspiration in the
lives of the people we touch. What stands in the way of people
seeing Christ's light burning in us? For some, it's our personalities, which need Christ's transformation; for others, it's privatism,
which keeps us from sharing our faith; for still others, it is simply
lack of loving concern. The psalmist reminds us of our calling:
"Let the redeemed of the LORD say so!" (Psalm 107:2).

Today I will exercise my influence for Christ.

"My" Gospel

Romans 16:25-27

...According to my gospel.
(Romans 16:25)

Authentic witnessing requires a **gospel that is personally and passionately ours**. Paul spoke of "my gospel." What is yours?

The word *gospel* means "good news." The word in Greek, *euaggelion*, had three uses in ancient times. It meant the bearer of good news, the good news itself, and the reward given to the bearer of the good news. All three have meaning for us. We are the communicators of the good news of the life, message, death, reconciliation, and resurrection of Jesus Christ. What He accomplished for our salvation, eternal life, and abundant living is the content of our good news. He Himself is our reward.

The gospel contains the truth of what Christ did and does. It is the declaration of the promise of life as it was meant to be. The content of the gospel is the message of the New Testament. It is to become my gospel and your gospel. The gospel according to you and me is the gospel that has been ingrained into our thinking, understanding, action, and attitude—biblical truth passed through the tempering of experience until it is an integrated part of us. We are not only to believe the good news, but are to be good news incarnate—the gospel on two legs walking. Only "our" gospel can make us contagious witnesses today.

The people around us need good news that is personal and near to us.

Dealing with Anger

Matthew 5:21-26; Exodus 20:13;
Deuteronomy 5:17; Mark 3:1-6

*If you bring your gift to the altar, and there remember that
your brother has something against you, leave your gift
there before the altar, and go your way. First be reconciled
to your brother, and then come and offer your gift.*

(MATTHEW 5:23-24)

This passage dealing with anger shows Jesus contrasting the written code and the deeper righteousness of the heart. The Lord forbids anger "without cause." He is concerned about the free-floating hostility caused by lack of the experience of God's healing love for ourselves. Where anger is uncreatively expressed, it eventually is turned on ourselves and is the major cause of anxiety. We also have a responsibility of diffusing anger in others. When we are the cause, we have the obligation to seek forgiveness and reconciliation.

Anger is not bad. It can be an expression of profound caring. But the Pharisees were more concerned about a regulation than they were about human need. Jesus' anger was an expression of love. He loved both the man with the withered hand and the Pharisees who were trying to trap Him. Anger must be expressed in a context of love in which people know that there is nothing that can make us stop loving them.

*Talk over your anger with Christ. Allow Him
to guide your expression of it.*

Straight Arrows

Matthew 5:33-37; 21:28-32

Let your "Yes" be "Yes," and your "No," "No." For
whatever is more than these is from the evil one.
(MATTHEW 5:37)

Our Lord challenges us to be "straight arrows." He wants us to be people on whom others can depend to speak the truth in love. He calls for integrity in our speech. In His time, oaths would be used to fortify the veracity of a person's statement because words could no longer be trusted as consistently true. The method of swearing by something or someone sacred was to alert others to the fact that the statement was absolutely true. Jesus demanded complete honesty and directness. All that was needed was a simple "Yes" or "No" without any embellishment.

Think of the ways that we can shade, confuse, or distort the truth by the way we say something or by what we leave out. We are to be people who are known for unvarnished, unambiguous truth. There's no need to swear by anything if we are known as people who mean what we say and say what we mean. What a great way to live!

Honesty isn't just the best policy; it is the
only policy for our communication.

An Artesian Flow

John 7:37-39; James 3:6-18

He who believes in Me, as the Scripture has said, out
of his heart will flow rivers of living water.
(JOHN 7:38)

What comes out of our mouths is dependent on what's in our hearts. We can speak no more than we've allowed the Lord to impute to our hearts. Jesus promises us that out of our hearts will flow rivers of living water—the Holy Spirit. When we allow the Spirit to live in us, He will speak through us. Our words take on power and love we cannot produce by ourselves. If we lack warmth and affirmation for people, the trouble is probably in our hearts. If words are used to manipulate and control, we need the Holy Spirit to fill our hearts and flow through our words.

James startles us with the power of our words. They can be used to heal or hurt, build up or destroy, encourage or dishearten. What a frightening power the Lord has entrusted to us! The key to this passage is in the gift of wisdom from the Holy Spirit. When we invite the Holy Spirit to dwell in us, we are given the gift of wise speech. When we ask for His wisdom, He gives it in abundance. We will be able to see with discernment and speak with directness.

The way from God to a human heart is through a human heart.
—S.D. GORDON

A Wordless Denial

Matthew 26:31-35,69-75; 1 Peter 3:13-17

*Sanctify the Lord God in your hearts, and always be
ready to give a defense to everyone who asks you a reason
for the hope that is in you, with meekness and fear.*
(1 PETER 3:15)

The account of Peter's denial is an alarming reminder of how we
can use words to deny our Lord. Often we do it in what we refuse
to say as much as by what we say. When we have an opportunity
to witness but remain silent, that's denial. Or think of the ways
we contradict what we believe by the way we talk! The very fact
that we talk so little about what we believe gives the impression
that we believe very little. This is an eloquent, wordless denial.
There's more than one way of saying, "I do not know the Man!"
It's then the cock crows.

But it is exciting to read Peter's own challenge many years later
in his letter to the early church. The disciple who denied the Lord
by what he didn't say, later became a bold apostle and encouraged
others to be ready to give an account for the hope that Christ had
placed within them.

Often I hear people say, "My witness is my life. I don't talk
with others about my faith." That is making quite a claim for our
life! But it is also a denial of people's right to know what is behind
our quality of life.

Let's make today a day to share the reason for the hope that is within us.

A Talent of Words

Matthew 25:14-30

To one He gave five talents, to another two, and to another one, to each according to his own ability; and immediately he went on a journey.
(Matthew 25:15)

Today let's think of the gift of words in the context of the parable of the talents. Our words can be used to multiply the kingdom of God—words of love, forgiveness, encouragement, and hope. We can use the talent of what He's done for us to share the adventure of new life with other people. They will listen to what Christ can do for them if there has been authenticity in our life and words. We will all have to make an accounting of what we did with the precious gift of words. The talent can be multiplied if we use words to share Christ's love.

There may be some of us who are more capable in communicating our faith, but we all have at least one talent. We need to dig it up and begin using it. The Lord has arranged relationships for all of us with people He wants to love through our expressions of words of love and explanations of what He means to us and can mean to them. I am a Christian because two friends in college used their gift of words to communicate affirmation and then tell me about the Savior. Think of all the people who may not live forever because our talent of words is buried!

Today is the day to dig up the talent of words and invest it in sharing love and hope with others.

Get to the Point!

Job 11:1-8

*Shall a multitude of words go unanswered, and
a talkative man be acquitted?*
(Job 11:2)

Jesus was never impressed with long, formal prayers that were
prayed to be heard and admired by people. He exposed and condemned people who misused the dynamic of prayer to gain spiritual status with others. We all know people whose oratory in
prayer must offend God. We do not pray to convince God, but to
converse with Him. Our prayer is a response to His Spirit at work
within us, creating the desire to pray. A multitude of words makes
little difference. Get to the point! Be simple and direct!

Note the people who arrested Jesus' attention. He was always
utterly available to the person in need who cried out the brief,
honest prayer, "Master, have mercy—help me!" A person full of
talk did not win Jesus' approval. He often shocked the verbose
and loquacious pretenders to piety who tried to create an impression with words. He pressed them beyond their words to their
moral condition. His radical moral demand brought reality and
honesty to the easy, word-oriented followers. Jesus demanded integrity of words and life.

*Some of us talk until we know what we want to
say. Christ helps us to get to the point.*

Giving and Forgiving Love

Matthew 5:38-40

*You have heard that it was said, "An eye for
an eye and a tooth for a tooth."*
(MATTHEW 5:38)

Don't miss the radical challenge Jesus made in this passage. The
Hebrews were very proud of their distinctive application of the
lex talionis, the practice of exact retribution. It had brought sanity
in the measurement of what a person could do to someone who
harmed or hurt him.

But Jesus outdistanced that a million miles. He called for no
retribution at all! It was no longer to be eye-for-eye and tooth-for-
tooth retaliation. The Master went way beyond the equal expression of anger and resentment. He drove home His point with
three very pointed illustrations: a blow with the back of the hand
(that's what happens when you turn your right cheek after your
left one has been struck with the palm of a right-handed person!),
giving a person who sues you for your tunic your only cloak, and
going a second mile with someone who compels you to go one.

The only way to live the way Jesus called us to live is by His
power. The life He challenges us to live, He more than exemplified Himself. His love is unchanging, unqualified, and unlimited.
It is giving and forgiving. Who in your life needs that quality of
love from you today?

What the Lord requires, He inspires.

Second-Mile Living

Matthew 5:41-42

Whoever compels you to go one mile, go with him two.
(MATTHEW 5:41)

The "second mile" has a fascinating background. The word *to compel* is from the Greek verb *aggareuein*. The noun form comes from the Persian word meaning a courier of the ancient postal system. Each road was divided into stages that took about a day to travel.

The custom was that a private citizen and his horse could be pressed into service to go a stage of the way. The word *aggareuein* is the word for such compulsive enlistment. Occupying troops could demand obedience by force. In Palestine, a Jew could be pressed into service at any moment. He had no recourse but to fulfill what was demanded of him.

What Jesus seems to be saying is that if a person asks you to go one mile and you do it, you are only fulfilling what is required in an occupied country. If, however, you keep the load and indicate willingness to go on in service, you surprise and impress others with your loving openness. The irreducible minimum does not impress Jesus. He calls His people to keep the load and press on.

Christ calls us to second-mile living with people.

Get Cracking!

Matthew 5:43-48

You shall be perfect, just as your Father in heaven is perfect.
(MATTHEW 5:48)

A man who celebrated his ninety-fifth birthday asserted that he had no enemies. "How do you live 95 years and have no enemies?" someone asked. "I've outlived them all!" was his answer. We laugh. But then we begin to wonder. Most of us are not that fortunate. We have people who disturb and distress us all through life. Who are your enemies? Think of them. Now consider Jesus' demanding words about loving our enemies.

We are to be perfect even as our heavenly Father is perfect. The Greek word used to translate Jesus' Aramaic word is *telios,* meaning "purpose." To be perfect is to accomplish our purpose. Just as our heavenly Father continually accomplishes His purpose moment by moment, so can we. That forces us to consider the reason we are alive. We were created to be loved and to love. Our goal is not perfectionism on our own strength, but to set our ultimate goal to receive and communicate God's love. That's top priority. All other lesser goals of life must fit into this purpose. What in your life gets in the way of this primary goal?

Today is a day to get cracking in accomplishing my real purpose.

Love Becomes Involved

Luke 10:25-37

He, wanting to justify himself, said to Jesus,
"And who is my neighbor?"
(LUKE 10:29)

The Good Samaritan expressed practical love. He did not give pious words of comfort and pass by on the other side. He helped the man change his painful condition and got him the help he needed. His love got him involved.

Words of love are cheap. Involvement that costs time, privacy, and money is love that counts. God got involved in Christ in the suffering of the world. It cost the cross.

When is the last time you were inconvenienced because of the needs of someone else? When has your pleasure of privacy been altered to give specific, costly love? When did you set your own plans aside to spend time with someone in need?

Most of us are like the Levite and the Priest. We say, "I sympathize." But do we? How much? The Good Samaritan gave what he had: wine and oil for the wound, his beast for transportation, his money for lodging in the inn. Also he knew the value of follow-up: He said he would come back. The need placed in his path had to be seen through to final healing, not just a passing concern.

Who in your life needs that quality of love today?

When God Is Our Audience

Matthew 6:1-4

You have no reward from your Father in heaven.
(Matthew 6:1)

It is dangerous to play to the wrong audience. Jesus was concerned about people who played their lives for the approval of others rather than God. The target of this passage was the hypocrites who did charitable deeds, giving alms for the adulation and approval of people rather than God. The classical meaning of the word *hypocrite* is an actor in a play who played more than one part. The hypocritical Pharisees were play-acting at religion for the wrong audience. Charitable deeds should be done out of praise to God for His grace and love, not for the applause of people.

We laugh at the picture of a person going to the Temple to give alms with a brass band leading the way to call attention to the gift and the giver. He will have the reward of people, but not of God. All that we have and are is a gift from God. The question is, "Who gets the glory?" We can never outgive God. The more we give to Him and His work in the world, the more He can entrust to us.

Write out a description of yourself as the person you want to be in Christ, eliminating any hypocrisy.

When Our Own Horn Is Flat

Matthew 6:2

When you do a charitable deed, do not sound a trumpet before you as the hypocrites do in the synagogues and in the streets, that they may have glory from men. Assuredly, I say to you, they have their reward.
(MATTHEW 6:2)

"Don't blow your own horn" is a colloquial saying with which we are familiar. It means, don't draw attention to yourself, your good deeds, your own accomplishments. We all have worked out subtle ways of letting people know whom we know, what we've done, and where we've been. We drop names, places, and possessions in our conversations.

Jesus uses a metaphorical image: "When you give alms, sound no trumpet before you!" A trumpet was used to call people to worship or to announce the times of prayer. Jesus had a sense of humor. His listeners could picture a man on the way to the Temple to give alms with a trumpeter going before him to announce to everyone that he was on his way to be piously generous.

Jesus was concerned about motive. He knew that our real motive for benevolence could be exposed, cleansed, and healed only if we give without any concern for reward. When Christ's love is our only motive, then the giving is itself our reward. Who needs more than that?

Any note blown from our own horn for our own glory is flat!

An Uninformed Left Hand

Matthew 6:3

*When you do a charitable deed, do not let your left
hand know what your right hand is doing.*
(MATTHEW 6:3)

How can we follow Jesus' advice to let our lights shine that men
may see our good works (Matthew 5:16) if we do not even let our
left hand know what our right hand is doing? Is this a contradiction? Not when deeply understood.

The key is found in giving God the glory. There are some things
that we do that we should freely share with others, while there
are other things that would only be ostentations to rehearse. The
question is—Who gets the credit? Do people praise us or God
at work in us? We often hide our motivating faith and parade its
manifestation. The result is that people think we are what we are
by our own strength and do what we do by our own self-generated
graciousness.

Let's experiment today. Every time we are tempted to hide
our faith, let's make a concerted effort to share the hope of our life,
and every time we are tempted to draw attention to what we have
done, let's consciously seek anonymity. The silent gift will radiate
in our being, and the outward gift will deepen our radiance.

*Be willing to share what God has done for you
and be silent about what you have done.*

Praying to People

Matthew 6:5-6

When you pray, you shall not be like the hypocrites. For they love to pray standing in the synagogues and on the corners of the streets, that they may be seen by men. Assuredly, I say to you, they have their reward.
(MATTHEW 6:5)

Prayer is the heart of fellowship with God. In it we open our total self to God in adoration, confession, thanksgiving, and supplication. Prayer is communion with God in which He speaks to us through the thoughts engendered in our minds and the decisions of our wills. How wonderful: We can share life with the Lord and Creator of the universe!

This is why Jesus was so critical of hypocrisy in attention-oriented public prayers. Three times a day a good Jew would stop his work and turn toward Jerusalem and pray. The professionally pious arranged it so that at the time of prayer they could be seen by others. Prayer became a formal duty used to gain the approval of others. They really were praying to people and missed the true purpose of prayer.

Often prayer is talking circles around the perpendicular pronoun "I" instead of glorifying God for who He is and what He has done. Right now, tell God how much you love Him and commit today to serve Him.

Prayer is conversation with God.

The Secret Place

Matthew 6:5-8; Isaiah 65:24

When you pray, do not use vain repetitions as the heathen do.
For they think that they will be heard for their many words.
(MATTHEW 6:7)

Prayer is the only source of authentic originality and creativity. Jesus said that we are to pray in secret. The idea behind this challenge was that people of wealth often had a place where their treasures and valuables were stored. They would go to this room to count their accumulations and to do their private business affairs. This suggests that Jesus wanted people to talk to God in the place where their real security was hidden.

Our inner hearts are our secret place. That's where Jesus wants to meet us. He was not talking about a place, but a quality. The "room" of which He spoke is more than a location. It is the dwelling place of real, personal self-purpose, plans, and perspective. The Lord wants to communicate with us there about who we are and where we are going. The reason many prayers are empty and ineffective is that they seldom come from the "secret place." We fear opening the door of that inner citadel to God—or even to ourselves. Today can be different. We can invite the Lord into the secret place where our real decisions about life and values are made. Start now!

I will invite the Lord into the secret place where my
decisions about my life and value are made.

The Model Prayer

Matthew 6:9-15

In this manner, therefore, pray.
(MATTHEW 6:9)

What we call the Lord's Prayer is really a Disciple's Prayer. Actually, it is a prayer of awesome depth for those who have come to know Christ, have turned the control of their lives over to Him, and are motivated by His indwelling Spirit to pray this radical prayer.

This prayer was meant as a model of prayer, not just as a memorized prayer. In it Jesus taught His disciples how to reverence God, how to pray for His rule in all things, how to acknowledge Him as the source of life, and how to ask for forgiveness and help in testing times. Our public worship and our private prayers should be guided by this prayer, but we wonder if we do not press people who are not committed to Christ to pray beyond their experience and belief by using it in public ritual. Its revolutionary content is soon blended into the general religious words and practices that most people do not take very seriously. Go over each word and phrase and ask, "What would it mean to live this prayer today?"

Lord, forgive me my faithless familiarity with Your prayer. Help me really mean what I pray.

The Fatherhood of God

Matthew 6:9; Galatians 4:1-7

In this manner, therefore, pray: Our Father
in heaven, hallowed be Your name.
(MATTHEW 6:9)

The Savior taught us to call God our Father. He is the source of limitless love, forgiveness before we ask, interventions when we need them most, hope for a million new beginnings. That's how much our Father loves us and why He sent Christ so we could know Him as He is.

When we pray "Our Father in heaven," we affirm that God is beyond us and other than we are, and yet He chooses to be with us in Christ. Heaven is the realm in which God is praised unreservedly and known completely. To know the Father in heaven is to have heaven begin now and know that death will be only a transition to complete union with Him. That enables us to hallow His name.

The word *hallowed* means "holy." A name signifies the character, nature, and power of a person. The name *Father* is holy. When we pray, "Our Father in heaven, hallowed be Your name," we are saying, "We accept Your unique place, affirm Your unlimited power, and are assured of Your nature of grace toward us. We will live in that confidence today."

God is willing to fill us with His love as water is
willing to flow into an empty channel.

The Key to Power

Matthew 6:10; 1 Corinthians 4:20;
Luke 13:18-21; John 3:1-5

Your kingdom come. Your will be done on earth as it is in heaven.
(MATTHEW 6:10)

The kingdom of God is the reign and rule of God in us, in our
relationships with others, in our circumstances, in society, and in
all future eventualities. This is an awesome prayer, which only a
disciple can pray. It means we want to surrender our minds, emotions, wills, bodies, relationships, and responsibilities to God for
His will to be done.

When we do His will, the kingdom of God becomes a reality.
This sentence in Jesus' model prayer is a promise and an admonition. We are assured that we can know and receive power to do
God's will. Our task is to ask, seek, and knock until we have the
inner assurance of God's best for us. In every situation, there are
usually three pressing possibilities: what we want, what others
want for us, and what God wants of us. To pray "Your will be
done" is to take the kingdom of God as Jesus revealed it as our
charter and make our decisions on that basis. That's how heaven
can begin on earth for us. Give the Lord a chance. He will show
us what we are to do and give us the courage to do it.

Dear God, reign in me, rule in me. You are Sovereign of my life!

Daily!

Matthew 6:11; John 6:1-58

Give us this day our daily bread.
(MATTHEW 6:11)

We are dependent on God for everything. We could not breathe a breath, think a thought, move a muscle, work a day, or develop our lives without His moment-by-moment provision. Daily bread is more than food to eat. Through the Bread of Life, Jesus Christ, all things we have and are become an evidence of unmerited favor from a Lord who knows our needs. Make this a day for "flash prayers" in which you repeatedly say "Thank You, Lord" for the abundant mercies in every moment of life.

The word "daily" reminds us that yesterday's blessings are not sufficient for today. The Greek word is *epiousion,* a combination of *epi,* "upon"; and *eimi,* "to be." So we are to pray for bread for what is to be. Bread for going on, or bread for the morrow. "Give us today the bread we need for tomorrow." We cannot live on the stale grace of our yesterdays. The Lord gives the day and shows the way. That's why we must seek His guidance and power for each new day. Thanking God in advance for His blessing for today frees us to live to the fullest today without worry over tomorrow. Have a great day—today!

Give us today the bread we need for tomorrow.

Let God Forgive You

Matthew 6:12,14-15; Mark 11:25-26

Forgive us our debts, as we forgive our debtors.
(MATTHEW 6:12)

This is the only segment of the Disciple's Prayer that Jesus found it necessary to explain and reemphasize. And with good reason. Forgiveness is costly—it was for God on the cross, and it is for us. But true forgiveness from us to others is not possible unless we have had fresh experiences of God's forgiveness. Out of gratitude for His forgiving love, we will want to make things right with others. The only person who is hurt by unforgiven hurts is us!

That leads us to some very serious thinking about three groups of people: those who need our forgiveness, those from whom we need to seek forgiveness, and those who need our help in forgiving others. Make a list of people in all three categories. Chances are that our longest list will be of people we need to forgive. It is frightening to ponder Jesus' words that we cannot be forgiven unless we forgive.

The years have taught me that when I'm really upset by others there is usually a need in me for fresh grace. When I receive it, then I'm ready to become a reconciler with and between people. What about you?

Today is forgiveness day!

Lord, Help Me!

Matthew 6:13; Hebrews 2:17-18; 1 Corinthians 10:13; James 1:13-14

Do not lead us into temptation, but deliver us from the evil one.
(Matthew 6:13)

God would not lead us into temptation. Then what does this petition mean? The implication is, keep us away from temptation; be with us when we are tempted; strengthen us in life's temptations. The second portion of the petition helps us understand the first. Evil is not abstract. It is rooted in Satan, the evil one, who is in opposition to our Lord and uses situations and people to entice us.

But we belong to Christ, who has overcome Satan through His death and resurrection. We become "overcomers" through Christ. He has sealed us from the power of evil and temptation that could entangle us. But we must cooperate with the Lord and accept His overcoming strength. When we pray this petition of the Disciple's Prayer, we admit our need and receive daily strength for life's temptations.

When the pressures are beyond us, He will intervene. Trust Him. All we need to do is cry out for help, and He will give us strength equal to the temptation.

When we do ill, the Devil tempts us;
when we do nothing, we tempt him.
—Thomas Fuller

All That We Need

Matthew 6:13; Jude 24-25; Philippians 4:13

Yours is the kingdom and the power and the glory forever. Amen.
(MATTHEW 6:13)

The last sentence of the Disciple's Prayer is an adoration and assurance. It ascribes to God the kingdom, power, and glory that are aspects of His nature. He is Lord of all, the source of all power, the One who manifests Himself in our lives.

To pray "Yours is the kingdom" is to make the Lord the King of our lives. It is an act of sublime submission. When we do that, power begins to flow through us. We become the riverbed of the Spirit of God. The word in Greek for power is *dunamis*, from which our words *dynamite* and *dynamic* come. The same power that raised Jesus from the dead is ours. We are no longer helpless victims of life. But the power is given to us to know and do God's will. We have come full circle in our prayer. Now we are ready to live for God's glory in all that we say and do. There is no limit of power available to a person who is willing to give God the glory and leave the results to Him.

Praise the Lord, His will is my will; the power to do it comes from Him, and the glory goes to Him. The antidote to pride is praise.

A Disciple's Prayer

Matthew 6:9-15; 7:7-12

*Ask, and it will be given to you; seek, and you will
find; knock, and it will be opened to you.*
(MATTHEW 7:7)

Let's recap what we've learned about how and what to pray from
our study of the Disciple's Prayer. The first section deals with how
we are to praise God, the hallowing of His name, the desire for
His kingdom, and the doing of His will. Only then can we consider our needs. God must be put at the center before we can lift
up our petitions. All-powerful praying begins by a commitment
to the majesty, purpose, and will of God. The second section of
the prayer deals with our petitions of supplication: food and daily
provision for today, forgiveness for the past, intervention for the
future. All our needs will be satisfied when they are surrendered
completely to our Lord.

The third section is a commitment to God. To pray "Yours is
the kingdom and the power and the glory forever" is to declare
our ultimate purpose. Thus, from the Disciple's Prayer we see that
prayer is adoration, confession, intercession, supplication, and a
dedication. Like the five fingers of our hand, each is necessary to
grasp and hold the promise of prayer. Now pray the Disciple's
Prayer, grasping one finger for each step of prayer.

Today I will live the Disciple's Prayer by the Lord's power.

The Window of the Heart

Matthew 6:6-18

Do not be like the hypocrites, with a sad countenance.
(MATTHEW 6:16)

Our face is the window of our heart. Or it should be. In our world of cosmetics and plastic surgery, we are not always able to look through the window. Even more serious, many of us develop a duality, so that our faces contradict our hearts. It is also true when we are sad and pretend to be glad. But it is also true when our joy is not expressed in radiance on our faces. What is on our faces, not our words, is the medium of our message.

Often our faces deny our faith. Our faces may be an introduction for others to Christ or a negation of what He could mean in their lives. Who would want to know Christ personally because of what is on your face? The Pharisees disfigured their faces or even smeared ashes on them to be sure people knew they were fasting. Fasting should have brought them closer to God and thus brought a radiance to their faces. The purpose of fasting had been so distorted that it was identified by a grim face. They had lost the joy! That leaves us with a question: How should our faces look because we have talked to God face-to-face?

The Lord bless you, and keep you;
The Lord make His face shine on you,
And be gracious to you.
—NUMBERS 6:24-25

Joy's Secret Place

Matthew 6:18; James 1:1-9

Your Father who sees in secret will reward you openly.
(MATTHEW 6:18)

It was obligatory for all Jews to fast on Yom Kippur and Rosh Hashanah. The Pharisees exceeded that by fasting on Monday and Thursday, the days they believed Moses ascended and descended Mount Sinai. The original purpose of fasting was self-denial and deeper communion with God. For many of the Pharisees, it became an outward display of piety and holiness. When the purpose of fasting was lost, the pretense of piousness began. Communion with God was displayed as a grim, unhappy thing.

Religion is considered to be that by many people. That's why it is so important to show on our face what is in our heart. The dominant note of Christianity is joy, an outward expression of the grace of God in our heart.

The truth is that joy is the unassailable, undisturbable, undeniable experience of those who know Christ in the midst of difficulty. Happiness is always dependent on our circumstances. Joy is way beyond that; it is the outward expression of the inner experience of God's grace. Joy cannot be dampened regardless of what has happened.

If you experience joy, tell your face!

Someone Is Watching You

Acts 6:8-15

*All who sat in the council, looking steadfastly at
him, saw his face as the face of an angel.*
(Acts 6:15)

There are times when our hearts ache with grief, suffering, or disappointment. It is then that joy, which is consistent through pain, shines through.

The elders and scribes at Stephen's trial and subsequent martyrdom could not take their eyes off him. And Saul of Tarsus would never forget. I have often wondered whether Stephen's radiant face remained in the gallery of Saul's mind as he set off to Damascus to further harass the Christians. He had seen what the living Christ could do for a person. I am convinced that the vision of Christ in the human heart and splendidly radiant on the face of a faithful disciple contributed to Saul's conversion. When he had a vision of the Lord, he saw the source of Stephen's face.

That leaves us with a question: Who in our life would want to know Christ because of what's on our face? Paul Tournier said, "Our task is to live our personal communion with Christ with such intensity as to make it contagious."

Someone's first look at Christ will be your face.

When the Lord Smiles at You

Psalm 27:1-14; 2 Corinthians 4:6

*When You said "Seek My face," my heart said
to You, "Your face, O LORD, I shall seek."*
(PSALM 27:8)

Seeking the face of the Lord transforms our faces. The only way to
have a radiant face is to meet the Lord face-to-face. The expression
"Seek My face" in this psalm means to seek the communion with
the Lord for which we were created. What is on our faces will come
naturally from that. The psalmist deliberately took his eyes off his
enemies and difficulties and turned to the face of the Lord. We behold God in the face of Jesus Christ. The more we know of Christ,
the more we know of God and what we were meant to be.

If we want a face that alerts people to what life was meant
to be, we will need to turn our eyes upon Jesus. Helen Lemmel
was right: "Turn your eyes upon Jesus, look full in His wonderful
face, and the things of earth will grow strangely dim in the light
of His glory and grace."

Close your eyes and see Christ's face looking at you in tender
mercy and confident assurance.

*Whene'er I shut my eyes to pray
Then let me see Your gentle face
That smiles upon me all the day,
So full of love and grace.*

The Anointed Heart

1 John 2:18-29

*You have an anointing from the Holy One,
and you know all things.*
(1 John 2:20)

The ancient custom was to anoint with oil as a symbol of joy and the Lord's blessing. The Greek word for anointing is *chrism*. When a Greek alpha is added it is *charisma*. *Chrism* must come before *charisma*. It is the anointing of the Holy Spirit that produces the winsome, winning radiance of authentic *charisma*.

We can know this deeper anointing. The anointing of the heart by the Holy Spirit results in extraordinary power, wisdom, and love. True anointing of the Holy Spirit enables confidence, courage, and conviction. When we refer to an "anointed" person, we speak of one who has been blessed, infilled, and empowered by the Spirit of God. May it be said of us, "You have an anointing from the Holy One, and you know all things."

Then we will know life's greatest satisfaction. We will astonish ourselves and amaze others by what the Lord has done with a human being completely yielded to Him.

You've got charisma!

Treasuring the Right Treasure

Matthew 6:19-21

Where your treasure is, there your heart will be also.
(MATTHEW 6:21)

We will live forever. But where, with whom, and how? Jesus speaks to that portion of us that will not perish. What kind of heart (or soul) will we have developed during the years of this life? That determines our eternal destiny. If we have not wanted Him and His kingdom now, why should our hearts change at death?

What we do with the earthly treasure will determine our heavenly treasure. Our life here is the container of the life that goes on forever. The word *treasure* meant the container, not the valued articles themselves. When Jesus said, "Do not lay up for yourself treasures on earth," He meant, "Do not invest your life in those things that debilitate and frustrate when you come to the demarcation point of death. Don't get so entangled that the one thing you will take with you—your true self—will be stunted and unfit for life forever." A surrender of our life to Christ will call for a daily relinquishment of our own will for our life and possessions. Then we can be sure of living forever in heaven.

My treasure, my soul, contains love for Christ,
with whom I will spend eternity.

What's Really Important?

Luke 16:10-13

*If you have not been faithful in the unrighteous mammon,
who will commit to your trust the true riches?*
(LUKE 16:11)

Treasure for earth or treasure for heaven? Christ mentioned three types of wealth people tried to amass on earth that caused them to miss a treasure in heaven.

There are things a moth can destroy. A portion of people's wealth consisted of fabrics in rugs, hangings, and clothing. Vermin and moths threatened this treasure. The beauty was easily destroyed.

There are things that rust can destroy. The Greek word *brosis* actually means "eating away." For us, the word *rust* is more applicable. Look at the junk heaps filled with old and smashed cars that once were the pride and joy of some family.

Then there are things that can be stolen. In this false category are all the treasures we collect in money, stocks, and bonds. If Jesus were to repeat His parable to us, He would talk about mortgage depreciation, market fluctuation, and financial insecurity. The point, however, would have been the same: Our values are distorted. The one thing we will take with us—our soul—often has the least of our care and concern.

Today I will care for the one part of me that will live forever.

The Indestructible Treasure

Titus 3:1-11

When the kindness and the love of God our Savior toward
man appeared, not by works of righteousness which we
have done, but according to His mercy He saved us.
(TITUS 3:4-5)

What are treasures in heaven? This phrase communicated more to Jesus' listeners than it does to us. A treasure in heaven for a good Jew meant the accumulation of good deeds recorded for him in heaven. This idea is not altogether dead among us. We often think of God as a tally keeper recording our good deeds against our failures. But we know this is not true, according to Jesus' message on forgiveness. Our good deeds flow from our experience of His love, and not to assure our eternal life. Yet it is interesting that often at Christian funerals we fall back into assuring a family that their loved one is with God because of his good life.

The other aspect of Jewish belief was that character was treasure in heaven. That comes closer to Jesus' teaching, but He went deeper. He concerned Himself with character in the depth of the soul. He believed that when a person lived in fellowship with God, God's own nature was imparted to him. The relationship of love and forgiveness through Christ nurtures a person's total being. Anything that encourages, depends, and develops this relationship is treasure in heaven, for this is the one thing that cannot be destroyed.

If your treasure is in heaven there's no need to worry on earth.

The Kingdom of Thingdom

Colossians 3:1-4; Hebrews 13:5;
1 Timothy 6:17-19

*Let your conduct be without covetousness; be content
with such things as you have. For He Himself has
said, "I will never leave you nor forsake you."*
(HEBREWS 13:5)

We live in a kingdom of thingdom! Much of our security is in things. We work and save and spend (often overspend) to keep our lives stabilized by things.

A friend recently had an experience that put things into perspective. On the way to a conference her bag was misplaced by the airline. She was frantic, not because she had no change of clothing for two days, but because she had foolishly placed her most precious jewelry in the inside pocket of the bag. The airline called and said the bag had been found, but also had been burglarized.

On the way to the airport she had to face how important these things had become. When she got her bag, she quickly checked to see what was missing. The thieves had taken everything of monetary value but had missed the pearls and the brooch, the only things of spiritual value, because of their sentimental value. The crisis had brought into focus her false master, which kept her from a deeper loyalty to Christ. What things dominate you? If they were lost or stolen, what would it do to you?

What things in your life may have become too important?

August

What Do You See?

Matthew 6:22-23

If…your eye is good, your whole body will be full of light.
(MATTHEW 6:22)

"What you see is what you get." In this passage Jesus is saying, "What you get is what you see!" What we receive from Him is what enables the eyes of our hearts to see clearly. When we accept Him as absolute Lord of our lives, then we can see all that we have and are as His gracious provision. We can worship the Giver and not the gifts.

That gives us the key to understanding good and bad eyes. The word for *good* in Greek means both "single" and "generous." When we are single-minded in our commitment, we see generously, with love and gratitude. The word for *bad* means "grudging" and "stingy." Sick spiritual eyes will make us judgmental and negative. How does this relate to the previous thought about treasuring the right treasure? How do you look with the eyes of your heart at what you have and have accomplished? What do you see? How does that make your eyes generous toward others?

*Absolute commitment to Jesus Christ makes us
generous people. We can give ourselves away.*

The Mammon Membrane

Matthew 6:24; Luke 16:1-8

You cannot serve God and mammon.
(MATTHEW 6:24)

The word *mammon* in Hebrew means "material possessions." Originally it meant money or possessions entrusted to someone else. The root of the word means "to entrust." As the years passed, the word changed from that which was entrusted to that in which a person put his or her trust. All we have has been entrusted to us by God. What would it mean to put the Lord first in our lives and trust Him as our Master in the use of what He has entrusted to us?

How often do we ask God's direction in financial matters? Do we pray about our budget? Do we give as much for the need of the community and world as we spend on our vacations, alcohol, personal appearance, and unnecessary comforts?

Do we follow the biblical admonition of the tithe? In our budgeting, are God's causes through the church and benevolent organizations in the world at the top of our budget? Do we take care of our tithe before anything else?

Well, how did you do in that inventory? Probably the answer is that we need to break through the mammon membrane!

What would it mean for you to put the Lord first in your life and trust Him as Master of how you use what He has entrusted to you?

When Possessions Possess Us

Luke 12:13-21

God said to him, "Fool! This night your soul will be required of you; then whose will those things be which you have provided?"
(Luke 12:20)

Possessions eventually possess us if they become our reason for being. The danger is that they become our "life," our dominant desire. The Lord becomes an addendum to our already full life. This parable flashes with meaning when we contrast verses 15 and 19. The word for *life* is *zoe,* meaning "essential life," eternal life as contrasted with death. The word for *soul* is *psuche,* referring to mental capacity. The rich fool was talking to his thinking process, not his soul. What he was really saying was, "Just think what I have achieved." His voice of self-assurance came from within himself, an echo of his frenzied accumulation. The voice of God interrupted his self-accolade: "Fool! Tonight you will die. Now who will get all you have acquired?"

What does that have to say to us? Is it possible to miss eternal life by making gods of the material possessions of life? A helpful way to answer that question is with a question. What dominates our thought most of the time? Our god is whatever controls our thinking and demands our allegiance. If we were to ask a family member or a really close friend to answer, what would be the response?

If I worry over too much or too little I am a fool
with a full barn and an empty heart.

Who Is Running Your Life?

James 4:13-17

What is your life?
(James 4:14)

The man was at a standstill spiritually. He believed in Christ, loved his church, and was a fine, responsible Christian business-man. Yet he had an anchor in the mud. He believed in Christ as Savior of his life but not as Lord of his life.

"What are the values that drive and shape your life? How do you decide between alternatives for your life? Just how much does Christ have to say about your daily life?" I asked.

"Very little!" he said. "I decide things according to what I think is best for everyone. But seldom, if ever, do I ask for specific direc-tion. I feel that's my business. God gave me some intelligence to work things out for Him."

That attitude is exactly what James is talking about in today's scripture. He is concerned about people who decide things for themselves without seeking the Lord's guidance. When we open ourselves to His guiding power, exciting things begin to happen, and we are released from the tension of running our own lives.

I will allow the Lord to run my life today.

Strangling the Soul

Matthew 6:25-29

I say to you, do not worry about your life.
(MATTHEW 6:25)

Worry is thinking turned toxic, the imagination picturing the worst. The word *worry* comes from the root "to choke or strangle." Worry does choke and strangle our creative capacity to think, hope, and dream. It twists the joy out of life. Worry changes nothing except the worrier. It becomes a habit.

At the core, it is a low-grade fever of agnosticism. When we worry, we express a lurking form of doubt that God either knows, cares, or is able to do anything. It is a form of loneliness—facing eventualities by ourselves on our meager strength. Worry is a distortion of our capacity to care.

In verses 31-34 is Jesus' description of worry and His diagnosis of what to do about it. Three sources of worry are enumerated: what we eat, drink, and wear. Jesus does an amazing thing in this passage. He tells us to exchange secondary worries with one great concern; He shows us the anxiety which can cure anxiety.

Our only concern should be to put God first in our lives. Then our only anxiety will be that we may miss the real reason we were born: to seek first the kingdom of God and to be right with Him.

Worry is interest paid on the trouble before it becomes due.
—WILLIAM R. INGE

God Really Cares

Matthew 6:30-33

Your heavenly Father knows that you need all these things.
(MATTHEW 6:32)

Morris Bishop has caught the yearning of human nature for identity in the midst of the secularized anonymity of our life in the poem "The Perforated Spirit."

> The fellows up in Personnel,
>   They have a set of cards on me.
> The sprinkled perforations tell
>   My individuality.
> And what am I? I am a chart
>   Upon the card of IBM;
> The secret places of the heart
>   Have little secrecy for them.
> Monday my brain began to buzz,
>   I was in agony all night.
> I found out what the trouble was—
>   They had my paper clip too tight.

Ever feel like that? Does anyone care?

God does. One of the most profound affirmations of Scripture is that the same God who is Creator and Lord of the universe, and the Source of all life, knows about each of us personally. He loves us as if there were only one of us.

God knows and cares about each of us and our needs.

The Father's Good Pleasure

Luke 12:22-34

Do not fear, little flock, for it is your Father's
good pleasure to give you the kingdom.
(LUKE 12:32)

Recently a man asked one of my sons a personal question: "What's your dad really like?" The man wanted inside information about me that only a member of the family could know.

Jesus gives us that kind of intimate information about God in today's scripture. Only the Father's Son could know and share His inner heart. And what He tells us has the power to change our lives. Be sure to listen to the amazing promise made in verse 32: Savor the word *pleasure*. The same Father who said about Jesus, "This is my beloved Son, in whom I am well pleased," is pleased to give us life in His kingdom.

But Jesus assures us that we will be given the desire and the capacity to want God's will and way in our lives. We get the feeling from Jesus that God is hovering over us, longing for us to want what He wants for us. He is not against us, waiting for us to measure up. We are His beloved. So why worry? What we need will be given at the time and in the way that is best for us.

Today I will live in the wondrous truth that in spite of all I
might just have said or done, the Father is unqualifiedly pleased
and wills to give me life in His kingdom. So why worry?

What Can I Say?

Matthew 10:1-42

*Do not worry about how or what you should speak. For it will
be given to you in that hour what you should speak; for it is not
you who speak, but the Spirit of your Father who speaks in you.*
(MATTHEW 10:19-20)

One of the great sources of worry for all of us is what we will say
in life's challenging moments. This passage is Jesus' assurance that
the Holy Spirit will give us the thoughts, words, and courage to
speak. Our only task is to open our minds in calm expectation of
wisdom beyond our own capacity. We need not worry. The Lord
will never let us down!

Note the progression in Jesus' challenge. The Spirit speaks in
us before He speaks through us. He gives us X-ray vision in discerning situations and people. When we calmly ask what He has
to say, He will speak in the deepest regions of our inner self. He
will infuse thoughts into our brains, love in our emotions so we
can "speak the truth in love," and incisiveness in our wills to dare
to communicate what He has revealed to us.

The Spirit-filled Christian has supernatural capacities. We are
equipped by the Lord for life's knotty problems and complexities.
Surrender the situation to Him, saying, "Lord, speak to me that I
may speak." And He will!

*I will listen to the Lord before I speak,
and then speak with boldness and love.*

Love Is the Antidote to Fear

John 6:15-21

It is I; do not be afraid.
(JOHN 6:20)

The account of the disciples in the storm at sea is an actual record of what happened, but also a parable of our life. How like these disciples we are. We struggle on the sea of life. The waves of problems and perplexities threaten to engulf us. Life seems like a perpetual night waiting for dawn.

Then Jesus comes. What He said to the disciples He says to us. The actual translation of verse 20 is "I am. Have no fear!" This is one of the great "I am" statements of our Lord. It is Jesus' undeniable claim to be Yahweh, God Himself. He could calm the water He had created. He is in charge of our lives. Nothing can happen to us that He cannot use for His glory and our growth. If we believe this and trust Him, worry is cut at the taproot. Watch! He is coming. Listen to Him: "I am. Have no fear." On the basis of that, we can stop worrying and start living! The secret to overcoming fear is to ask for and receive more of Christ's perfect love. Today is the day to start!

*We are "more than conquerors," not through our own
valor or stoic resolution, not through a creed or code or
philosophy, but "through Him who loved us"—through the
thrust and pressure of the invading grace of Christ.*
—JAMES S. STEWART

Sure Anchors in the Storm

Acts 27:13-44

*Fearing lest we should run aground on the rocks, they dropped
four anchors from the stern, and prayed for day to come.*
(Acts 27:29)

What are your anchors for the storm? What do you have within
you to stabilize the ship of life through the winds of doubt, sorrow's bitter sea, temptation's jagged rocks?

During Paul's voyage to Rome under Roman guards a north-
easter caught hold of the ship. In the frenzy Paul alone was confident. While the ship was driven across the sea nearing the coast
of Malta, the sailors sounded the fathoms and, fearing for rocks,
let out four anchors. But Paul had four of his own anchors.

He had the anchor of *trust* in the present help of God. God
had been faithful in each new crisis. Then he had the anchor of
hope. The Lord had seen the apostle through great difficulties.

But Paul also had the anchor of *purpose.* He knew his work
was not finished. He was to stand before Caesar. God would finish what He had begun. A purpose liberates our fears and gives
us courage. Lastly, there was the anchor of *fellowship.* God always
provides some people who know and understand, listen and love.
These are our anchors until the dawn of a new day.

Put out the anchors and ride out the storm.

Creative Anxiety

Luke 15:11-24

I will arise and go to my father, and will say to him, "Father,
I have sinned against heaven and before you."
(Luke 15:18)

There is a creative anxiety. Jesus seems to be saying that we ought to be much more anxious about living in the kingdom under God's guidance than anxious about things that do not ultimately count.

Jesus' listeners thought they had it made spiritually. They took God for granted and misused their election to be His people. They had grown careless and had tried to manipulate God for their own purposes. They had shelved Him, and they took Him off the shelf only when they needed Him.

Jesus is saying, "Don't be so sure you can use God that way; without knowing it, your anxiety about little things is really caused by the anxiety of separation from God." Anxiety of this deeper kind is God's gift. It tells us something is wrong, missing, out of joint. The uneasiness we feel in quiet moments, our disquiet inside when all is quiet around us, our loneliness in a crowd, our deep insecurity even when all seems outwardly in order—that's creative anxiety because it presses us back to God. The Father is waiting!

The Lord has a tight grip on us. He will
never let us go. Not now; not ever.

Today Is All We Have

Matthew 6:34

*Do not worry about tomorrow, for tomorrow will worry about
its own things. Sufficient for the day is its own trouble.*
(MATTHEW 6:34)

One of the most disturbing aspects of anxiety is concern for the
future. Soren Kierkegaard said, "What is anxiety? It is the next
day." It is the unwritten chapter of our lives that distresses most
of us. Jesus gives us the key: Let tomorrow take care of itself; live
today to the full.

The point is that if we live the way He suggested today, tomorrow will be more glorious than we ever dared to imagine.
The reason for this is that what we do today will be inseparably
related to what can happen tomorrow. We can have something
to say about what will happen by how we handle what's happening. Jesus' advice is that there is sufficient opportunity today
to see His power at work over evil and trouble. Concentrate on
that, and tomorrow will be a succeeding opportunity. Once our
ultimate "tomorrow," or eternal life, is secure, we can live without
reservation each day.

The seeds of tomorrow's harvest are today. How we cultivate
them will determine what we will reap.

Don't forget to live…today.

The Boomerang of Judgments

Matthew 7:1

Judge not, that you be not judged.
(MATTHEW 7:1)

What's wrong with judging? We can't help making judgments. Evaluations, appraisals, and ethical verdicts are a part of everyday life. Are we to overlook wrong in society or people in some kind of sentimental, mushy acceptance of evil? Are we not responsible for ourselves and those for whom we care, to see things for what they are and speak truth about them? What did Jesus mean?

He was concerned about judgments of condemnation. Whenever our judgment depreciates another human being, it is wrong. This happens when we write off another person for what he has said or done. We judge him as useless.

Also, Jesus wanted us to know that we are judged by God. If we can be as gracious to others as God has been to us, our criticism will be creative. If we first examine our own hearts before God on the same subject, we will not be as anxious to blast another person. What we give we will get. That's the boomerang of censure.

It is in an environment of friendship—Christ-inspired and Christ-guided—that people change blaming boomerangs. Our calling is to provide friendly relationships in which people can share and face their problems and change. That's our calling.

Plankated Vision

Matthew 7:3-5

*Hypocrite! First remove the plank from your own eye, and then
you will see clearly to take the speck from your brother's eye.*
(MATTHEW 7:5)

Jesus had a sense of humor. We see this in His use of hyperbole,
an overstatement to drive home a basic truth. One of the best ex-
amples of this is our scripture today. For Jesus' listeners, this must
have been a source of laughter.

The word *speck* is really the word for a splinter of wood. *Plank*
can also be translated as "beam." A plank of timber is grossly big-
ger than a splinter. The sin in us is more serious to God than the
sin in another that we criticize. The sin of negative judgment, in
God's eyes, is larger than the sin in the person we criticize. It is
easy to criticize if we have never comprehended how deadly a sin
this is. It eats away at us and breaks down not only our relationship with the people criticized, but with God.

The point of this pithy parable is that if we busy ourselves
with the plank in our own eye, we will have less time and inclination to criticize. If our sour minds are sweetened by God's forgiveness, we will have less negativism about others.

*Looking at the faults in others which I had a secret
consciousness were in myself…has more hindered my
progress in love and gentleness than all things else.*
—F.D. MAURICE

When Analysis Brings Paralysis

Matthew 7:2

With the measure you use, it will be measured back to you.
(MATTHEW 7:2)

Jesus does not condemn honest value judgments between truth and falsehood, right and wrong. He does not counsel us to abandon analysis and evaluation. We have been given powers of discernment to know what is right and to do it. The question is, With what kind of spirit do we evaluate the lives of others? What Jesus condemns in this passage is a censoriousness that ends up in playing God. When we become censorious judges of others, we constantly find fault and are negative and debilitating. We have plankated vision.

The only way to develop a nonjudgmental, noncensorious spirit is to consider what we have done with the gift of life ourselves. Jesus is very humorous in His parables of illustrations—a speck in someone's eye, a plank in our own. A censorious spirit is an unloved and unlovely spirit. We are condemnatory in our judgments when we have refused to allow God to love us sufficiently. A gracious person is one who has been loved profoundly by God and then by himself or herself.

Today, take responsibility for the way you share your insights so there will be no question of the depth of your love.

Dear God, take from my heart a censorious spirit.

The Context of Criticism

Ecclesiastes 3:7

A time to be silent and a time to speak.
(ECCLESIASTES 3:7)

Creative judgment requires timing and relationship. We dare not blurt out our judgments without an ambience of mutual acceptance, love, and sensitive timing.

In every relationship there are those things that disturb us about others. However happy a marriage, family, friendship, or business association may be, eventually there will be some friction. That's natural. We are all different and bring to every relationship all that we have been and are. The deeper two people grow together, the more of their individuality is exposed. The problems that arise between people may not indicate an inadequate relationship, but rather that each person needs to be able to say what he thinks and observes about the other so both may grow.

This is done through affirmation and timing. When we know that nothing can break our relationship with a person, we are free to say what we think. But at the right time. If we ask God to judge our judgment and guide our timing, our insights can open a new stage of growth for another person.

He has a right to criticize who has a heart to help.
—ABRAHAM LINCOLN

Before You Criticize

James 2:8-13

So speak and so do as those who will be judged by the law of liberty.
(JAMES 2:12)

Judgments often relieve us of responsibility—or so we think. But this is not really so. We categorize people in limiting preconception, expose their weakness, condemn their failure, ridicule their inadequacy, and go on our way. Judgments are careless unless we are willing to be part of God's solution. If not, we become part of the multiplication of the problem.

"All right, what are you going to do about it?" should be our response to ourselves and critical others. Talk and analysis are cheap: Action is costly; caring is demanding. What constructive thing can you do and say about the need you have cut open?

This gives us pause to think! How can we say what we have to say in such a way that people will feel our love and willingness to help? Judgments debilitate and often leave people immobilized for any constructive action. We add to the burden rather than lift it. Conversely, the way we word our insight, the spirit of love with which we communicate, can enable a person to say, "Well, I'd never thought of that! Thank you."

We have been given the mind of Christ to understand; the grace of Christ to express encouragement; and the power of Christ to act in the most creative way and at the right time to help people with the very things we might criticize.

Stumbling Block

Romans 14:1-13

*Let us not judge one another anymore, but rather resolve this, not
to put a stumbling block or a cause to fall in our brother's way.*
(ROMANS 14:13)

Paul gives us a formula for freedom from negative judgmentalism.
The thing he wants us to be sure about is that Christ, and
not we, is the stumbling block. He talked about Christ as a stumbling block. "Why? Because they did not seek it by faith, but as
it were, by the works of the law. For they stumbled at that stumbling stone" (Romans 9:32). The Greek word *skandalon* means "a
snare, a trap, or a cause of tripping." Christ tripped up our efforts
at self-justification. The cross short-circuits our desire to be right
with God on our own adequacy and performance. We must trip
before we can fall into His arms of loving forgiveness. Our pride
must be snared.

Once we have stumbled and been caught up in the everlasting arms of the Lord, our task is to be sure there is nothing in our
personalities, character, or attitudes that is a stumbling block as
people move toward Christ. It is frightening to consider all the
people who may never stumble creatively over Christ because
they stumbled over us!

*I will not be a stumbling block today—so that if people do
stumble, they will be caught in the arms of the Lord.*

The Cure of Negativism

Romans 14:14-23

Happy is he who does not condemn himself.
(ROMANS 14:22)

I shall never forget the time I discovered that I could never love anyone deeply until I learned to love myself. I had always been taught that self-appreciation was conceit and was to be avoided at all costs. An inverted pride of pretentious selflessness and self-negation filled the void. I could not take real delight in being myself and enjoying the gifts and opportunities God had given.

What a joy it was to begin to appreciate myself! When I accepted Christ's uncalculated, unchanging love for me, I found I had a new patience with myself and a new excitement at being me! Lots of people had greater gifts, many had superior skills, and most outdistanced my ability, but suddenly I was overcome with the realization of the tremendous potential God placed within me. I decided to use all I had as loved by Christ and to stop negating what He had given.

I had new love because I had learned to love myself. Judgmentalism was worked out of my soul by forgiving and affirming love. I longed to be to others what Christ had been to me.

We hear the saying, "Have a heart!" How about having a heart for ourselves and relating to our inner person with the same love and forgiveness Christ has shown us?

A Major Cause of Criticism

Romans 2:1

*You are inexcusable, O man, whoever you are who
judge, for in whatever you judge another you condemn
yourself; for you who judge practice the same things.*
(ROMANS 2:1)

A father paced the bedroom floor while his daughter took what
he thought was far too long to say good night to her boyfriend in
the living room below. "I don't see why it takes that young man
so long to say good night. I don't know about this younger generation!" he said. "Oh, come to bed," his wife said. "Weren't you
young once?" "Yes, I was, and that's just why I'm worried and
can't come to bed!"

The overworried father's statement expressed real insight into
himself. His judgment of his daughter and her young man was
based on his memories of what he had done in living rooms
a generation before. The problem was that he had projected these
memories into worry in the present. His judgment did not fit the
new situation but was based on his own concern.

Whenever we are overcritical we should ask ourselves and
each other, "Why does that bother you?" There are some things
that need to be questioned in loving concern for another person,
but when our judgments are rash or emotional or severe, it usually
indicates that part of the problem is still within us.

What we criticize in others may be unresolved in us.

Mercy Triumphs over Judgment

2 Timothy 4:1-5; James 2:1-13

*Judgment is without mercy to the one who has shown
no mercy. Mercy triumphs over judgment.*
(JAMES 2:13)

Mercy triumphs over judgment! That's the answer to the judgmental times we live in. Anyone who has true mercy will have little condemnatory judgment. We all make judgments about things, situations, and people, but the deprecatory judgments that relegate and debilitate are healed by the expulsive power of mercy.

Mercy is the very nature of God. It is His love in action. In Christ, God has identified with us in our plight. He does not condemn us, but comes that we might have life. This kind of identification cuts negative judgment at the taproot. Once we feel with another person what he is going through, our judgments will be less severe. A good test of the extent of mercy in our lives is how much we judge others. We will know that something is amiss in our relationship with Christ if this urge to undercut others is present in our hearts.

The only way to overcome judging is to go deeper in God's mercy. Calculate anew what God has put up with, gone through, forgiven, repaired, and healed in your own life.

*A renewed sense of God's mercy will inevitably
fill you with mercy for others.*

Spiritual Snobs

Romans 2:1-11

*Do you think this, O man, you who judge those practicing such things,
and doing the same, that you will escape the judgment of God?*
(ROMANS 2:3)

"What a snob I am!" a woman cried out in a moment of honest
confession. "I am beginning to realize that one area my faith in
Christ has never touched is my prejudice and reserve with people
who don't meet my standards. I just seem to gravitate to people
with education, Ivy League clothing, and culture. I don't dislike
others, but I just never get around to them. I must admit that
people in power, with popularity and position, are the ones I am
attracted to. I used to say that they need Christ's love as much
as others, so why fight it? Now I am beginning to wonder why I
can't love people who don't measure up."

Well, what do you think of that? Sound familiar? Ever feel
that way? Most of us have, in one way or another. And think of
the people we miss because of it! God's surprises often come in
people with strange wrappings. He has a great deal to give us from
unusual people, many of whom are not great by the world's standards. So let's resign from being spiritual snobs!

We will be judged for our judgments.

Lifting Up Each Other

Galatians 6:1-10; 5:22-23

Bear one another's burdens, and so fulfill the law of Christ.
(GALATIANS 6:2)

"Why should I tell anyone else my troubles? I caused them, I am responsible, and I must work it out for myself. Anyway, who can I trust?" is an often repeated statement. Not unlike it is the statement of another: "I am afraid to let people know about my sins. If people really knew what I am like, they wouldn't like me!"

These statements hit wide of the mark of Christian fellowship Paul is talking about. We are to bear each other's burdens. That requires an openness with each other that does not pretend by leading from strength all the time.

When we have failed or sinned, another person is needed to mediate and communicate God's grace. We were never made to know God alone. His word of assurance of forgiveness is to be given by another.

The other day a man poured out his heart to me. After we talked I said, "My friend, God loves you and forgives you." Then he said, "You know, I knew that, but I needed to hear it from someone else."

When we listen to people with empathy, we earn the right to share with them what Christ has done for us and is ready to do for them.

The Danger of Too Much Self-criticism

Romans 8:1-5

There is therefore now no condemnation to those who are in Christ Jesus,
who do not walk according to the flesh, but according to the Spirit.
(ROMANS 8:1)

The young woman was critical of her grades even though they indicated real improvement. Her father's comments were encouraging and enthusiastic.

"How can you be so hard on someone I think is so great?" the father asked his daughter. "Well, Daddy," she said, "you don't have to live with me all the time like I do."

Some of us are harder on ourselves than others, or even God, would be. We are critical of our best efforts and can't believe in ourselves. We negate God's love for us and can't believe He accepts us as we are. Only if we measure up to our impossible standards could He or anyone else love us. This is just another way of running our own lives. We are still in control, however bad we think we are.

We have not accepted ourselves as forgiven. This becomes a sick pattern of life and keeps us from loving others. It is self-centeredness in the worst form. We become inverted on ourselves. Be careful that genuine self-analysis and healthy introspection do not turn into self-condemnation.

Christ helps us get up when we get down on ourselves.

When to Offer the Pearl

Matthew 7:6

Do not give what is holy to the dogs; nor cast your pearls before swine, lest they trample them under their feet, and turn and tear you in pieces.
(MATTHEW 7:6)

The parable of the pearls and the swine in this verse is another example of Jesus' illustrative use of hyperbole—an overstatement of contrast to make a point. A pearl has no nutritional value for a pig. That's the issue. Not until a person knows our love and God's acceptance can we communicate what He, the Lord, has given us for them.

This has meaning for our witness to others. The pearls of our advanced thinking and experience of Christ cannot be digested by those who have not met Christ. We need to be simple, but not simplistic. People are yearning to see how Christ can make stepping-stones out of their struggles. What they need to hear and see is the difference Christ can make in a person's life. There is a winsome contagion in a person who shares the adventure of life in Christ. But there will be times when a person is resistant and hostile. That's the time to lovingly witness with affirmation and assurance. There will be a time when the person is ready and receptive. God will make sure of that!

*People are like islands—you need to row around
them before you know where to land.*

God's Best Gift for My Life

Matthew 7:7-12; Luke 11:13

*If you then, being evil, know how to give good gifts to
your children, how much more will your Father who is
in heaven give good things to those who ask Him!*
(MATTHEW 7:11)

The deep meaning of this passage is unlocked when it is studied
with Luke 11:13: "If you then, being evil, know how to give good
gifts to your children, how much more will your heavenly Father
give the Holy Spirit to those who ask Him!" The emphasis in both
renderings (Luke and Matthew) is on the amazing generosity of
God. He longs to give His best gift—Himself—the Holy Spirit.
But only to those who ask, seek, and knock.

This is more than an exercise in importunity; it is the expression of a dominant desire. To *ask* is to have our needs clarified
by God; to *seek* is to have those needs corrected in keeping with
His will; to *knock* is to seek entrance into the abundant life filled
with His Spirit. We come with our wants; the Lord shows us our
deepest need, then we can knock with assurance.

The impact of this passage is that the will and desire to ask,
seek, and knock are all gifts of God! He motivates us to desire
what He is waiting to give.

*Listen to God: "I am Jehovah-Shammah, The Lord Is
There. And wherever you are, be more sure of this than
you are of your next breath—I will be there."*

Fruitfulness

Matthew 7:15-20

By their fruits you will know them.
(MATTHEW 7:20)

This is an awesome passage. It is more than a warning against false prophets or wolves in sheep's clothing. The bottom line of the whole impact is that every one of us is a prophet. We are all models to others of what we believe—in our actions, attitudes, words, and lifestyles. Inadvertently we are reproducing our quality of Christianity, or lack of it, in the people who observe us.

This passage leads to an honest evaluation of our fruitfulness. In the New Testament, fruit is used in several ways: the character of Christ reproduced in us; the fruit of the Spirit; the fruit of the branch connected to Christ the Vine; the fruit of good works; the fruit of new life in others through witness and evangelism. Eventually we must confront the issue that the people in our lives are beholding in us what it means to be a Christian. We can lead people only as far as we have gone ourselves. They are deciding for or against Christ by what they observe He means to us.

A saint is one who makes it easy to believe in Jesus.
—RUTH BELL GRAHAM

God's Best Enables Our Best

Matthew 7:21-23

Not everyone who says to Me, "Lord, Lord," shall enter the kingdom of heaven, but he who does the will of My Father in heaven.
(MATTHEW 7:21)

Our Lord is deeply concerned about our influence on others. His great concern is that we will expose to others a mediocre level of discipleship that honors Him with words while we run our own lives. The contradiction between what we say and are is the focus of this passage. Is it possible to call Jesus "Lord" and not allow Him to be Lord of our lives? Look at history. Look at the church through the ages. Look at yourself! The secret of producing good fruit of authentic Christianity is in the words, "but he who does the will of My Father in heaven." What areas, situations, circumstances, relationships in your life need to be brought under radical obedience to the will of God?

Augustine's prayer helps us to know how to pray:

When I vacillated about my decision to serve my God, it was I who willed and willed not, and nobody else. I was fighting against myself...All You asked was that I cease to want what I willed and begin to want what You willed.

Productive Branches

Luke 3:7-20; John 15:1-8

Bear fruits worthy of repentance, and do not begin to say to yourselves, "We have Abraham as our father." For I say to you that God is able to raise up children to Abraham from these stones.

(LUKE 3:8)

Our scripture today is both a warning and a promise. Jesus warns that those who do not bear fruit will be cut off. What is the fruit of which He speaks? The fruit of one Christian is another. We were meant to be reproductive. Can you look to any one person as your child of the faith? Have you ever helped someone else know Christ and trust his life to Him?

The function of an ethical life and service to others is to put us in the position of sharing with another person the source of life we have in Jesus Christ. We do not draw attention to ourselves so others will say, "My, what a fine person you have made of yourself" but rather, "Now that's the way I want to live! What's the secret of your joy?" Do people say that to you?

That leads us to want to pray:

Lord Christ, I can look to so few people who have come to know You because of Your life in me. Help me to be reproductive! Make me sensitive today to all the people who are anxious to know You if I would only point the way. Amen.

Faith on the Job

Ephesians 6:5-9

…Not with eyeservice, as men-pleasers, but as bondservants
of Christ, doing the will of God from the heart.
(EPHESIANS 6:6)

The key to being a Christian on the job is to bring meaning to our work, not to try to find life's ultimate meaning in our work. For example, the major cause of vocational burnout is that men and women make work their god. Titles, positions, salaries, significance, and recognition become a lust of life. We work all the harder to assure success and power. Fear of failure grips us. Then exhaustion and fatigue creep up on us. Usually when we are run down, we take on more. The love of work becomes a compulsion. Overburdened, we become irritable, defensive, cynical, paranoid, and depressed. Creativity eludes us. It happens so subtly that we do not know it's happening until it's too late.

And yet, for a Christian, it's never too late. The Lord is ready to begin again whenever we realize that our work has become more important to us than our relationship with God. He helps us to draw back and get things into perspective. Then we can surrender our work to Him and ask Him to guide us in making our work an expression of, rather than an exception to, our faith.

Go to work for Christ on the job!

Our Wills to Make Them God's

Psalm 40:1-17; 143:1-12

I delight to do Your will, O my God; Your Law is within my heart.
(Psalm 40:8)

*Teach me to do Your will, for You are my God; let
Your good Spirit lead me on level ground.*
(Psalm 143:10)

If we are to be Christians who do more than say "Lord, Lord" in wordy religiosity, we will need to desire God's will more than anything else. The psalmist shows us how to have a passion for God's will. Memorize these key verses. Repeat them in times of indecision and uncertainty. Make this a day to focus your consciousness in deliberate longing for God's direction and determination to follow through. Tennyson was right: "Our wills are ours, we know not how; our wills are ours, to make them Thine."

That's it! To want what God wants is the secret of true happiness. If we want that with all our hearts, specific guidance in our decisions will not be long in coming. Robert Louis Stevenson said, "I came about like a well-handled ship. There stood at the wheel that steersman whom we call God."

Who is at at wheel of your ship?

Take the wheel, Lord!

Lord, What Do You
Want Me to Say?

Mark 13:9-13

When they arrest you and deliver you up, do not worry beforehand, or premeditate what you will speak. But whatever is given you in that hour, speak that; for it is not you who speak, but the Holy Spirit.
(MARK 13:11)

"What can I possibly say in a situation like this? How will I ever find the words to explain, give comfort, offer challenge, and express love in a circumstance like that? What should I say?"

Jesus gave us a promise that dispels our fears.

Preparation for times of trial and testing comes long before the situation. Jesus Christ, who knows what we will face, is at work imputing into us the wisdom that will give birth to the right words for each troublesome and challenging time. When the moment comes and we are on the spot, we will have power to speak with maturity beyond our years, love beyond our capacities, and insight beyond our knowledge. He will use us to speak the right word, which will convict, comfort, and challenge. We will be amazed! All He needs from us is the willing mind and tongue.

If we dare to pray, "Lord, what do you want me to say?"
He will answer, and we will know what to say.

True Stability

Matthew 7:24-25

*Whoever hears these sayings of Mine, and does them, I will
liken him to a wise man who built his house on the rock.*
(MATTHEW 7:24)

How would you describe a stable person? What words would you
use? At the conclusion of the Sermon on the Mount, Jesus gave
a parable to illustrate a stable person, whose life was built on a
rocklike foundation. The man who built his house upon a rock
was one who heard the Master's words and did them. Hearing and
doing were the inseparable combination for great character. Jesus
Christ is able to help us hear His message and live it.

That kind of stability will show in our countenance, be reflected in our voices, and radiate in our convictions. The world
desperately needs stable Christians: those who know who they are,
whose they are, and what they are to be and do. The storms of
life may beat on us, but we do not change. The winds of change
blast away, but we do not collapse, because the One who is able
has taken control of our minds so we can think His thoughts, of
our emotions so we can be calm in life's distresses, of our wills so
we can discover and do His will, and of our bodies so they can be
strengthened by His Spirit.

*No one ever gets ready for a crisis in the midst of one.
Christ makes us stable today for whatever comes.*

Not What But Whom

Matthew 7:26-27

Everyone who hears these sayings of Mine, and does not do them,
will be like a foolish man who built his house on the sand.
(Matthew 7:26)

Jesus lived in a time not unlike our own: Great beliefs were held
but not applied. That's why He ended the Sermon on the Mount
with a "Do it now!" thrust. The parable of the foundations—one
on rock, the other on sand—teaches us the integration of hearing
and doing. The Lord's conclusion is very direct: What are you going to do about it? Take an inventory—how have your actions and
behavior been changed by the days of this review of Jesus' teaching? Today is a day to listen to Christ and do what He says.

John Oxenham reminds us that Christ and obedience to Him
comprise the only sure foundation of a great life:

> …Not what I do believe but whom!
>> Who walks beside me in the gloom?
> Who shares the burden wearisome?
>> Who all the dim way doth illume,
> And bids me look beyond the tomb
>> The larger life to live?
> Not what I do believe
>> But whom!
> Not what but whom!

Today is a day to hear and do!

An Astonishing Life

Matthew 7:28-29

He taught them as one having authority, and not as the scribes.
(MATTHEW 7:29)

The difference between Jesus and the scribes was that He demanded action. Ultimately He was crucified not only for what He said but for what He did. He didn't just talk about love; He loved. He not only proclaimed God's power to heal; He healed the people. He didn't say the kingdom of God would come someday; He announced its reality as present and called people to live in it presently. He did more than theorize about forgiveness; He forgave. That's why people were "astonished at His teaching."

The astonishing life will be one in which word and deed, idea and character, thought and action, belief and obedience are one. The words *astonished* and *amazed* are used often in the Gospels to describe people's reactions to Jesus' life and message. We are to live in Christ in such an abandoned way that people will be astonished by what we are and do. The test of how astonished they are will be the urgency with which they desire to know our secret of true happiness. Who has asked you lately?

Christians should be blessed question marks prompting people
to ask how they became the astounding people they are.

Over the Rainbow

Genesis 9:1-17

I set My bow in the cloud, and it shall be for a sign
of a covenant between Me and the earth.
(GENESIS 9:13)

The rainbow is a **sign** of the end of the storm. It has been a special symbol of God's faithfulness to His people through the ages. Noah had been obedient before the flood. He followed the Lord's instructions completely and was the source of the survival of humankind. In affirmation, the Lord gave the rainbow as the sign of the covenant. I never see a rainbow without remembering what God can do with people who do what He says. As George Matheson put it, "I climb the rainbow in the rain and know the promise is not vain that morn shall tearless be."

It is in the storms of life that we need to remember the rainbow. When the rains fall and the winds blow in the adversities of life, we need the courage to remember that the storm will end and the rainbow will appear. Only the covenant that God has made with us can give us that kind of fortitude. God is committed to be our God. Our hope is not that we can be adequate enough to deserve His love, but rather that He has chosen to be our God.

Over the rainbow is the cross. Greater than a sign in the
heavens, the cross is an assurance of a new covenant of grace.

Dare to Risk

Genesis 12:1-9

The LORD appeared to Abram and said, "To your descendants I will give this land." So he built an altar there to the LORD who had appeared to him.
(GENESIS 12:7)

It was an awesome promise that required audacious risk. The Lord astounded Abram with the promise that he would be the father of a great nation. All the families of the earth were to be blessed through him. But the cost was high. He had to leave Ur of the Chaldeans, security, familiar surroundings, and prosperity. Abram became the patron of people who discover that being obedient means risk.

In contrast, think of how hard we work to eliminate the risks of life. We labor, save, plan, and accept only safe responsibilities. Then we settle into the ruts of sameness and complain that life is no longer exciting.

However, as long as we are alive, there will be a next step in our adventure with the Lord. He constantly calls us out from where we are to a new level of risk. There will never be a time when what we've done or been can be our security. Where is the element of creative risk in your life? What would you do if you trusted God completely?

A life without risk is like a bird without wings.

Old Ways in a New Life

Genesis 12:10-20

Pharaoh called Abram and said, "What is this you have done to me?"
(GENESIS 12:18)

Abram failed the first opportunity to discover God's intervening power. He was afraid of what might happen to Sarai in Egypt, and he fell back on his old methods of manipulation and lying. How very honest the Bible is about its heroes! Abram fled and implicated Sarai in his lack of trust in God. His fear was that the Egyptians would see how beautiful Sarai was, take her, and kill him. He told his wife to lie and tell the Egyptians that she was his sister.

Everything happened as he had suggested. Sarai was taken to the Pharaoh, and Abram was treated like royalty. But the Lord had greater plans for Sarai than to be one of the many women of the Pharaoh. God sent a plague on the ruler's house, and he sent the two dissemblers away from Egypt.

We all have some difficulty living the new life in Christ, with vestiges of the old person still controlling our responses. Raw dependence on the Lord to take care of us is a moment-by-moment risk. But He's worthy of the trust. He will step in and make old ways unnecessary.

Daily risk requires daily dependence.

The Parable of
the Red Volkswagen

2 Timothy 3:1-9

They will maintain a façade of "religion"
but their life denies its truth.
(2 TIMOTHY 3:5 PHILLIPS)

A woman bought a new red Volkswagen. One day she took her children to the zoo and left her car in the parking lot near the elephant show. When she returned, she was dismayed to see that her car was smashed in on the roof and side.

An elephant had gotten loose. It had been trained, as part of its act, to put its foot on a big red drum. Dutifully, after years of training, it had put its great foot right down on top of the VW! The woman was frantic.

On the way home she and the children were stopped by a policeman, who accused her of having left the scene of an accident. He saw the damage but did not know the unusual circumstances. "But officer, I have not been in an accident!" she explained. "An elephant put his foot on my car." His response to this was to give her a drinking test and take everyone to the nearest police station. Eventually the officer called the zoo, and the woman was released. She held on to the truth even when she was misunderstood. No façade needed!

To be and not to seem—that is the issue.

Oh, Really?

1 Corinthians 4:6-13

Who sees anything different in you?
(1 Corinthians 4:7 rsv)

One Sunday I finished my sermon with a flourish, with my hand outstretched in a triumphant gesture. At that very moment a ham radio operator was carrying on a conversation somewhere that invaded the public-address system in the sanctuary. As I stood before my people, arm outstretched, his voice was heard all over the sanctuary. "Oh, really?" he said in his conversation. We all laughed.

That's not a bad question to ask at the conclusion of any sermon or anything we do in the church. "Oh, really?" points us to the credibility gaps of what we say so eloquently and forcefully from the pulpit and throughout the life of a church. What difference will it make?

The same question needs to be asked about the follow-through of our grand beliefs in daily discipleship. "Who sees any difference in you?" is another way of asking "Oh, really?" Who could tell that Christ lives in you because of your attitudes, actions, and reactions in life's tight places?

*The world is watching and listening. Is what I say
and do congruent with what I believe?*

Walk Through the Promise!

Genesis 13:1-18

*Arise, walk about the land through its length
and breadth; for I will give it to you.*
(GENESIS 13:17)

We wonder why the Lord wanted Abram to walk through the land
that He had shown him would be his and his descendants! Wasn't
seeing enough? No, the Lord wanted Abram to relish each acre of
His gift, claiming what He had promised as true.

The same is true for the Christian life. When we read through
the Gospels we are amazed by what our Lord had told us He
would do for us. He promised an abundant life now and an eternal life forever. All power would be given to us. He would be
with us. Our hearts were to become His home. The things He
had done we were to do, and even greater things. Through Him
we would be able to love, forgive, heal the needs of people, and
introduce them to Him. Our problems would be the prelude to
receiving fresh power. He would make us like Him in our character and actions. Death would be a transition in living, and heaven
would be our eternal home.

We capture how Abram must have felt as he began to walk
through the promise God had made. To claim what Christ has
offered is our challenge.

*There is a great difference between sitting on our
problems and standing on the promises!*

It's Going to Be a Great Day!

Psalm 118:1-29

This is the day which the LORD has made;
let us rejoice and be glad in it.
(PSALM 118:24)

I greeted a cab driver early in the morning in Austin, Texas. "How are you?" I asked sleepily as he drove me to the airport. "Just great—and it's going to be a mighty fine day!" I asked him why he was so hopeful about the day ahead. "The way it began," was his reply. He had come to work at 4:00 AM and made several trips already. "When a day starts right, it stays right. If it starts slow, it stays slow," he said prophetically.

The Lord never sleeps. He's awake waiting for us to talk to Him and give Him our day. Jeremiah discovered that the mercies of God are new every morning. God has divided our time into days and nights so we can ask for fresh power for each day. When we begin the day with a quiet time with the Lord, it's like reporting in for duty, getting the strategy for the day, and hooking into power to make each day maximum.

Attitudes determine so much of how we handle life's pressures and challenges. When we surrender a day to the Lord and spread out before Him all that we anticipate, suddenly the day is a delight and not a drudgery.

God's best for my life makes any day the best day of my life.

By Faith Alone

Genesis 15:1-21

He believed in the LORD; and He reckoned it to him as righteousness.
(GENESIS 15:6)

We all have an inner longing to know God and be in a relationship with Him. There is no inner peace without being right with God. What can we do? Our key verse for today is one of the most crucial verses in Scripture. Two words in it are interdependent: *believed* and *righteousness*. Abram believed that God existed, and he trusted his life to His guidance in accomplishing the promise He had made. Faith in God is the only basis of righteousness. Abram was made right with God, not on the basis of character refinement or what he did for God, but by faith alone. That faith spurred him on in obeying God, but his goodness was not his status with God.

In Romans, Paul used Abram's faith as the example of what God requires of us. It is not good works but faith that makes a person righteous. The apostle looked back on Abram's faith from the other side of Calvary.

Our faith also is a response to love revealed on the cross. How wonderful it is to live by faith alone.

The just shall live by faith—alone!
—LUTHER

Marching to a Different Drummer

Romans 3:1-31; 1 Corinthians 12:6-11

*Where is boasting then? It is excluded. By what
law? Of works? No, but by the law of faith.*
(ROMANS 3:27)

Authentic faith is the work of the Holy Spirit in us. He alerts us
to the emptiness inside our souls, creates a hunger for truth, em-
powers the communication of the gospel to us, and gives us the
power to respond. True faith is the Spirit's power in us releasing
us to surrender our mind, soul, and will to the Lord. We accept
God's control over all our affairs. We march to a different drummer. We have primary faith.

Then added to this primary faith is a quality of pertinacious
faith. The faith given to us in the beginning is to believe in God;
the special gift of faith after we've become a Christian is to courageously trust God with situations, circumstances, people, and
impossibilities. The same Holy Spirit who gave us faith to respond
to God's grace initially, gives us the capacity to dare to believe that
all things are possible if willed by God. We should pray for this
special gift of faith listed in the gifts of the Holy Spirit and thank
God in advance for it. The gift gives us a daring, all-stops-out
boldness to expect miracles.

I will march to the cadences of Christ, my new Drummer.

When and When Not to Laugh

Genesis 17:1–18:33

The LORD said to Abraham, "Why did Sarah laugh,
saying, 'Shall I indeed bear a child, when I am so
old?' Is anything too difficult for the LORD?"
(GENESIS 18:13-14)

There's a great difference between laughing *at* God and laughing *with* Him in joy over what He is able to do with life's seemingly impossible situations. Abraham and Sarah laughed at God over the promise that they would have a son to carry on the Lord's legacy of blessing. Sarah was 90 years old! No wonder they laughed. What would your response have been?

The question must be answered. Is anything too difficult for the Lord? No, not if He wills it and we are willing to accept it. When confronted with that, Sarah claimed she had not laughed. Why was it important to the Lord for her to admit that she had laughed? Why did He retort with the demand for honesty: "But you did laugh." The birth of the child of promise was absolutely necessary for the fulfillment of God's plan for His people. Sarah's age was secondary to that. God does not squander His miracles. He can, and will, do anything that is strategic for our eternal welfare.

I will stop laughing at God's possibilities so I can
hear His laughter and laugh with Him.

Who or What Is Your Isaac?

Genesis 22:1-13

Abraham said, "God will provide for Himself the lamb for the
burnt offering, my son." So the two of them walked on together.
(GENESIS 22:8)

Imagine the panic that gripped Abraham when the Lord made
this ultimate test of his obedience and unquestioning faithfulness.
What turbulence tumbled about in his heart? What was God doing? Why would He ask for the sacrifice of the only hope of the
fulfillment of His promise?

Listen to the imploring love of Isaac. He trusted his father im-
plicitly. His question, "Behold, the fire and the wood, but where
is the lamb for the burnt offering?" must have cut Abraham to
the core. He ached with pain in his heart too great to bear as he
bound his son.

Envision it: It was just as Abraham was about to thrust the
sharp blade into his beloved son's chest that the Lord intervened:
"Abraham, Abraham!" The commanding voice from heaven so
shattered and shocked Abraham that he dropped the knife. Then
he saw the ram the Lord had provided for the sacrifice.

Why did God put Abraham through it? It was because He
wanted Abraham, not Isaac.

Our Isaac is not ours until surrendered to the Lord.

The Lord Will Provide

Genesis 22:14-24

Abraham called the name of that place The LORD Will Provide, as it is said to this day, "In the mount of the LORD it will be provided."
(GENESIS 22:14)

Abraham had been faithful and obedient. He had been willing to give up his cherished son. The Lord intervened at just the right moment and provided the ram for the sacrifice. He had all of Abraham that there was. The altar Abraham built in memory of the crisis of obedience and the Lord's intervention gives us one of the greatest names for our God: *YHWH-jireh*, "Yahweh will provide."

I once had a frightening dream. In it, the Lord asked me to hand over all my loved ones, my church, and my ministry as if never to have them again. I felt the anguish of the loneliness and depletion of all my efforts to serve the Lord.

It seemed like an eternity before He returned them to me. I will never forget the words He spoke in my dream: *All that you have and are are Mine! I entrust them back to you as My gifts. Never again think of them as your possessions. They are a trust from Me to you. As long as you put Me first in your life, and keep the cross as your only security, you can enjoy them for My glory.* I know in some small way what Abraham went through, and that the Lord does provide!

All that we have belongs to the Lord.

Great Parents of Great Children?

Genesis 25:1–26:35

He built an altar there and called upon the name of the LORD,
and pitched his tent there; and Isaac's servants dug a well.
(GENESIS 26:25)

Would you rather be a great parent or the parent of great children? That depends on what we mean by "great." The challenge all parents face is to communicate the vitality of their faith. The family accomplishes its purpose if children are able to hear and see in their parents the evidence of an authentic relationship with the Lord. If children can witness how parents deal with the delights and difficulties of life, with both bringing them closer to the Lord, they will discover a faith that is their own.

Abraham was both a great man and a great father. He shared the promise and destiny God had given him so that Isaac grew to be a strong, quiet, consistent man. He trusted God, acknowledged His faithfulness, stood firmly against his enemies, and worked hard in the simplicity of his pastoral life. Isaac is remembered for little else than that he was Abraham's son and Jacob's father, and that he dug wells. There were no acts of valor. But a good life can be a great life. Isaac fulfilled his purpose in God's unfolding strategy. What parent could want more than that?

One of life's greatest joys for a parent is to have a
child commit his or her life to Christ.

Making the Willful Willing

Genesis 27:1–33:20

*Jacob named the place Peniel, for he said, "I have seen
God face to face, yet my life has been preserved."*
(GENESIS 32:30)

Jacob is like many of us—impetuous, strong-willed, and gifted,
but slow to acknowledge the Lord as the source of our blessings.

Jacob could not wait for the providence of God to give him
his father's blessing. Along with the connivance of his mother, he
manipulated events to steal the blessing. God would have worked
that out, but Jacob could not wait. When Isaac blessed him and
sent him to Paddan-aram, the Lord extricated him from the syndrome of sibling rivalry so He could make him into the man He
destined him to be.

The blessing of the Lord in the dream at Bethel gave Jacob
the assurance he had tried to manipulate. How gracious the Lord
was to him! In Laban's land, he was given Rachel and eventually
great wealth. But the memory of his deception prompted him to
return to make restitution with Esau. On the way, the Lord again
appeared to him. Jacob wrestled with the angel of the Lord. The
limp that resulted never allowed him to forget that he had to lean
on God. What has the Lord said to you in Jacob's story?

The Lord makes us willing to be made willing.

When Circumstances Contradict Our Vision

Genesis 37:1-36

Here comes this dreamer!
(GENESIS 37:19)

So often, circumstances contradict our dreams. We get a vision of what is ahead and then seem to face difficulties that contradict the dream. While Joseph rode along on the Ishmaelites' camel, he probably felt the disappointment we all feel at times.

But God was working His purposes out. When Joseph arrived in Egypt, he was sold to Potiphar, the captain of the Pharaoh's bodyguard. There he rose to power. His natural talents, multiplied by the Lord's blessing of him, resulted in position and authority in Potiphar's household. That too was part of the plan that would lead to accomplishing God's purpose to use Joseph as a source of blessing, as the one through whom He would eventually bring Jacob and his sons to Egypt.

Hold fast to the vision God has given you for your life. The difficult things we go through are to prepare us for the realization of the vision on God's timing and by His power!

Don't deny the vision God has given, even when
circumstances seem to contradict it.

God Uses Everything

Genesis 39:1–41:57

The LORD was with Joseph and extended kindness to Him.
(GENESIS 39:21)

Joseph would not deny his loyalty to Potiphar or his faithfulness to God. It landed him in jail on the charge of doing what he had refused to do! The term in jail also had its purpose in God's plan. There were others in that jail by divine appointment. The pharaoh's cupbearer had fallen into disfavor and was thrown into prison along with Joseph. He had a dream which Joseph interpreted by God's power.

When the cupbearer was released, he was more than ready to tell the pharaoh about the mysterious Hebrew he had met in jail. The ruler of Egypt had had a perplexing dream about seven fat and seven lean cows and seven good and seven thin ears of grain. Joseph was called on to interpret. The dream predicted seven prosperous and seven lean years ahead for Egypt and the surrounding territory. The interpretation won for Joseph the position of regent of Egypt, the next in power and command to the pharaoh.

God can weave in His plans despite the evil that people do to and around us. The hurts people do and say are not beyond the providential workings of our God! Nothing can deter the plan of God.

God can use the difficulties you are facing right now to
get you one step further in His plan. Trust Him!

Life Makes Us Bitter or Better

Genesis 42:1–49:33

*I am your brother Joseph, whom you sold into Egypt. Now
do not be grieved or angry with yourselves, because you sold
me here, for God sent me before you to preserve life.*
(GENESIS 45:4-5)

The account of the intrigue involved in the visits of Joseph's brothers to Egypt reads like a good mystery story. What Joseph put his brothers and Jacob through was so they could share in the real purpose of his original dream.

His brothers did indeed bow down before him, but he was a very different man from the one they had sold to the Ishmaelites. Note his compassion and tenderness when he finally revealed his identity to his brothers. Instead of an arrogant dreamer, he now saw himself as God's agent of preserving life. The Lord had given him the wisdom to realize that he had enabled the succession of miraculous interventions in his life to get his family to Egypt.

A sense of being a cooperator in God's strategy gives us accepting love and forgiveness for people who may have blocked His plans with us. How easy it would have been for Joseph to say, "You did terrible things to me. Now don't expect any kindness from me!" Instead, his repeated expressions of God's kindness made him tender and gracious.

Life can make us either bitter or better.

God Knows What He Is Doing!

Genesis 50:1-26

Do not be afraid, for am I in God's place? As for you, you meant evil against me, but God meant it for good in order to bring about this present result, to preserve many people alive.
(GENESIS 50:19-20)

All that Joseph had been through had brought him to this profound conviction that God can bring good out of evil. What he said to his brothers could be a good motto for our daily living. It should be memorized, and remembered when things go wrong, people hurt us, or our dreams are dashed. God does know what He's doing.

This passage affirms God's control and our free will. He loves us so much that He wants us to be people, not puppets with no freedom. The choice to give us freedom was awesome. God knew what we would do with it. Yet He also knew that there can be no freedom to choose to love Him unless we are given free will. He gave us the sublime opportunity to use our freedom of choice to respond to His love and love Him and others in return. It is with this same freedom that we choose what our attitude will be to people who have misused or mistreated us.

Lord, I believe in Your providential power to use the worst for the best. Teach me and help me to grow to be a person who dreams and is mature enough in You to realize the dream.

God Is Faithful

Exodus 1:1–2:25

*The sons of Israel sighed because of the bondage, and they
cried out; and their cry for help because of their bondage
rose up to God. So God heard their groaning; and God
remembered His covenant with Abraham, Isaac, and Jacob.
God saw the sons of Israel, and God took notice of them.*

(EXODUS 2:23-25)

Have you ever had the feeling that God had forgotten you? We've
all experienced it. It happens when we face difficulties, pray about
them, and there seems to be no answer.

The people of Israel felt like that. Their bondage in Egypt was
excruciating. Did God know or care? Had He forgotten His covenant with Abraham, Isaac, and Jacob?

At the very time the people doubted Him most, God was
preparing for His big move. The passage of Exodus we read for
today vividly communicates three things: the condition of the
people of Israel, the faithfulness of God to His covenant, and
His preparation of Moses to be the liberator of His people. The
Lord had not forgotten.

It is usually just before we give up that the answer comes.
Probably we were not ready before. We would have used the answer as a reason for pride, thinking we had accomplished it. Be
sure of this: God never forgets.

God will act when we are ready and His timing has arrived.

One Thing That Is Certain

Exodus 3:1-22

Thus you shall say to the sons of Israel: "I AM has sent me to you."
(Exodus 3:14)

Moses' experience of God in the burning bush came at a time of weakness and despair in Moses. He was an exile from Egypt. He had tried to take things into his own hands, had made an effort to help his people, and had failed. He had learned about the God of his people, but he did not know Him. The plight of the people was on his heart that day as he tended the sheep. Where was this God? What was He like? Why didn't He do something about the suffering of His people? It is when we are feeling the weakest and are filled with questions about the Lord that He comes to us. A burning-bush encounter is for those who have tried and failed and are ready to receive power beyond their own.

We've all said to God, "Who am I to go? Who will believe me? When they ask who sent you, what shall I say?" The Lord's response to Moses was, "Tell them 'I AM' sent you." That name really means, "I will be what I will be." The divine name *YHWH, Yahweh,* signifies the One who makes things happen. That's all Moses had to go on. But what more did he need? The Creator, the Father of Abraham, Isaac, and Jacob, would be with him, and He would make things happen, indeed!

God will make things happen for your good and His glory today.

Be Careful What
You Call Impossible

Exodus 14:1-31

*Moses said to the people, "Do not fear! Stand by and see the
salvation of the LORD which He will accomplish for you today."*
(EXODUS 14:13)

The Lord set up Moses and the people of Israel for a miracle of
His grace. He led them into an impossible position. Following instructions, they traveled down to the foot of the mountain range
on the western shore of what we know now as the Gulf of Suez.
They were trapped by the mountains on one side, Migdol (a gar-
rison outpost of Pharaoh's troops) on another side, and the north-
ern extremities of the Gulf of Suez. Nor could Moses lead the
people east because of the approaching chariots of the pharaoh's
armies, which were now in hot pursuit. The people of Israel were
like a mouse in Pharaoh's trap. But the Lord had led them there.

It was when the situation reached crisis proportions that Moses, confident of the I AM of the burning bush, said, "Fear not,
stand firm, see the salvation of the LORD." There's a three-point
strategy for life's struggles! The Lord opened the Red Sea for the
people to pass through at just the right time. He had allowed an
impossible situation to teach them that if they would trust Him
nothing would be impossible. That's the assurance we all need.

Do not suffer dismay; the Lord will show the way!

Anything's Possible

Mark 6:30-56

*They had not understood about the loaves,
because their heart was hardened.*
(MARK 6:52)

Here is one of those passages that must be read in the light of how it ends. The key is what Jesus says when He comes to the disciples in a tempestuous sea when they were rowing against the wind. He walks across the water and says, "Take heart; it is I—have no fear!"

That day Jesus had fed the five thousand with the multiplied five loaves and two fishes. After that the disciples should not have doubted that nothing was impossible. They should not have forgotten so easily...nor should we in our crises. The Lord gives His present miracles, not only to help us now, but to give us lively confidence for the future.

What impossible thing do you need to see Jesus do in your life? Great Christians are daring. What is it that makes us pull back and say, "Everything is possible for our Lord...but not that... or this!" That then becomes the very thing we must trust to the Lord's limitless possibilities.

Lord, break open my hardened heart and help me trust You!

By Whatever Name, Remember!

1 Corinthians 11:17-26

Do this in remembrance of me.
(1 CORINTHIANS 11:24)

On the first Sunday of October all of Christendom celebrates Worldwide Communion.

It is the Lord's Supper. We remember the historical event when Jesus celebrated the Passover meal with His disciples. There Jesus broke bread and shared the cup as a portent of His broken body and shed blood on the cross.

It is the covenant in Christ's blood. "Covenant" means a relationship of promise. Through the shedding of the blood of the Lamb of God, Christ, a new covenant of forgiveness and grace has been established.

It is a Eucharist. This became the official name for the sacrament from Ignatius in AD 115. The word means "thanksgiving." Our hearts are filled with gratitude for what our Lord has done to reconcile us and set us free from sin and guilt.

It is a communion. We experience the living Christ in the broken bread and the wine.

It is a sacrament. The word comes from the Latin word for *pledge*—a *sacramentum,* an outward sign of a deep and inward bond.

We don't just "take communion." It takes us to Christ!

Stale Grace

Exodus 16:1-8

Behold, I will rain bread from heaven for you; and the people shall go out and gather a day's portion every day.
(Exodus 16:4)

Most of us live on stale grace. Old experiences, outworn ideas, tattered religious memories have become the false basis of our security, rather than a fresh realization of God's grace for each situation and each new day. God wants to give us a new portion of His power and wisdom for each crisis so we may discover the unique thing He seeks to do in each situation and with each person.

This was the Lord's promise in the miracle of manna. *Manna* was a sticky, honeylike substance that exuded in heavy drops from a shrub found in the desert. During the night under the heavy dew, the manna would be provided by God. In the morning there would be left on the ground a sweet, flaky substance that provided adequate nourishment for the people of Israel in each day.

If the people tried to hoard the manna from one day to the next, except in preparation for the Sabbath, it would rot and be filled with worms. The Lord sought to help His people depend on Him by giving them just enough food for each day.

He wants us to trust Him day by day for strength.

The Royal Order of Aaron, Hur, and Joshua

Exodus 17:8-16

It came about when Moses held his hand up, that Israel prevailed, and when he let his hand down, Amalek prevailed.
(EXODUS 17:11)

We belong to each other. We are the Lord's gifts to one another in the battles of life. We were never meant to fight alone without the Lord's help and the encouragement of one another.

As the people of Israel pressed on into the wilderness, they were attacked by the Amalekites. The Lord gave Moses the secret of fighting His battles for His people. All Moses had to do was hold his rod high in the air, and the armies of Israel would win against the Amalekites. The rod of God used to open the Red Sea would be the symbol of His presence and His power for victory in battle.

But the battle was long and hard. Moses' arms grew weary. It was then that Aaron and Hur became strengthening agents. They held Moses' arms up while Joshua fought the battle. What a team! I like to call it the royal order of Aaron, Hur, and Joshua. It is impossible to win in life's battles without faithful friends who pray with us, uphold us, and fight our battles as if they were their own.

Who holds your arms up? Who needs you to do that for him or her today?

The Everlasting Arms

Exodus 19:1-8; Deuteronomy 32:8-12

*You yourselves have seen what I did to the Egyptians, and how
I bore you on eagles' wings, and brought you to Myself.*
(EXODUS 19:4)

At the end of Moses' life, he looked back on how God had cared for His people. He had been like an eagle training its eaglets to fly. The Lord stirred up the nest in Egypt, making it so uncomfortable that they had to move on to the plans He had for them. An eagle will do whatever is necessary to get an eaglet out of the nest when it is time to fly. Then it will push the eaglet off the edge of the nest so that it can use its unfledged wings.

The word "hover" in our Scripture reading is the same Hebrew word used in the creation account of God "hovering over the waters" (NKJV). In this case it is the eagle's watchful eye caring for the first-flight attempts of the eaglet. And then when the eaglet is in danger of falling too far, the eagle swoops down, spreads its wings, and catches it on its pinions.

That's the way God deals with us. He will not allow us to stay in any comfortable nest. He presses us out to discover our potential. And yet He hovers close by, over us, keeping us from falling too far.

*The eternal God is a dwelling place, and
underneath are the everlasting arms.*
—DEUTERONOMY 33:27

I'll Do It His Way!

Exodus 20:1-17

You shall have no other gods before Me.
(Exodus 20:3)

Words from a well-known song—"I did it my way"—appeal to our desire to carve out a life of independence and self-reliance. I think of the song each time I review the Ten Commandments. The Lord gave us the commandments so that we could "do it His way." There is no other way that really works. We don't just break the commandments; we break ourselves on them when we sidestep the Lord's ordained plan for living. The commandments are like natural law—they are principles by which we are able to realize the purpose for which we were created. But they were never meant to be obeyed on our own strength. The same Lord who gave them offers to give the strength to live them.

When we take the commandments seriously, we realize how difficult it is not to break them in one way or another—if not in acts, so often in our thoughts. A Christian dares to live by the commandments by the power of grace through Christ. When we are faithful in "doing it His way" we are given strength and courage each day.

With Christ's love and power, I'll do it His way!

The Cloud Where God Was

Exodus 20:18-21

*The people stood at a distance, while Moses
approached the thick cloud where God was.*
(EXODUS 20:21)

There are times when God seems to be clouded, beyond our reach, mysterious and aloof. Other translations use "thick darkness" for the thick cloud. It is often in those dark times that God is most at work in our lives. The words *darkness* and *God* seem contradictory. But He uses the dark times of discouragement as well as the bright times of victory. He is with us in the dark clouds of life's difficulties.

When we accept that basic fact, we are ready to grow through what happens to us. God has not left us. The mist has come in for a time, and we must walk by faith. The mist will lift and we will look back on the experience, wondering why we questioned what God was doing. And we will know something else: The Lord never forsakes us. His answers will not always be what we think best, but the friendship He longs to have with us will be deepened.

The only way to live with freedom and joy is to accept that there are dark, cloudy days. Without them we would never appreciate the bright days when the answer we asked for in the darkness is given.

The Light of the World is with us even in the dark days.

When We Get Tired of Waiting

Exodus 32:1-29

*When the people saw that Moses delayed to come down
from the mountain, the people assembled about Aaron
and said to him, "Come, make us a god."*
(EXODUS 32:1)

One of the most difficult challenges in living is knowing when to act
and when to wait. We all abhor lack of courage and boldness. But
equally so, we are disturbed by people who constantly take things
in their own hands and act without guidance from the Lord. The
secret is to discover how to act in His timing, on His power, and
under His guidance. And that requires waiting for Him.

The people were tired of waiting for Moses. He had been on
Mount Sinai for 40 days. "What are we waiting for?" they asked.
"Who is this tyrant of Sinai who makes us wait? And where is Moses? We want a god to live on our level, go before us, and lead us to
our destination when we want it. We are tired of waiting around!"
The golden calf was the result. Impatience is the illegitimate child
of faithlessness and willfulness.

Anything we do without waiting for God's guidance and timing becomes a golden calf. We overlook the fact that God has
promptly met our needs and graciously denied any wants that
would hurt us. But if we remember and wait for Him, He will
grant us guidance, exactly when we need it.

God is on time, in time, for our times of need.

A Broken Sentence
from a Broken Heart

Exodus 32:30-35

> *Moses returned to the LORD, and said, "Alas, this people has committed a great sin, and they have made a god of gold for themselves. But now, if You will, forgive their sin—and if not, please blot me out from Your book which You have written!"*
>
> (EXODUS 32:31-32)

We can empathize with Moses during that long night of the soul when he contemplated the sin of his people, who had built and worshiped the golden calf. Three undeniable realities burned within him: the righteous holiness of God, the idolatrous sin of his people, and the judgment of God on the sin. Then he remembered a new word the Lord had used 11 times in the instructions about the Day of Atonement. The thought of the sacrifices for the sins of the people seized his mind. He would offer himself!

It has been called literature's most pathetic broken sentence. God did not seem to be impressed. No person can assume the sins of another. Only God can do that. And that's exactly what He did when He came in Jesus Christ.

> *We can't atone for another person,*
> *but we can share Christ's atonement.*

The Ultimate Prayer

Exodus 33:12-23; 34:29-35

Moses said, "I pray You, show me Your glory!"
(EXODUS 33:18)

What could Moses do? He does the only thing any of us can do when life becomes difficult and people around us are problems: He goes to God with all his troubles. He tells the Lord he wants to know Him better and understand His ways. He reminds Him that the people are His people. Then the Lord promises that His presence will go with them. Moses is shocked. He had never considered leading the people without the Lord. "If Your presence does not go with us, do not lead us up from here." He wanted nothing to do with leading the stiff-necked people without God!

Then Moses felt the courage and confidence to pray the ultimate prayer. "Show me Your glory!" he pleaded. The Hebrew word for *glory* means "presence." It is the total impact of the person and power of God. That was Moses' greatest need. With God's glorious presence, he could attempt anything.

We all need deep times with our Lord in which His glory is infused into us. The ultimate prayer, "Show me Your glory!" is always answered. Any answer to prayer that does not bring us into the Presence is no answer at all.

More than answers, we need the answer: the glory of God.

Face-to-Face

2 Corinthians 3:2–4:6

We all, with unveiled face, beholding as in a mirror the glory of the Lord, are being transformed into the same image from glory to glory, just as by the Spirit of the Lord.
(2 CORINTHIANS 3:18)

Paul underlines the astounding difference between Moses' and our experience of the glory of God. We can remove the veil and look the Lord in the face through Jesus Christ. God has graciously revealed His presence, His glory, for us to behold in Christ. And the result is that we can be changed into Christ's image, from one degree of glory to another.

That's what we all need, isn't it? We all long to be more like Christ in character, attitude, action, and reaction. Human personality can be changed. Day by day we can know Paul's assurance that the "glory of God in the face of Jesus Christ" can have lasting radiance on our faces. The more we concentrate on Christ, the more, by His grace, we are refashioned into His image.

Do you really want that? Tell the Lord you do. He is more ready to answer that prayer than we are to ask. We will notice the difference in our relationships and responsibilities. Christ's love and forgiveness, peace and power, hope and courage, will be unmistakable.

The Christian life is transformation into Christlikeness.

Things Become What They Seem

Numbers 13:25-33

Caleb quieted the people before Moses and said, "We should by all means go up and take possession of it, for we will surely overcome it."
(NUMBERS 13:30)

There was a majority report of fear and a minority report of courage. The majority report of the spies sent in to survey the land of Canaan was grim. The negative reporters viewed themselves as grasshoppers in comparison to the Canaanites and became that in their own sight.

Now look at Caleb's courage. He saw the same giant warriors in Canaan, but he also knew the Lord was with His people. Praise God for people like Caleb! They have the capacity to multiply limited human resources by the unlimited power of God and turn it into vision and hope.

We face challenges today, with the alternatives of the majority report or the minority report. There are more than enough people around us who are afraid and negative. We need a Caleb to give us assurance that, with the Lord, we can move forward. Now the crucial question: Are you more like Caleb or more like the men who became grasshoppers in their own image? How would your family, church, the people with whom you work, answer that?

Dear God, make me a Caleb today!

Willing to Receive Wonders

Joshua 3:1-7

*Consecrate yourselves, for tomorrow the LORD
will do wonders among you.*
(JOSHUA 3:5)

There's an inseparable relationship between today's consecration and tomorrow's wonders. The Lord was ready to do wonders. What He needed was the unreserved consecration of the people to His plans and purposes. Consecration is yielding all we know of ourselves and our resources to all we know of God. There is no limitation on what He can do with people who have given Him control of their total lives.

Joshua was elevated into an awesome position of leadership as Moses' successor because the Lord had all of Joshua there was. The Lord was his passion and purpose. Joshua was completely sold out in a surrender of his will to the Lord. He had learned his lessons well from Moses. The leader of the Exodus had given him the secret of power: absolute obedience.

What wonder would you long for the Lord to do tomorrow? He gives us today to focus the wonder we need tomorrow. When we relinquish our tenacious control of our future, the Lord can step in and do wonders beyond our imagination.

Tomorrow's miracles begin with today's consecration.

The First Step Is the Hardest

Joshua 3:8-17

*It shall come about when the soles of the feet of the
priests who carry the ark of the LORD, the Lord of all
the earth, rest in the waters of the Jordan...*

(JOSHUA 3:13)

That's a great promise! The priests carrying the ark of the Lord
held the key to realizing it. They represented the tribes of Israel
and were to be participants in the realization of a great miracle.
All they had to do was get their feet wet! They had to take the first
step into the Jordan River, and then the Lord would roll back the
waters so the people could pass through. The first step was the
hardest; the Lord did the rest.

Often the first step to realizing a miracle of God in our lives
is to ask for guidance, receive a promise, and then act as if it were
ours. I find that the formula of asking what to ask for, then asking, and thanking the Lord with praise really works. The crucial
thing about the miracle of the rolling back of the waters of the
Jordan is that this is exactly what the Lord told Joshua would
happen if the priests were courageous enough to believe and take
Him at His word.

There will be no miracle until we get the soles of our feet wet.
Have you acted on what He's told you to do? If you loved Him
with all your heart, what would you do? Do it today!

Lord, the soles of my feet are wet!

Take Courage!

Matthew 9:2; Mark 10:49; Psalm 31:1-24

Be strong and let your heart take courage,
all you who hope in the LORD.
(PSALM 31:24)

Courage grows from faith. Courage is ours for the taking. The psalmist discovered that. The Lord said to him, "Be strong and let your heart *take courage*." It must be claimed and appropriated. This is the salient thrust of Jesus' offer to His disciples on the night before the crucifixion. I like the accurate rendering of the Greek in the New American Standard Bible: "These things I have spoken to you, so that in Me you may have peace. In the world you have tribulation, but *take courage; I* have overcome the world" (John 16:33). We can take courage only because the Lord has taken us. He has a tight grip on us. Then we will have courage to discover and do His will.

"How can I know that what I want is what the Lord wants for me?" There is only one way: the conversion of your "wanter." Questions about knowing the will of God reveal a great need for intimacy with God: Bible study and prolonged periods of prayer with the Lord. We should be in constant conversation with Him. Longing for the will of God is really longing for Him!

If God is on our side, who can ever be against us?
—ROMANS 8:31 TLB

The Secret of Spiritual Power

Judges 6:1-27

Surely I will be with you.
(JUDGES 6:16)

Gideon was pressed into the Lord's service at a very difficult time in Israel's history. The people had entered the Promised Land and began to learn the disciplines of being an agricultural people. They made a fatal mistake. They adopted the local fertility worship and placed Baal shrines in their fields.

Their agrarian success was short-lived. The Midianites swept down at harvesttime to rape and ravage the products of Israel's pluralistic religion. God's people had become syncretistic—they worshiped Yahweh and the Baal gods all at the same time. Syncretism is the worship of more than one god, the blending of religious loyalties. At a time when all seemed hopeless, the people cried out to God, but kept the Baal shrines intact.

That's when God stepped in. He came to Gideon with a promise and a command. He promised to go with him, and He told him to tear down his family's Baal shrine and its female counterpart, the Asherah.

God always begins a reformation in us before He can use us to accomplish one around us. Gideon had to take a stand. And so do we.

God is ready to do great things through us
when we put Him first in our lives.

Contagious Courage

Judges 6:28-33

They said to one another, "Who did this thing?" And
when they searched about and inquired, they
said, "Gideon the son of Joash did this thing."
(JUDGES 6:29)

We need more parents like Gideon's father, Joash, today, parents
who are willing to support their children's obedience to God. Joash
stood with his son and the Lord against the people who wanted
their false gods kept intact. His ridicule of Baal's impotence was
magnificent. If Baal was as strong as the people thought, let him
defend himself against Gideon. Joash's affirmation was expressed
in giving his son a new name, Jerubbaal, meaning "Let Baal con-
tend against him." He released his son to battle for the Lord.

We all have false gods we syncretize with the Lord. We believe
in Him, and yet we draw our meaning and purpose from people,
possessions, positions, and our human power. We worship at the
shrine of success, human achievement, and culture. What is it for
you? What competes with your obedience to the Lord? The promise of His presence and power for Gideon was dependent on the
tearing down of the pagan altar. When Gideon did that, the peace
and power of the Lord were promised for future challenges. The
magnificent things Gideon did to save Israel were accomplished
because the Lord had all that there was of Gideon.

On the throne of our heart, there's only room for God.

Christ Clothed in Us

Judges 6:33-35

The Spirit of the LORD came upon Gideon; and he blew a trumpet.
(JUDGES 6:34)

The meaning of the Hebrew of our key verse for today could be translated, "The Spirit clothed Himself with Gideon and he blew a trumpet." What a vivid image! The Spirit of God comes within us, clothes Himself with us, and gives us courage to sound the trumpet, calling others to seek His best for their lives.

God's best for our lives is His Spirit. All that we ask Him for or ask Him to do for us in our prayers is not His best. He is the best Himself. The Lord's Spirit is all we need. The glory of God is a person fully alive through the infusion of His Spirit.

All that Christ said and did was to prepare a new people who would be His clothing in the world. When He clothes Himself with us, we are made like Him, given His character, and empowered to live the life He lived. That's what He meant when He promised, "These things which I do, you shall do also, and greater things." Our life should demand an explanation. How can we be the people we are? Then we can explain: Christ is our motive, message, and might.

*My mind, emotions, will, and body are the
wardrobe of the Spirit of Christ.*

Go for It!

Ephesians 5:15-21

Be filled with the Spirit.
(Ephesians 5:18)

There are three ways to live. The first is to do our will on our own power. That's humanism. The second is to do our will on Christ's power. That's religion. The third is to do Christ's will with Christ's power. That's the abundant life.

Paul's five-word admonition "Be filled with the Spirit" spells out the secret to power. The Greek tense is in the continuous present imperative: "Go on being filled with the Spirit." Throughout the New Testament there are two uses of being filled with the Spirit. The first is initial at the time of conversion, and the second is for the challenge and opportunities of ministry.

Christ creates in us a sense of emptiness, makes the good news of the gospel impellingly clear, engenders desire to receive forgiveness and a new life, gives us the gift of faith to receive Him as our Lord and Savior, takes up residence in us, and then gives us exactly the gift we need to launch out into the adventure of the abundant life. That's why we need "to go on being filled." Each new possibility or problem presents us with an opportunity to be given fresh power for the immediate situation, circumstance, or relationship. We need not be afraid. Our confidence is not that the Lord has joined our team, but that we have joined His.

Our motto is "Go for it!"

God's Peace Is Our Fleece

Judges 6:36-40

> *Then I will know.*
> (Judges 6:37)

It is some comfort to us to know that even after Gideon's decisive encounter with the Lord, he needed further assurance that God would deliver Israel through him. How like most of us! We want to be sure. There needs to be some sign. Our lack of confidence demands an undeniable revelation before we will get on with what the Lord has told us plainly we are to do.

Gideon needed not one but *two* reaffirmations just to be surer. The amazing thing is that God was willing to meet the frightened leader at the point of his need. The fleece was wet and then dry according to the precise requirements of Gideon's two tests.

We wonder about that. What would it take to convince us that the Lord is with us and will give us power to accomplish His guidance? The point is that He loves us so much He is willing to enter into dialogue with us in prayer and give us a sign that a particular direction or action is what He wills. He uses the thoughts of our minds, the feelings of our emotions, and the arrangement of circumstances to assure us. When we surrender our wills and ask for guidance well in advance of a major decision, He will get through to us. Be sure of that!

An inner peace is our fleece.

The Rudder of Guidance

James 3:4

Look also at ships: although they are so large and are driven by fierce winds, they are turned by a very small rudder wherever the pilot desires.
(JAMES 3:4)

The fleece was fine for Gideon at that stage in his spiritual development, and the Lord answered in a way to make him sure. The great difference for us is that we can have the mind of Christ. We live in a new dispensation of grace. Through the cross we are reconciled with God and have access to Him in a much more profound way. So many of our questions are answered in the message and mandate of Christ. As new people in Christ and in intimate fellowship with Him, each of us can ask these questions.

Will this decision enable me to grow in grace? Is it God's best for my life? Is it in keeping with the life and message of Jesus Christ? Can I do this and seek first His kingdom and His righteousness? Does it will the ultimate good for me and all around? Is it part of the long-range goals the Lord has already revealed to me?

There's no better fleece than answering those questions. But finally, raw trust in the Lord is our only fleece. And not even our wrong choices are beyond His forgiveness and innovative power to provide His best for our lives.

Our Pilot has the rudder in hand.

The Audacious Assumption

Proverbs 16:1-9

The mind of man plans his way, but the LORD directs his steps.
(PROVERBS 16:9)

"Isn't it a bit audacious to think that God cares or is concerned about the decisions of our daily life?" Paul would have answered this person's question with a resounding "No!"

The word *audacious* can be taken in two ways. It can mean "intrepidly daring, bold, adventurous, venturesome"; it can also mean "presumptuous, saucy, and impudent." The two divergent uses of the word focus on the different attitudes of people about God's guidance. The rank-and-file Christians do not expect to be guided by God. They think it petulant personalism to think that God either has a plan for their lives or has the inclination or interest to communicate to individuals a particularized providence. They feel that the idea of God guiding us makes the Almighty a messenger boy, the Bible a Ouija board, and contemplation of the implications of circumstances like reading a horoscope.

But there are others whose audacity is rooted in a humble belief that the habitual response of a God-centered mind to the responsibilities and opportunities of life, can find guidance from God for specific decisions.

Ask boldly, follow obediently, and live abundantly.

A Daring Adventure

Judges 7:1-25

The LORD said to Gideon, "The people who are with you are too
many for Me to give Midian into their hands, for Israel would
become boastful, saying, 'My own power has delivered me.'"
(JUDGES 7:2)

The odds were not good when Gideon prepared for battle: 32,000
Israelites against 135,000 Midianites. With the Lord's help, perhaps he could win. No wonder Gideon was shocked when the
Lord made two cuts in his army! He lost 22,000 when he followed the Lord's instruction to tell those who were afraid and
trembling to go home.

The test of the remaining 10,000 was to march the soldiers
through the riverbed. Those who stopped, took off their armor,
and put their mouths into the water to drink were eliminated.
Only those who kept their eyes on Gideon while reaching down
for a little water in their cupped hands, then lapping it like a dog,
were qualified. The issue was commitment to battle and not their
own temporary thirst. Only 300 men survived this test. But with
these the Lord accomplished victory over Midian.

The Lord wants loyal, committed followers who keep their
eyes on Him. He can do the impossible with people whose only
security is in Him.

I will attempt something that only
God could accomplish through me.

Criticizing After the Battle

Judges 7:24–8:3

*The men of Ephraim said to him, "What is this thing you
have done to us, not calling us when you went to fight against
Midian?" And they contended with him vigorously.*

(JUDGES 8:1)

Amazing! After the worst of the battle was over, Gideon gave the
armies of Ephraim an opportunity to be a part of the mopping-
up action of completely defeating Midian. They were given the
chance of sharing the victory and the glory. How grateful they
should have been! Not so. They complained that Gideon had won
the battle without them.

We are left to wonder: What does it take to satisfy some
people? Ever have the problem? Of course, we all have. We do
our best and we try to be considerate of the ego needs of others,
but still something is always wrong. The Ephraimites were not
unaware of Gideon's battle against Midian. Why did they wait
to be called? Were some of their army those who were afraid, or
those who could not pass the Lord's test in the river? My experience of human nature wants to read that into the account. But
true or not, it would be consistent with people through the ages
who can't take the heat of the battle and then find some reason
for complaining after the victory is secure. Know anyone like that?
God forbid that anyone would ever say that of you or me!

Lord, give me patience with the careless critic.

The Listener

1 Samuel 3:1-21

The LORD came and stood and called as at other times, "Samuel, Samuel!" And Samuel said, "Speak, for Your servant is listening."
(1 SAMUEL 3:10)

The theme of the life of Samuel's character was, "Speak, Lord; Your servant is listening." Samuel's name was interpreted by his mother to mean "God hears." Biblical scholars also suggest that the name means "The Name of God." Both were expressed throughout Samuel's life. No person in the Old Testament lived more completely in the confidence that God does hear and that in His name is power and authority for His people. The words he spoke in response to the Lord's call provide us with the secret to making this an exciting day in our lives. Because the Lord hears, we can say what's in our hearts and then say, "Speak, Lord; I'm listening."

Samuel was the architect of the rebuilding of Israel's spiritual and social life. The "Lord's listener" was used to communicate God's call to Saul and David, and he anointed them as kings. The prophet was the father of the prophetic office in Israel's life from his time forward. He was a God-sensitive man who was so open to God that he could hear God speak and then acted on what he heard. Let's make this a day to listen—to God and then to people.

My mind and heart have ears to listen to the Lord.

Raise Your Ebenezer

1 Samuel 4:1–7:17

Samuel took a stone and set it between Mizpah and Shen, and named it Ebenezer, saying, "Thus far the LORD has helped us."
(1 SAMUEL 7:12)

Samuel became a mighty source of courage and guidance to the armies of Israel in their battles against the Philistines. It was a time of military crisis. The Lord met the people's need in Samuel. The prophet was totally dependent on Him to show each step of the way.

This is exposed in a beautiful way in today's key verse. After victory over the enemy, Samuel built an altar and called it *Ebenezer*. The Hebrew word is very significant. It means "thus far the Lord has brought us." What had been the site of Israel's defeat was now a hallowed memory of victory. They did not have to retreat. The stone marked the place where the Lord had brought them under His watchful care and intervening strength.

The hymn "Come, Thou Fount of Every Blessing," by Robert Robinson, uses this word *Ebenezer*: "Here I raise my Ebenezer, here by Thy great help I've come, and I hope, by Thy good pleasure, safely to arrive at home. Hitherto Thy love has blessed me; Thou has brought me to this place; and I know Thy hand will bring me safely home by Thy good grace."

I will raise Ebenezers today along the way.

Our Awesome Power to Limit God

1 Samuel 8:1–15:35; 1 Chronicles 10:13

Saul died for his trespass which he committed against the LORD,
because of the word of the LORD which he did not keep.
(1 Chronicles 10:13)

Saul had great potential. He was handsome, and endowed with immense talent. But the signs of his weakness were evident from the beginning. Why didn't he know about Samuel? Was he unaware of the soul-sized issues gripping his people? He was so engulfed in his own affairs that he was not a part of the struggle of Israel to be the faithful people of God. He was totally undone by the fact that the Lord would choose him to lead in a struggle he had never made his own concern. When he had a moving experience of God, the people were equally amazed. "What has come over the son of Kish?" they asked. And yet God chose him through the voice of the people. But where was he? Hiding among the baggage!

The first evidence of Saul's deeper problem was exposed when he blundered ahead in making a sacrifice without Samuel and then led the people into battle without clear guidance. Saul found it difficult to trust God to be his only strength. He never got his heart into the rhythms of the Lord's guidance. He lived on the level of talent rather than the Lord's gifts. God was never really personal to him. In Saul we see our awesome power to limit God.

There is no substitute for habitual obedience, constant
trust, and God's resources for our needs.

God Uses the Ordinary
to Do the Extraordinary

1 Samuel 16:1-23

He sent and brought him in. Now he was ruddy, with
beautiful eyes and a handsome appearance. And the
LORD said, "Arise, anoint him; for this is he."
(1 SAMUEL 16:12)

We can imagine that there was no small stir in Bethlehem when Samuel appeared and said that the voice of God had directed him to the house of Jesse to find a king of Israel. Jesse had eight sons, and he did not think to call David, his 14-year-old. Surely the Lord would not want David! Yet Samuel said, "Are all your sons here?" Jesse was amazed. "There remains yet the youngest, who keeps the sheep." "Send and fetch him," said Samuel.

The moment Samuel looked, he knew David was the one. This lad who had roamed the hills, keeping watch over the flocks, playing on his shepherd's harp, gazing at the stars at night, and dreaming of the future—this was God's chosen to lead His people. God was to make him one of the greatest men of history, but not without trial and conflict. The hammer blows of experience were to shape him into the man God wanted and needed.

The story of the life of David tells us the exciting truth of how God takes frail, ordinary human beings and makes them great for His purposes.

We never dare say, "Who, me? Why me?"

A Person After God's Heart

Acts 13:16-25; Psalm 89:20;
2 Samuel 11:1–12:31; Psalm 51:1-19

*When He had removed him, He raised up for them David as king,
to whom also He gave testimony and said, "I have found David the
son of Jesse, a man after My own heart, who will do all My will."*
(ACTS 13:22)

David was a man after God's own heart because he abounded in thanksgiving. In the psalms there is such a mixture of confession and thankfulness. Only a sense of unworthiness can issue in profound thanksgiving. David's life challenges us that it is not our perfection but our thankful dependence that counts. We can identify with David in his fallible humanity, and we can see what God can do with a person who confesses and thanks God for His forgiveness.

The Bible paints the dark story of David's transgression and sin. God waited long for him to repent. After his adultery with Bathsheba and his cruel sending of her husband, Uriah, into war to die, God sent Nathan the prophet to judge his sin. A deep, penetrating parable was given and then the challenge "You are the man!" David knew! His repentance is for history to read in Psalm 51. And God took him at his word. The infinite mercy of God lifted him up and used him in His further purposes for Israel. Amazing grace, indeed!

We are called to be persons after God's heart.

Affirming the Gifts of Others

1 Samuel 17:48–18:16

Saul has slain his thousands, and David his ten thousands.
(1 Samuel 18:7)

Saul's reaction to David smiting Goliath was very human: "Inquire whose son the stripling is." He wanted to use him to accomplish his purposes without seeking the source of his power. David was successful in battle wherever Saul sent him. And then, as David became popular and the people grew to love him, Saul became angry and jealous. Saul was more concerned with his own image than with getting God's work done. What a sorry analysis Scripture gives us: "Saul was afraid of David, because the Lord was with him and had departed from Saul."

Often what we cannot use for our own purposes and manipulate for our own plans, we grow to hate. The history of God's people is black with stories of godly people who could not work together to accomplish God's will. The church, Christian groups, families, and friends are often split because they cannot bear to affirm what the Lord is doing through another.

Christian maturity leads us to care most that God's work is done; who does it and gets the credit is not important.

Today I will affirm others who do God's work differently from me, and I will get on with what He has called me to do.

Saul's Problems
with Saul—Called David

1 Samuel 18:1-30

When Saul saw and knew that the LORD was with David…then Saul was even more afraid of David. Thus Saul was David's enemy continually.
(1 SAMUEL 18:28-29)

Saul had a problem with Saul he called David. His own insecurities became fastened on how the Lord was using David. That exposes that his greatest concern was not the battle with Israel's enemies, but with his worry over his own status and recognition. Why couldn't he rejoice that David was victorious over the Philistines? Any wise king should be able to affirm a general's success for him. Not Saul. He could not see that David was fighting for the Lord *and* for him. Saul's unstable relationship with the Lord made him jealous of one who was able to do what he could no longer do.

The poison of jealousy keeps us from sharing the glory. When we do, we can take delight in the way God works in others and in us. Commit this day to affirm the way He is using others, and praise Him. The old Gaelic blessing is needed for that: "Belong to God and become a wonder to yourself and a joy to your friends."

I will not sip the poison of jealousy until my soul is dead.

Misplaced Praise

Song of Solomon 8:6-7

Jealousy is as severe as Sheol; its flashes are flashes
of fire, the very flame of the LORD.
(SONG OF SOLOMON 8:6)

Jealousy is the result of an unstable state of grace. It hits us when we are out of the flow of the Lord's grace, do not delight in our own uniqueness, and fail to express thankfulness for what we have received ourselves. Comparison of ourselves with others takes our eyes off the Lord.

In today's scripture, Solomon depicts the grimness of jealousy. It is like hell, here called Sheol. Sheol was the place where the dead continued to exist, a region of shadows, misery, and futility; there the faithless lived forever in misery and futility. Jealousy is a living hell.

Most of all, jealousy is misplaced praise. That's the meaning of "the very flame of the LORD." The flame of God in us is misspent and misused in envy of another person or his gifts and possessions. The capacity of praise is misdirected and used to want to be or have what is someone else's. The antidote to jealousy is to focus on the Lord and His goodness and then on ourselves as blessed and loved by Him. The more we praise Him for our uniqueness, the more we can affirm another's specialness without wanting to steal it for ourselves.

I will praise the Lord, accept His gifts to me,
and affirm others today.

The Alarm Signal

Galatians 5:16-26; James 3:16

The works of the flesh are evident…jealousies…envy.
(GALATIANS 5:19-21)

*Wherever you find jealousy and rivalry you also
find disharmony and all other kinds of evil.*
(JAMES 3:16 PHILLIPS)

There's a great difference between the works of the flesh and the fruit of the Spirit in today's passage. The works of the flesh are human nature apart from the Lord. They are what we are without the regeneration of being born again and the rejuvenation of being Spirit-filled. When we surrender our minds and emotions to the Lord, He takes up residence in us. He actually displaces the tendencies of flesh (humanity separated from Him) with His own character. It's impossible to imagine Jesus Christ being jealous! Paul lists jealousy as a work of the flesh, a natural tendency of human nature that has not been transformed.

But what about jealousy after we are converted? It is an alarm signal that we are taking our measurements from other people rather than Christ. The way to win in the battle with jealousy is to go deeper into Christ and the realization of His fruit in us. Christ's love for us is the only medicine that heals jealousy. When you are jealous, take His prescription!

I let go of false comparisons and accept the Lord's delight in me.

Helping People Deal
with Their Feelings

James 5:13-18

*Confess your trespasses to one another, and pray
for one another, that you may be healed.*
(JAMES 5:16)

The young wife stood talking to friends at a party. The room was jammed with wall-to-wall people. Suddenly she was distracted from the pleasantries of her conversation. Through the forest of people she spied her handsome husband talking to a very attractive young woman. A surge of jealousy pulsed through her.

As the husband and wife drove home, the wife's stony silence provoked the question she hoped for: "Is everything all right? You seem upset." She tried to share how she had felt at the party and confessed she was engulfed with a feeling of jealousy. He exploded with defensive consternation, sidestepping the moment of understanding that could have healed the whole thing. "Of course not! Your insane jealousy is going to ruin this marriage."

We all have feelings of jealousy at times. We need to be able to get them out in the open. A true mate or friend is not shocked or judgmental. He or she understands and empathizes. Then we can be helped to tell God.

*The Lord cures our jealousy by unqualified love and a special
gift of new delight in the person we are, as cherished by Him.*

Whom Shall I Fear?

Psalm 27:1-14

The LORD is my light and my salvation; whom shall I fear?
The LORD is the defense of my life; whom shall I dread?
(PSALM 27:1)

In this great psalm, David reaffirms that God is his sure defense. Light for darkness and deliverance for battle were his hope. The Lord would show the way, would light the path, would give mental illumination and emotional courage. Why be afraid?

Note how this psalm teaches us to pray. First, it teaches us to begin with a simple review of what we know of God and His nature. Second, it shows us that we are to pour out whatever is on our minds and hearts in complete self-emptying of concern. Third, we are to affirm again that the one thing we wish above all is to do God's will and ask God to teach us His ways. Fourth, we are to leave the problem or opportunity with Him, acknowledging His goodness in our lives. Last, we are to wait in patient confidence to see what He directs.

The Lord's constant word to us is "Fear not!" There are 366 "Fear not!" verses in the Bible—one for every day of the year and an extra one for leap year! Most of the admonitions are followed by a firm reminder of an aspect of His nature—such as His faithfulness, goodness, lovingkindness, and intervening power.

God's personal word to us is "Fear not, I will help you."

Glorify and Enjoy God!

2 Samuel 6:1-5,12-19

David was dancing before the LORD with all his might.
(2 SAMUEL 6:14)

The story of David is filled with human pathos, but it is also filled with divine joy. David knew how to rejoice. There are dark days of failure and repentance in David's story, but we must also see this man of deep emotion praising God out of sheer, uncontainable joy.

We are thankful for the picture of David dancing before the ark of God. He let himself go in unreserved praise: "David played before the Lord and danced before the ark, and the earth shook." There's a dimension of adoration we too need to discover as a part of our life. The Westminster Catechism says, "Man's chief end is to glorify God and enjoy Him forever." We are to enjoy God!

God is not a cosmic policeman looking to arrest those who enjoy themselves. The Christian faith is not dull and drab. It is delight with God, with life, and the gift of others. Let yourself go in praise and adoration. David did, and so should we.

But do we? Many of us are grim Christians. We have the distorted idea that being a Christian is only thinking right, acting decorously, and being responsible. We need enthusiasm and excitement.

Franz Joseph Haydn put it this way:

*When I think of God my heart is so full of joy that notes leap
and dance as they leave my pen; and since God has given
me a cheerful heart, I serve Him with a cheerful spirit.*

The Affirmation of Life

Psalm 18:25-30; 1 Kings 2:1-4,10-12

*I am going the way of all the earth. Be strong,
therefore, and show yourself a man.*
(1 Kings 2:2)

There is no human emotion or problem that David did not experience. He could not look back on it all without thanking God for the gift of life and say that it was good to live. Now at length the sunset and quiet of eventide had come for David. His dependence upon God was always a sure defense against evil, his victory in battle was always a fresh opportunity for praise to God, and his personal failures were always the prelude to a new sense of forgiveness and mercy. At the end of all his trials, this was still his verdict as it had been before: "This God—His way is perfect; the promise of the Lord proves true; He is a shield for those who take refuge in Him."

The only good life is the God-life. A life lived in fellowship with Him will enable us to grow in grace in the triumphs and victories as well as the failures and defeats. God is in control, and He has given us the gift of the abundant life as it was meant to be in Jesus Christ.

*The Spirit of God is within me…O how good it was
to live! I thank You, God, You who gave me life.*
—Arthur Honegger,
concluding words from his oratorio *King David*

God Can Make Us Wise

1 Kings 3:1-28

Your servant is in the midst of Your people which You have chosen,
a great people who are too many to be numbered or counted.
(1 Kings 3:8)

It was an awesome thing the Lord asked young King Solomon: "Ask what you wish Me to give you." There are so many things Solomon could have asked for: the favor of the people, military might, trusted officials, strength like his mighty father, David. But Solomon had learned the profound lesson from his father. He observed that as David walked before the Lord "in truth and righteousness and uprightness of heart," he had been richly blessed.

Solomon did not presume he had been given the throne because of his own ability or temperament. He knew that the opportunity was a gift of God's providence. Therefore, he asked for the one gift he needed most: wisdom. "And it was pleasing in the sight of the Lord that Solomon asked this thing."

Wisdom is the mind of God implanted in the tissues of our brain. More than the talent of a sagacity or insight, it is God's thought controlling our thought. It results in an immense discernment and knowledge beyond our own human capacity.

But we know so much more about what to ask for than even Solomon. Paul said that Christ is "the wisdom of God." Dynamic Christianity is Christ living in us to think His thoughts through us.

Lord, give me the gift of wisdom!

Let Me Go!

1 Kings 11:14-22; Matthew 19:16-21

Pharaoh said to him, "But what have you lacked with me, that behold, you are seeking to go to your own country?" And he answered, "Nothing; nevertheless you must surely let me go."

(1 KINGS 11:22)

Hadad and the rich young ruler had the same problem: The kingdom of thingdom had trapped them. They both needed a metamorphosis of their materialism. Hadad found the answer. His story is vivid and exciting. He had escaped the slaughter of the males of Edom and fled to Egypt. There the pharaoh took a special liking to him and gave him all the material blessings that Egypt could offer. The sumptuousness of Egyptian society was at his fingertips. Yet when he learned that his people were leaderless and that God needed him in Edom, he asked the pharaoh to release him.

The rich young ruler could not make that choice. He had conditions in his response to the Master. When Jesus discerned that the bind of materialism was upon him, He told him to go sell all he had. He could not do that, and so turned away.

The implications of this are for all of us, whether rich or in need. There may be something, someone, some memory, or some uncommitted plan that Jesus would expose and demand we surrender to Him.

When we consider the joy of life in Christ now and eternity with Him forever, we say, "Oh world! Only let me go!"

We Are Never Finished

1 Kings 18:1–19:3

Ahab told Jezebel all that Elijah had done, and how he had killed all
the prophets with the sword. Then Jezebel sent a messenger to Elijah,
saying, "So may the gods do to me and even more, if I do not make
your life as the life of one of them by tomorrow about this time."
(1 Kings 19:1-2)

The battle with the priests of Baal on Mount Carmel left Elijah
depleted. He had fought for the Lord and won. That should have
settled the question of who was God in Israel once and for all. But
what Elijah thought was the final battle with evil, Jezebel regarded
as a skirmish. Elijah had only touched the peak of the iceberg of
evil in the land. Jezebel was more dangerous than ever after the
defeat of her priests, and Elijah was never more vulnerable to
discouragement than after his spectacular victory. The emotional
high of his triumphs clouded his perception of his emotional,
physical, and spiritual exhaustion.

Jezebel's vitriolic threat undid him: "So may the gods do to
me and more so if I do not make your life as the life of one of
them by this time tomorrow." And Elijah was afraid.

We've all had times like that. We battle life's problems and
win, work hard for the Lord and know superhuman effectiveness,
and then suddenly a small threat or mishap throws us into a tail-
spin. That's when we need the Lord's perspective and power.

The Lord replenishes our strength for each new battle.

Fire out of the Ashes

1 Kings 18:1–19:21

*It is enough; now, O LORD, take my life, for
I am not better than my fathers.*
(1 KINGS 19:4)

Note carefully how the **Lord healed Elijah's depression.** He gave
him rest and sleep. The prophet had to be rebuilt physically. Then
the Lord fed him with nourishing food. When he was rested and
refortified, the Lord asked the shocking question that broke the
bind: "What are you doing here, Elijah?" He wanted Elijah to get
in touch with what was happening to him. Then the Lord sent
outward signs of His power: wind, earthquake, and fire.

But the assurance of the Lord's presence came in a still, small
voice. Elijah was finally quiet, rested, and ready to hear. His status with the Lord was not dependent on his spectacular feats of
victory, but on the Lord's love and acceptance. The same fire that
had won the victory on Mount Carmel now burned in his heart.
Then the Lord sent Elijah back to work, not on his own strength,
but with the Lord's. He gave the prophet a new image of himself,
a new task, and a new power. Discouragement was turned to new
courage. The Lord will do the same for each of us when we take
ourselves and our failures too seriously and forget to take Him
seriously enough.

The Lord sets a new fire in our hearts when we are burned out.

Where Is Your Nineveh?

Jonah 1:1–4:11

Should I not have compassion on Nineveh…?
(Jonah 4:11)

Jonah was astonished by the call from God to go to the Ninevites to proclaim the sovereignty and power of the Lord as the God of the world. Jonah lived in Gath-hepher in the Zebulun territory, which is now Galilee. The Ninevites were archenemies of the Hebrews, and Nineveh was symbolic of everything they had been taught to abhor and hate. And yet the Lord told Jonah to go to these people with a message of judgment and forgiveness. He resisted the Lord at every turn.

Jonah ran away from his calling. He went to Joppa and took a ship in the opposite direction. Tarshish could not have been farther away from Nineveh. And yet the Lord intervened to get him back to where He wanted him. In Nineveh the people were very responsive to the petulant prophet. From the king down, the people repented.

Jonah ran from God and got into trouble; he ran with God and had great success; and finally he ran into the loving arms of God. The message of the book of Jonah is that we can keep our faith only when we give it away—even to people we don't like but who are infinitely loved by our Lord.

*It is better to be in Nineveh with the Lord
than in Tarshish without Him!*

14

His Love Knows No Limits

Hosea 1:1–14:9

The LORD said to me, "Go again, love a woman who is…an adulteress, even as the LORD loves the sons of Israel, though they turn to other gods."
(HOSEA 3:1)

The heart of God is filled with limitless love. Hosea discovered this out of an excruciating personal experience in his marriage. His heartbreak put him in touch with the things that break the heart of God. Hosea's wife, Gomer, became unfaithful in the most abhorrent way. She not only became a harlot, but participated in the sacramental fornication of the orgies of Baal and Ashtaroth worship. And yet, the prophet saw that what Gomer had done to him, the people of Israel had done to the Lord.

And then Hosea discovered something far greater than his pain: He encountered the grace of God. As God loved His people in spite of their sin and willful rebellion, so too Hosea must love Gomer.

In this poignant life story we are ushered into the cross-shaped love of the heart of God. Eventually, long after Hosea's discovery, God would pay the price of ransoming His people. Calvary was the place. His own Son was the cost. And now, in spite of anything we do or say, His love is offered to you and me.

His love has no limits, His grace has no measure, His power no boundary known unto men.
—ANNIE JOHNSON FLINT

A Gifted Life

1 Corinthians 12:1-31

There are diversities of gifts, but the same Spirit.
(1 CORINTHIANS 12:4)

In 1 Corinthians 12, Paul tells the Christians at Corinth that the qualities of life for which they long most are not humanly produced but divinely imputed. He lists the gifts of the Spirit as wisdom, knowledge, faith, power to heal, power to work miracles, prophecy, discernment, speaking in tongues, and interpreting tongues. These were sought-after qualities in the church. Paul simply says that these gifts are the operation of the Holy Spirit, who distributes them to people in His church in order that the ministry may be done by all the people.

In chapter 13, Paul clarifies what is meant by love. Most important of all is the fact that it is a gift. We can receive it and be a communicator of it, but we cannot produce it. We cannot love in a giving, forgiving, free, unmotivated, unchanging, uncalculating way until the gift is given to us.

The Spirit is love. When He lives in us, we are able to love because He loves through us. Have you received the Holy Spirit? This week we will consider the nature of the love-gift of the Spirit. Make a list of the relationships and responsibilities in which you desperately need this quality of love. Ask for the gift. The Lord will be faithful.

The need before us calls forth the gift God puts within us.

The Gift of Love

1 Corinthians 13:1-3

*Though I speak with the tongues of men and of angels, but have
not love, I have become sounding brass or a clanging cymbal.*
(1 CORINTHIANS 13:1 NKJV)

Paul takes all the honored human qualities and exposes them one
by one as inadequate unless we have received the gift of love.

Eloquence, humanly motivated or divinely inspired, is nothing without love. What priority we put on clarity and beauty of
speech! But does it communicate love? Unless it does, it is no
more than the noise of blaring brass or crashing cymbal, like an
orchestra that only tunes up but can never play the melody of
the score.

Prophecy was a cherished gift. To tell the truth about contemporary situations and to foretell God's truth about the future
were considered great. Paul says that insight into life and discernment of the future mean absolutely nothing if we do not have
the gift of love.

Absolute faith cannot compare with love. The power to do
miraculous things is nothing if we lack the power to love another
person as God loves us. Even if this faith becomes sacrificial, and
gives itself in radical acts of obedience, but does not communicate
the imputed gift of love, the Christian has lost his purpose.

We are nothing and have nothing if we do not have the gift of love.

The Gift of Gratitude

1 Corinthians 13:4; Ecclesiastes 4:4;
1 Timothy 6:1-21

Love does not envy; love does not parade itself, is not puffed up.
(1 CORINTHIANS 13:4 NKJV)

Jealousy grows out of the distance between what we are and what others have become, between what we have and others have, between our inadequacies and others' achievements. It breaks down relationships, destroys families, splits churches, and hinders the growth of the kingdom.

When we receive God's love for us, we have a profound experience of self-acceptance and appreciation. We no longer need to compare jealously or blow our own horn boastfully. We accept ourselves as accepted and loved by God. Our concern is to use what gifts we have, not in competitive comparison, but in thankful enthusiasm. Jealousy and boasting melt before the truth of God's generosity. We become able to praise God for our own and others' gifts. Dante's Virgil was right: "Envy bloweth up men's sighs. No fear of that might touch ye if love of higher sphere exalted your desires."

The love of the higher sphere has been given us in the gift of love through the Holy Spirit. Have you received Him?

Love is not jealous or boastful.

Patient Love

1 Corinthians 13:4

Love suffers long.
(1 Corinthians 13:4 nkjv)

Love is patient because God is patient. An essential quality of His nature is given to our character. If we substitute the name of Christ for each time the word *love* is used in this passage, we get close to its meaning. In Christ, God's patience with us is exposed. He is not limited by our standards of time and emergency. Above time He sees the eternal, big picture. Love will always issue in a patience with people's slowness to learn, respond, or grow. Patience can be real only if we see things from God's point of view and live on His timing. We live only for the fulfillment of His purposes in people and programs. If He can wait, why can't we?

This patience issues in kindness. This is an active expression of love. The self-restraint of patience prepares to express kindness. Involvement with people in their needs and frustrations is an expression of kindness. It is love getting its hands dirty. Because we are freed by God's patience, we can love without plans and demands that people become something for our satisfaction. We are to help relate them to God and seek His purpose for them. A patient Christian is also kind to himself and his own failures. When he is, he inadvertently finds that he is much more understanding of others.

Love is patient and kind.

Love with Sensitivity

1 Corinthians 13:5; Luke 18:9-17

Love…does not behave rudely.
(1 CORINTHIANS 13:5 NKJV)

What's really important? What makes a person important? Who are God's VIPs? The greatest danger is that we will strive to become important for the wrong reason. We all love recognition and the rewards of position and power. What goes wrong is that importance becomes a detriment instead of a gift.

No one can determine himself important. This is for others to do. We are to do our work as well as we can and leave the results to God. Self-appointed importance is the root of arrogance. At the heart of it is the desire to "play God" over others and our realm of life.

The result of this is lack of consideration and rudeness toward others. We run roughshod over others and their rights because we believe we are in control. Love liberates us from arrogance because it heals our need to be important. It gives us new energies to care infinitely for people and to work diligently. The outcome is that without seeking it, God uses us in His strategy of the kingdom. A person who has been made important no longer has to convince other people of his importance. He no longer has to push other people around to be sure they know he is important. They will know by our life and the power of our love!

Love is sensitive to the needs of others.

Christian Maturity

1 Corinthians 13:6-7

*...Bears all things, believes all things,
hopes all things, endures all things.*
(1 Corinthians 13:7)

An authentic mark of a mature Christian is a graciousness that is free and flexible. J.B. Phillips translates our scripture as suggesting that love is not touchy or quick to accuse or make judgments. When our own ideas or rights are so crucial to us that we cannot listen and adjust to others, we are not living by the power of God's love. Yet how many of us are like a powder keg, ready to explode when things don't go our way? We are edgy and quick to be offended.

A man in whom Jesus Christ's love has penetrated is slow to judge and accuse. He waits with caution and concern. Knowing how fallible and vacillating he is himself, he can understand the weakness and frailty of others. There is a loving acceptance about him. Judgments are irrelevant because even after our haughty judgment is made, we still must love and forgive. There is nothing we can learn about each other that gives us a right to exclude or reject. The person we condemn still needs our love. We cannot escape the responsibility.

Love is not touchy and does not gloat over the weakness of others.

Love Does Not Give Up

1 Corinthians 13:8-13

Love never fails. But whether there are prophecies, they
will fail; whether there are tongues, they will cease;
whether there is knowledge, it will vanish away.
(1 CORINTHIANS 13:8 NKJV)

The indefatigable quality of **God's love** is amazing. Wave upon wave, in spite of our resistance or indifference, God loves. His love is not dependent upon our response or acknowledgment. He loves us in spite of everything. And that's the kind of love He can give us through His own indwelling Spirit! Everything we think is important will pass away; love alone persists.

That love never ends is the theme of the whole New Testament. God has come in Jesus in spite of humankind's sin and because of it. With mature forgiveness, He offers Himself and meets us "eyeball to eyeball." Nothing that we can do stops His love. Even the final rejection of the cross becomes the ultimate triumph of God. He came back and picked up with men and women where they had left off at Calvary. He could not be dismissed or diminished. The love that had guided His people, sent the prophets, dwelt in Jesus, and brought Him from the dead was the same love that returned in the resurrected Lord. And He is loving still, utterly available to those who will believe and receive.

Love never ends.

When the Bind Is Broken

Romans 6:20-22

Now having been set free from sin, and having become slaves of God, you have your fruit to holiness, and the end, everlasting life.
(ROMANS 6:22)

They had come to an impasse. Their marriage was in deep trouble. Each had clearly delineated what the other would have to do to make things right to fulfill the other's need. There was now no question of what would be the cost to save their marriage. Yet neither could begin until the other proved that he or she would also begin. The multiplied rejection of the years immobilized both of them. They were stuck on dead center, immovable because of pride and the need to be sure the other would follow through.

Sound familiar? Of course it does, because it describes an experience most of us have had in marriage, in the family, or with some other person. We desire things to be different, and we even know what will make them different, but we are stuck. We have lived under reciprocal love, give-and-take barter, so long that to give and forgive initiatively is almost impossible. We need to be able to say, "Resolved first: I will give myself in costly love and do the thing I know will communicate love in the language that will be understood. Resolved second: I will, even if the other person never does."

To love means to will someone's ultimate good and put yourself on the line to help make it possible.

Take No One for Granted

Matthew 25:31-46

Then He will answer them, saying, "Assuredly, I say to you, inasmuch as
you did not do it to one of the least of these, you did not do it to Me."
(MATTHEW 25:45)

We all have people in our lives who are the "least." They are the
emotionally, spiritually, physically needy people in our families,
among our friends, in our places of work, as well as in the more
obviously indigent pockets of poverty in our communities. Be
careful of the either/or. We can miss the needy in the community
by preoccupation with our immediate circle; but we can also miss
the needs closest to us by overinvolvement in the more obvious
needs in the community.

The danger is if we miss one or the other by lack of balance.
The "least" often changes for us. It may be a spouse, a child, or a
close friend; at another time it may be someone who is segregated
or debilitated socially; or again, it may be someone who is lonely
or hung up by life. How shall we know who it is for each of us?
Ask Christ who the particular "least" is for you. The wonder of
prayer is that He will show us.

We are to be committed to serve the "least" as
we are to serve Christ Himself.

Good Comfort

Philippians 2:19-24; 1 Thessalonians 3:1-13

I have no one like-minded, who will sincerely care for your state.
(PHILIPPIANS 2:20)

What Paul had to say about Timothy becomes a personal challenge to us. "He really cares about you. Everyone else is concerned only about his own affairs, not about the cause of Jesus Christ." Timothy had been to Philippi with Paul on his first visit and had gone ahead for a second visit. Now he was to be sent back again to give comfort.

Timothy means "good comfort," and he had lived out his name. He was the only one left with Paul who was free enough of concern about his own affairs to give himself to the cause of Christ, spelled out in the Philippians' needs. Others were too busy, but Timothy knew there was enough time in any day to do the things God wanted him to do. Note the same emphasis about Timothy's visit to Thessalonica and Paul's love for his friends.

Most of us are overconcerned about our own affairs. Our time fills up with a daily round of demands and responsibilities. How do we know what's important? For Timothy, it was the cause of Christ. Could that be said of you and me?

Who needs you to be a Timothy in his or her life today?

A Friend Who Won't Go Away

Ruth 1:1–4:22

Now, my daughter, do not fear. I will do for you whatever you ask, for all my people in the city know that you are a woman of excellence.

(Ruth 3:11)

The little book of Ruth communicates a great truth. Ruth was a Moabitess. She married one of the sons of Naomi, a Hebrew who sojourned in Moab with her husband, Elimelech. When both her husband and father-in-law died, Ruth was indefatigably loyal to Naomi. She journeyed with her to Bethlehem of Judea. Even when Naomi gave Ruth freedom to leave her, she responded with the now-famous and oft-quoted words of fidelity, "Where you go I will go, and where you lodge I will lodge. Your people shall be my people, and your God my God. Where you die I will die, and there I will be buried. Thus may the Lord do to me, and worse, if anything but death parts you and me" (Ruth 1:16-17).

The author of the book of Ruth stresses the commitment of Ruth to the Lord. Though she is a convert to the Hebrew faith, she expresses the faithfulness he longs for his readers to have to their God and to one another. Ruth's integrity and consistency of friendship to Naomi is rewarded by her courtship and marriage to Boaz. A commitment to friendship with the Lord spells commitment to be a true friend to others.

Are we dependable? Do people know that we love them with an unchanging faithfulness? Are we a friend who will not go away?

Happy Thanksliving!

Psalm 18:1-50

You have also given me the shield of Your salvation, and Your
right hand upholds me; and Your gentleness makes me great.
(PSALM 18:35)

A little boy in a Vietnamese immigrant family was learning English. He had a particular problem with "g's" and "l's." On Thanksgiving Day he attended church services with his family. After the service he shook my hand and said, "Happy Thanksliving!" Not a bad description of real thanksgiving. When we are truly thankful, it radically affects our living.

In today's scripture David acknowledges that the gentleness of the Lord had made him great. The original Hebrew word translated here as "gentleness" actually means "condescension." That sparks profound thought. God has condescended to create us, to offer us a relationship with Him, and to care for us so graciously. David had discovered a liberating truth: All that he was, had, and did was because God condescended to bless him. No wonder this psalm ends with a crescendo of thanksgiving!

God's grace, plus our gratitude, equals greatness. When we give God the glory, greatness grows in our character. We become affirmers of others. When is the last time you told the people in your life that you are thankful for them?

Thanksgiving: God desires it, we require it for
humility, and others never tire of it.

Before We Can Love Others

Mark 12:28-34

*"You shall love the LORD your God with all your heart, with
all your soul, with all your mind, and with all your
strength." This is the first commandment. And the second, like
it, is this: "You shall love your neighbor as yourself."*
(MARK 12:30-31)

Jesus' second great commandment, to love our neighbors as
ourselves, is not easy to fulfill. Why is it so difficult to love people
without any demands, standards, and images of what we want
them to be? The reason is in the commandment itself: We are to
love others as ourselves. But that's the difficulty. Often we do not
love ourselves. The mark of Christian maturity is when a person
can say, "All right, this is who I am; these are my talents; these are
my liabilities, my quirks, and my gifts." Each of us is uniquely gifted by God, and each of us has talents to be used for His glory.

A little girl received a new dress. She danced joyously about
the room singing, "I'm glad I am me!" What a simple, untar-
nished, unblemished, and healthy self-appreciation! How many
of us could say this? How many of us are glad we are who we are
and where we are?

*Lord God, give me the healthy self-appreciation to say, "I am glad
I'm me!" Help me to see all You have given me and how You have
blessed and guided me through the years. And then, with real
freedom, help me to enjoy the life You have given me. Amen.*

The Other Half of Grace

Amos 7:1-9

He showed me, and behold, the Lord was standing by a vertical wall with a plumb line in His hand. The LORD said to me, "What do you see, Amos?" And I said, "A plumb line." Then the Lord said, "Behold, I am about to put a plumb line in the midst of my people Israel."

(AMOS 7:7-8)

Amos was a prophet of righteousness and justice. In the midst of religious apostasy and neglect of human suffering, his theme was, "Let justice roll like waters, and righteousness like an overflowing stream." The Lord told him that righteousness and justice were His plumb line that measured and exposed the crooked structures of religious institutionalism. The issue was that belief in God had to be expressed in personal righteousness and social justice. Amos' cutting message slices through any religion that does not result in discovering and doing the Lord's will in our relationships and responsibilities.

The Lord's plumb line is lowered on each of us and our churches. Our bland toleration of anything that contradicts His love is exposed. Judgment is a part of grace. When the plumb line is lowered we can see what is out of line. Then we can ask Him to help us put the crooked straight. Judgment is an expression of grace.

What does the plumb line tell you is wrong that He is ready to help you make right? List the people and situations.

"You Are Mine"

Isaiah 5:1-7; Mark 12:1-9

*What will the owner of the vineyard do? He will come and
destroy the vinedressers, and give the vineyard to others.*
(Mark 12:9)

The parable of the vineyard tells us that God will have the final
word, and that word is *love.*

Here is the picture of rejected trust. The Lord had entrusted
Israel with the gift of life. They had rejected the overtures of God's
loving judgment in prophet and priest. As we read the parable,
Amos, Jeremiah, and Isaiah march before our mind's eye. The history
of God's people is red with the blood of rejected prophets.
But God was not done in by humankind's rejection. He sent His
own Son. In allegorical language Jesus clearly predicts His own
suffering and death. Do you sense the persistence of God in the
parable? He will not take "No" for an answer.

The parable is a word of truth and hope for us today. We now
are the stewards of the vineyard. We are responsible to God for
what we do with the gift of life. We belong to Him. He will not
let us go. Think of the many ways we reject His claim upon us. We
take things into our own hands, we run others' lives, we misuse
our gifts. But still He comes. In experiences, in other people, in
the quiet of our own soul, we hear Him say, "You're mine!"

*Judgment leads to grace, and grace enables us
to be faithful as stewards of the Lord.*

20/20 Hindsight

Mark 12:10-12

Have you not even read this Scripture: "The stone which the
builders rejected has become the chief cornerstone…?"
(MARK 12:10)

What people rejected, God elevated. Just to be sure the leaders of Israel did not miss the point, Jesus quoted a familiar messianic text to clearly identify the Son of the parable as the Messiah and Himself as that long-anticipated Messiah. The rejected Jesus would be elevated to the keystone of the arch of God's revelation.

This was the confidence with which Jesus faced His death—that God would use the cross as the focal point of history. He trusted His Father to bring good out of evil.

Most of us have 20/20 hindsight. We can see how God has worked in the past, but it is difficult to see how He can use for any good the raw material of present crisis, of dreaded future uncertainty. Yet we are given the vision that can sing, "Oh God, our help in ages past, our hope for years to come."

Do you have this kind of confidence? Can you say, "Whatever comes, God will bring final victory"? Worry about what is to come robs us of joy in the present. Jesus Christ, who was, is now…will be forever. Give Him your concerns about the future, and God will give you 20/20 foresight of trust.

God is His own interpreter, and He will make it plain.
—WILLIAM COWPER

A Realistic Reason for Hope

Lamentations 3:1-66

*This I recall to my mind; therefore I have hope. The
LORD's lovingkindnesses indeed never cease.*
(LAMENTATIONS 3:21-22)

Realism and hope. They are difficult to keep together at times.

Jeremiah was both honestly realistic and authentically hopeful. His appraisal of conditions in Jerusalem under the rule of the Babylonians was filled with anguish. The ruin of the city and the Temple as well as the deportation of the best citizens to Babylonia broke the prophet's heart. Most of all, the people failed to connect what had happened and the judgment of God on their apostasy. Chapters 1, 2, and 3 through verse 20 express hopelessness. "So I say, 'My strength has perished, and so has my hope from the LORD'" (3:18).

Then note in verse 21 a shift in mood and spirit. Jeremiah not only remembers all the tragedy but now remembers the Lord's lovingkindness. His spirits begin to rise, and then soar in exuberant joy. The Lord is not finished with the prophet or with His beloved people. Jeremiah bases his hope on the Lord who is good to those who wait for Him, seek Him, and completely trust in Him. When we do that, we will be able realistically to see things as they are, but also hope for what God will do.

*Realism gives us an honest appraisal of what we need
to surrender to God. Hope comes from that!*

Stand Up, Stand Tall, Stand Ready!

Ezekiel 2:1–3:27

Son of man, stand on your feet that I may speak with you!
(Ezekiel 2:1)

There are three things the Lord did for Ezekiel that He wants to do for us today. He got him on his feet, filled him with His Spirit, and fed him with His Word.

The Lord first told Ezekiel to stand on his feet so He could speak with Him. The image is vivid. He wanted Ezekiel at full attention, ready to hear what the Lord had to say. That's what He does for us right now. He gets us on our feet, ready to listen and then move on in obedience. He says, "Stand up! I'm going to get you moving again!"

But note the second gift. The Lord entered into Ezekiel and enabled His own command. The Lord provides for what He guides. Once He gets us on our feet, He gives us power to get moving.

The third command may seem strange to us. "Eat the scroll, and go speak to the house of Israel." The scroll was the sacred Scripture. The Word of the Lord had to be thoroughly digested so Ezekiel could speak with authority. After we are on our feet and receive God's Spirit, we need to feed on His Word. Daily Bible study is the only way to stay standing.

Get on your feet, get power, get fed, get going.

Before You Give Up

Ezekiel 37:1-28

*"Son of man, can these bones live?" And I
answered, "O LORD God, You know."*
(EZEKIEL 37:3)

There are times when we are tempted to give up—on some person,
group, situation, ourselves. This was the mood of God's people in
the Babylonian exile. But God gave them a prophet who could
see the worst and the best. Ezekiel had a vision of the dry bones
in the valley of Jezreel, symbolic of the dried-up vision and hope
of the people. The prophet forces the people to realize they had
brought their plight on themselves by turning from the glory and
holiness of God. When the true cause of the condition was acknowledged, the promise would be given. The bones were going
to come together and live!

The message of this for us has two parts. Before we give up,
we need to confess what brought us to the time of discouragement. Instead of asking, "Why did this happen to me?" we must
ask, "What did I do to cause this to happen to me?" Then we are
ready for the most crucial question: "What is the Lord saying to
me in what has happened to me?" That leads to a surrender of
what is tempting us to give up. In response, the Lord gives us a
new heart.

*When Christ takes up residence within us, we are
filled with His heart. And He never gives up!*

Twice Born

John 3:1-8

*That which is born of the flesh is flesh, and that
which is born of the Spirit is spirit. Do not marvel
that I said to you, "You must be born again."*
(John 3:6-7)

Jesus put His finger on Nicodemus's deepest need. He was deeply impressed by His mighty works, but Jesus swept aside his compliments and got down to the Pharisee's real problem. He needed to be born again, to start all over, by a quickening to a new life by the Spirit of God.

It happened! What Jesus explained to Nicodemus that night actually took place later. The leading Pharisee became a secret follower, then an open defender of Jesus. He risked status and position to help bury Jesus, and according to historical tradition became a leader in the church after Pentecost. The crucifixion must have had a profound impact on him. But it surely was the experience of the resurrected Lord that brought back the full meaning of what He had told him about being born again.

Put yourself in Nicodemus's skin. Experience what he experienced when the risen Lord fulfilled His own prediction and Nicodemus became a twice-born, Spirit-filled person.

*New birth is a sure beginning of life in Christ;
growth in Christ is a sure sign that the beginning was real.*

Born Again to Hope

1 Peter 1:3-4; Romans 6:3-23

If we died with Christ, we believe that we shall also live with Him.
(ROMANS 6:8)

Paul presses us on in our understanding and experience of the new birth. We are born again when we die with Christ and are resurrected to new life in Him.

Throughout his epistles Paul tells us about the new birth as a death-and-resurrection experience. We die to our self, our plan, our purposes, our presuppositions. By the power of God we are raised up to a new life. How is your life radically different because of this experience?

Our own present resurrection from death of self to a deathless life gives us courage to face life's problems and disappointments with the sure conviction that our Lord will intervene and infuse His power in our times of need. We can face anything with that assurance. Hope provides patience. We are able to take the long view of things. The shortness of time and the length of eternity give us patience with the trifles of life. A born-again person knows he or she belongs to Christ. Christ's nature is being reproduced in them. Would the people around you say that your rebirth has made you a contagiously hopeful person?

What oxygen is to the lungs, such is hope for the meaning of life.
—EMIL BRUNNER

6

New Wine in Old Bags

Mark 2:20-22

*No one puts new wine into old wineskins; or else the new wine bursts
the wineskins, the wine is spilled, and the wineskins are ruined.*
(MARK 2:22)

New wine expanded and pushed out the wine bag. The bags were
made of sheepskin and were flexible for expansion as the wine
expanded. Old bags would crack and split open and would not
be able to contain the new wine.

Our Lord warned His followers that the new teaching He proclaimed could not be contained in the old customs and practices.

The message of the new wine in old bags is applicable to us
as individuals and to our churches. Jesus Christ must be the *basis*
of our life, not an addition. Most of us want all this world offers
and heaven too. We want the security of our background, education, financial position, talent, ability, friends, and future plans.
But we want Jesus also. The difficulty is that Jesus Christ is not
satisfied with this. Conversion means a break with the old and a
fresh start with Christ.

Christ's message and His indwelling power are like new wine.
This new wine requires a new bag of fresh commitment to Him
each day.

*Old ways, customs, and habits will burst with the pressure
of Christ's tumultuous reformation of our lives.*

An Authentic Encounter

Romans 10:5-13

If you confess with your mouth the Lord Jesus and believe in your heart that God has raised Him from the dead, you will be saved.
(ROMANS 10:9)

The teenager had been to camp. The challenge of the lordship of Jesus Christ over all of life had been presented. At the close of the camp, an opportunity to let Christ run her life was given in a very simple but direct way. The young woman had given as much as she then knew of herself to as much as she then knew of Jesus Christ and was determined to trust Him to guide her in the midst of the ambiguities and complexities of today's world.

"Well, what did you do at camp?" was the traditional question almost thoughtlessly asked by the girl's father at the dinner table after she returned home. "I have decided to let Jesus Christ run my life!" was the direct answer, followed closely by a gentle but powerful question: "Have you ever done that, Daddy?"

The father was challenged. That would mean praying about decisions, expenditures, investments! It would mean getting Christ's help for relationships, plans, and programs! No, he had never done that. Christ was not very real. His daughter's newly found joy in Christ forced him to realize he was a religious man who needed Christ.

There is a great difference between knowing about Christ and actually knowing Him as personal Savior and Lord.

A Fourth in the Fire

Daniel 3:1-30

*Our God whom we serve is able to deliver us from the furnace of
blazing fire; and He will deliver us out of your hand, O king. But even
if He does not, let it be known to you, O king, that we are not going
to serve your gods or worship the golden image that you have set up.*
(DANIEL 3:17-18)

Four words give us faith for the fires of life: "If He does not." The
faith of Shadrach, Meshach, and Abednego was firmly rooted in
God's sovereignty over all creation and His righteous care for His
people in Babylonia. But even if He did not choose to extricate
them from the fire, they would not worship the golden calf of
Nebuchadnezzar.

The story of what happened to Daniel's friends is a source of
courage and confidence for us today. We are never left alone in
our fires. The Lord is with us when we feel the blasts of difficulty
and testing. He is ready to join us in the heat of life if we can say,
"He can and will help me in this situation, but even if He chooses
not to intervene in the way I want, I will not give up, for I am alive
forever. Nothing in this life can separate me from His love."

There is a wonderful breakthrough to power and peace whenever we are sure that no fire will have to be endured without the
Lord and nothing can destroy our relationship with Him.

*Our hope is not based on getting God to do what we want
but in wanting Him regardless of how events work out.*

No Longer Part of the Problem

Psalm 24:1-10

*The earth is the LORD's, and all it contains, the
world, and those who dwell in it.*
(PSALM 24:1)

Who hasn't at some time felt the icy-cold sword of doubt about the ultimate purpose of God cut into his or her very soul? Each of us has at some time in his or her life faced situations for which he or she could find no logical explanation or solution. We have questioned, "What did I do to deserve this?" "Why did this happen to me?" "Why does God allow things like this to happen?" Often this tangled world makes no sense, and doubts "rap and knock and enter into the soul," as Browning put it. In the deep recesses of the soul, "the deep heart's abode," we want to know.

The answer comes from the psalmist: "The earth is the LORD's, and all it contains, and those who dwell it it." History is an account of humankind's inhumanity. But God has given us freedom to accept Him or reject Him. What we have done to ourselves and each other breaks His heart of love. In Jesus Christ He came and comes today. The only answer to the riddle of life is in Him. Through His power we can be what we were created to be and live as part of His solution, rather than as part of the world's problem.

*God is not finished with our world. Those
who trust Him can change history.*

The Final Assurance

Psalm 56:1-13

*You have taken account of my wanderings; put my
tears in Your bottle. Are they not in Your book?*
(Psalm 56:8)

"How can God know and care about me with all the billions of people?" We've all wondered about that at times…on a crowded street or when thinking about the immense number of people in the world. We must dare to think magnificently of God. If He could create the universe out of nothing and make humankind, if He could reveal His light and love for us to see and experience in Jesus Christ the Mediator, we can dare to assume that He knows and cares about us individually. But the gospel goes way beyond that! It tells us that God not only knows and cares, but that He has chosen us to be His beloved. That's the one final assurance!

Jesus tells us what He told the disciples: "You have not chosen Me, but I have chosen you." By the mystery of election we are called, appointed, chosen people of the Lord. A sure sign of our election is our amazement that He should choose us. Paul constantly was astounded the Lord had elected him. The Lord's call was a source of humbling delight. We know how he felt!

*Aim at heaven and you will get earth thrown in.
Aim at earth and you get neither.*
—C.S. Lewis

Old Measurements for a New Life

Zechariah 2:1-13

*I said, "Where are you going?" And he said to me, "To measure
Jerusalem, to see how wide it is and how long it is." And…the
angel…said, "Run, speak to that young man, saying, 'Jerusalem
will be inhabited without walls…For I,' declares the LORD, 'will
be a wall of fire around her, and I will be the glory in her midst.'"*

(ZECHARIAH 2:2-5)

An alarming picture invaded Zechariah's vision. He saw a young
man measuring Jerusalem so it could be rebuilt according to the
old measurements of the Holy City before it was destroyed in
586 BC. There were two things wrong with that: The old measurements were too small, and no wall could ever be a defense.
Only the Lord was a sure defense and His presence the source
of lasting glory.

Zechariah had the rebuilding of Jerusalem in his heart. The
returned exiles wanted to rebuild the city to its original grandeur.
They had not learned from the past. Their vision was limited.

It is our problem also. So seldom do we learn from past mistakes. We fail to trust God, we get into trouble, and we miss what
the mistake has to teach us. We all have compulsive, repetitive
patterns that get us into the same old problems again and again.
The Lord wants to change that.

We can overcome the past, not repeat it

Heresickness

Job 36:1-33

Elihu continued and said, "Wait for me a little, and I will
show you that there is yet more to be said in God's behalf."
(JOB 36:1-2)

There's a pointed story of a young man who was sent away to boarding school. He was lonely, he found it difficult to make new friends, and he was challenged by his studies. A teacher sensed he was having a difficult time. "What's the matter, John?" The teacher asked with empathy. "Have you got a bit of homesickness?" The boy thought a moment and then answered, "No, sir, I don't have homesickness—I have heresickness!"

For "heresickness" God offers "now-help." He comes to us to help us learn, grow, and mature. Often He sends a person into our lives to help us ask the right questions and deal with reality. When there is no place to go, the Lord intervenes to help us maximize where we are.

Elihu was that kind of friend to Job. He forced Job to discover God's presence in the present. He enabled him to love God for God and to know that his Redeemer lived.

After we have experienced the incisiveness of an Elihu sent from God, we are ready to go to someone we know is suffering from a bad case of "heresickness." Who is it for you?

You can be a "heresickness" healer today.

The Boast That Banishes Burdens

Psalm 44:1-26

In God we have boasted all day long, and we
will give thanks to Your name forever.
(PSALM 44:8)

One of the great women of our time was Corrie ten Boom. I noticed that she was able to praise God for the way He used her. Some years ago I asked her how she handled compliments and adulation from people.

"Oh, Lloyd," she responded, "that is no problem. Every time a person praises me for something I've said or done, I just accept it as a flower. Then at the end of the day I put all the flowers together into a lovely bouquet, get on my knees, and say, 'Here, Father, this bouquet belongs to You! The lovely things people have said about me, they were really saying about You. Thank You, Father, for using me.'"

I complimented a friend of mine for a message he had given at a conference. "Isn't that wonderful!" he responded. He knew that the Lord had blessed, and he gave Him the credit.

Today is a day to boast in the Lord. There will be no problem of false pride when we boast in Him and what He's doing. Each time something good happens and you're tempted to take the credit, add a flower to the bouquet to give to God at the end of the day.

All of life is a lovely bouquet to present to the Lord in gratitude.

With the Help of Our God

Nehemiah 1:1–6:19

*The wall was completed on the twenty-fifth of the month Elul, in
fifty-two days. When all our enemies heard of it, and all the nations
surrounding us saw it, they lost their confidence; for they recognized
that this work had been accomplished with the help of our God.*

(NEHEMIAH 6:15-16)

Nehemiah returned from the exile in Persia in 445 BC with determination. He had two goals: to call the people back to faithfulness
to the law and to rebuild the wall around Jerusalem. Nehemiah
is an example of courageous leadership. He clarified goals, demanded accountability, engendered enthusiasm in people, and
got in and worked with them.

But, like any outstanding leader, Nehemiah had his enemies.
Therefore, work on the wall had to be done under hazardous
threats of attack, and the progress was slow. Nehemiah's life was in
danger. Friends begged him to come down off the wall and enter
the protection of the precincts of the Temple at night for safety.
His response was, "Should a man like me flee? And could one
such as I go into the temple to save his life? I will not go in."

Courage is as contagious as fear. Nehemiah had charisma
rooted in a firm trust in God's faithfulness. He was sure of His
guidance and His strength for the task.

*God gives us impossible tasks so we can show others
that with Him nothing is impossible.*

Ready for Christmas

Isaiah 40:1-31

A voice is calling, "Clear the way for the LORD in the wilderness;
make smooth in the desert a highway for our God."
(ISAIAH 40:3)

It happened again. I had promised myself it would not happen again last year, but it did. I'm a last-minute, day-before-Christmas shopper. The department stores that had stayed open for me and my fellow procrastinators looked like a Sherman tank had been driven through them. The tired clerks looked as picked over and worn out as the merchandise.

In one store, a long line of exhausted people stood waiting at the cash register checkout with arms filled with frantically selected gifts. A woman in front of me had a frazzled, "if I can only hold out until after the holidays" look on her face. The public-address system played a tired recording of "God Rest Ye Merry, Gentlemen" that must have been replayed thousands of times since Thanksgiving.

When she reached the man at the register, he asked her that thoughtless, innocuous question we hear repeated ad nauseam during the days before Christmas: "Well, ma'am, are you ready for Christmas?" Her exhausted reply was, "As ready as I'll ever be!" How would you have responded?

What would it mean to be ready for Christmas and
ready to live Christmas all through the year?

Open Before Christmas!

John 1:1-18

He came to His own, and His own did not receive Him.
(John 1:11)

Many people spend the month of December buying, wrapping, decorating, and preparing for the festivities of the holidays but are not ready for a transforming Christmas, nor free to experience its real impact for all of life.

My greatest concern is that it won't make any difference, that we will go back to the same old life as the same people as we were when it all began. It's possible to celebrate Christmas and miss Christmas!

Imagine a time around the Christmas tree in which you opened all your presents except those from one particular person. Feel the hurt of that rejection. Look at it from God's point of view. What do you think He wants to give you? Picture Him waiting for you to open and enjoy His gift.

The gift I want to share with you during the days leading up to Christmas is marked a bit differently. The tag has your name on it. It says, "To be opened in preparation for Christmas and enjoyed all through the year!" The heart of Christmas is the heart. God's heart in Christ offered to you and me.

Don't go through the Christmas season and never open and accept God's gifts of love, joy, hope, and peace that flow from His heart to ours!

The Crèche and the Cross

1 Timothy 1:12-17

This is a faithful saying and worthy of all acceptance, that Christ Jesus came into the world to save sinners, of whom I am chief.
(1 TIMOTHY 1:15)

Christmas is the experience of unqualified love. We all need that more than breathing, eating, or sleeping. There's a love-shaped emptiness in all of us. Our deepest need is to be loved, to love ourselves, and to be free to love others. That's rooted in feeling special. The shepherds felt very special on that first Christmas. The good news of Christmas is that you and I are special to God!

The words of the angelic chorus are better translated "Glory to God in the highest, and on earth peace among men with whom He is pleased" (Luke 2:14 NASB). Let that soak into the love-parched place in your heart. In spite of all that we have done or been, God is pleased with us. We are His beloved; we belong to Him; nothing we can do or say will make Him stop loving us.

Christmas is your special time. God has something to say. Listen! Put the personal pronoun in the familiar words: "God so loved *me* that He gave His only begotten Son, that believing in Him, *I* should not perish but have everlasting life. For God did not send His Son into the world to condemn *me*, but that *I*, through Him, might be saved."

Our hearts leap. God is for us and not against us. His love is unconditional.

The Gift of Self-esteem

Romans 8:1-11

There is therefore now no condemnation to those who are in Christ Jesus.
(ROMANS 8:1)

Christ came into the world when we least deserved Him or wanted Him. And He keeps coming. There's nothing we can do to earn His loving forgiveness or make Him stop loving us. From the crèche to the cross, an open tomb to His impelling presence with each of us, we hear His imploring love: "You belong to Me. You are My loved and forgiven person. I came for you, lived for you, died for you, defeated death for you, and am here now for you."

That's God's Christmas gift to us. Don't leave it unwrapped! Open it and enjoy the healing, liberating, motivating power. There is no problem, perplexity, or potential facing you and me that cannot be conquered if we accept the gift. Love plus forgiveness equals freedom!

We will be free to love and forgive ourselves. Christ came so that we can get up when we are down on ourselves. What is it for you? What memory of failure haunts you and makes you negative and hostile to the most important person in your life—the inner you? Be gracious to yourself this Christmas. Give yourself a gift. Forgive yourself.

Have you ever thought that in every action of grace in your heart
you have the whole omnipotence of God engaged to bless you?
—ANDREW MURRAY

A Christmas List of What to Forget

Ephesians 4:25-32

*Be kind to one another, tender-hearted, forgiving each
other, just as God in Christ also has forgiven you.*
(EPHESIANS 4:32)

The litmus test that we have accepted God's gift of love and forgiveness is that we will be free to be initiative communicators
of what we have received. Paul warns against grieving the Holy
Spirit. That is to deny the reason God came in Christ: to love us
and make us lovers. Billy Graham said, "God has given us two
hands—one for receiving and the other for giving." We need to
celebrate Christmas with both hands!

Who in your life is suffering from emotional malnutrition because you are holding back approval, acceptance, and affirmation?
Whom do you need to forgive? Whose forgiveness do you need to
seek? Imagine what Christmas could be now if all the hurts could
be expressed and real reconciliation experienced!

Many of us are burdened by the inner tension of the "if only's"
and the "what might have been's" of life. I am convinced that the
frustration many people feel at Christmas is because of lovely
things we do and give that contradict how we really feel. Perhaps
we need two kinds of Christmas lists: one list of the gifts we want
to give and the other of people whom we need to forgive or from
whom we need to seek forgiveness.

Who is on your forgiveness list?

Tidings of Great Joy

John 15:9-17

These things I have spoken to you, that My joy may
remain in you, and that your joy may be full.
(JOHN 15:11)

The recurring note of the Christmas message is joy. Joy is the outer expression of the inner experience of being loved. Robert Louis Stevenson was right: "To miss the joy is to miss all." I have a friend who has a favorite saying each time he closes a conversation and says goodbye. He takes hold of a person's hand and says, "Don't miss the joy!" A sure sign that we have allowed Christmas to happen to us is an artesian joy that lasts all through the year.

Joy is not gush or ho-ho jolliness. Joy grows in the assurance that God will use everything that happens to or around us for our ultimate good and for His glory. True joy is what Paul calls a fruit of the Spirit—a result of the Lord living in us. We sing the familiar carol's words, "O come to us, be born in us, O Christ Immanuel." Christmas is not only accepting the love of Christ's birth in Bethlehem, but opening our hearts for Him to be born in us today.

The authentic mark of a Christian is joy. More than circumstantial or dependent on people's attitude or words, joy is constant and consistent in life's changing problems. It is unassailable and vibrant. "Joy to the world, the Lord is come."

Don't miss the joy!

The Hope of the World

Lamentations 3:21-26

Therefore I have hope.
(LAMENTATIONS 3:21)

Christmas is a festival of hope. And there is nothing our world needs more desperately than authentic hope.

But hopelessness is also profoundly personal. People disappoint us when we place our hope in them. It's heartbreaking when they fail us or are unable to be our source of happiness. We place hope in our careers, our financial planning, and our abilities. Life's reversals shock us with the realization that our hope has been misplaced. Our plans for the future may pull us on to tomorrow with the longing that things will happen as we've dreamed. But things seldom work out as we've planned. Circumstances, people, ourselves, and our talents are not reliable sources of hope.

What we need is a hope that's more than wishful thinking or blind expectation that everything will work out smoothly. We need a hope that is vibrant in pain, consistent in grief, indefatigable when people break our hearts, unassailable in disappointment, and unflagging in life's pressure. Do you have a hope like that? Is your hope ultimately reliable?

True hope grows out of two basic convictions: that God is in charge, and that He intervenes. This is why a true experience of Christmas gives us lasting hope.

22

An Anchor of the Soul

Hebrews 6:9-20

This hope we have as an anchor of the soul,
both sure and steadfast.
(HEBREWS 6:19)

The Lord is faithful. His promises are sure. We can never drift off the solid anchor of His care. We are never alone. There is no situation, circumstance, or problem too big for our Lord. That's the tonic we need to fire our blood and give us courage. The Christmas present to be opened every day of the year is written in the Lord's own hand: "Lo, I will be with you always."

The deep conviction of my life is that the Lord is always on time—never early, never late. We can let go of our worried grip on life. If we hang on to yesterday's troubles, tomorrow's fears, and today's anxieties, we will overload and blow the circuits.

But now, because of Christmas, we can identify our deepest needs and surrender them to our Lord. Don't let Christmas come and go without an experience of release from tension. Our hope is built on our Lord's faithfulness. He's there with you now. Trust Him. And then expectantly anticipate that at the right time and in the way that's most creative to you and all concerned, He will intervene and infuse you with exactly what you need. What an exciting way to live!

Set your anchor in the faithfulness of God.

Peace for Broken Pieces

Isaiah 9:1-7

His name will be called...Prince of Peace.
(ISAIAH 9:6)

We've heard and seen a lot about peace during the preparation for Christmas. The word has been artistically embossed on cards we've sent and received. Banners on street lights, placards on store windows, and advertisements in newspapers expose our longing for peace. We ache for peace on earth, in our relationships, and in our hearts. International crises force us to feel the pulse beat of the heart of God when He grieved over Israel long before He sent Immanuel. "They have healed the wound of my people lightly, saying, 'Peace, peace,' when there is no peace" (Jeremiah 8:11 RSV). When we get in touch with the turbulence in our world and the anguish in people, or identify our own conflicts, we realize how much we need Christ's peace.

Peace is righteousness—right relationships with Him, ourselves, and others. It is a cleansed conscience and a future surrendered to Him. Why is there so little peace? To reword a great saying, "It is not that the world has tried the peace of Christ and found it didn't work; the world has never tried the peace of Christ!" How would you like to give up the broken pieces of your life and allow the Christmas Christ to give you an unbreakable peace?

Christ is our peace.

Christmas Peacemakers

John 14:25-31

Peace I leave with you, My peace I give to you.
(John 14:27)

True peace is available only in knowing Christ intimately. All that He said, did, and does is to bring peace in our hearts. He was born to bring it; He taught to explain it; His life modeled it; He died on the cross to establish it; He rose from the dead to defeat all the enemies that rob us of it; and He is with each of us now to give the gift. It pervades our hearts when we put Him first in our lives.

Then we can be peacemakers, combating negativism, criticism, gossip, and innuendos that destroy relationships. We will become active in working for peace between us and others, between people who need to understand, forgive, and accept one another, and in our society. Think of what the future could be if your sole purpose were to bring reconciliation among your family, friends, and people in your community. Picture what you would be like as a peace-possessed person. Then use your imagination to focus what you will be like as you communicate Christ's peace in active peacemaking. Thank the Lord that it shall be so by His power in you.

Peace is ours only as we give it away.

Christmas Day

The Experience That Changes Everything

Luke 2:1-20

*Let us now go to Bethlehem and see this thing that has
come to pass, which the Lord has made known to us.*

(LUKE 2:15)

The account of what happened to those lonely shepherds is a
before-and-after story. We can identify with the before; we need
to become involved in the after; and in between is the experience
that changes everything!

Like the shepherds, we live in two worlds now at Christmas.
Get in touch with your feelings. We all suffer from future jitters
over our war-weary world gripped in soul-sized issues. None of
us is free of difficult situations and impossible people. And inside
are the hopes and hurts, disappointments and discouragements,
fears and frustrations we all feel.

Suddenly, piercing the silence is a magnificent sound, and
dispelling the darkness is a glorious splendor that makes the night
as day. No wonder the shepherds crouch in fear, clutching one another, looking and listening with astonishment. Hear the angel's
words as if for the first time: "Don't be afraid—I bring exciting
news for you and everyone. A Savior, Christ the Lord, has been
born in Bethlehem! This is the sign: you will find a Babe wrapped
in swaddling clothes, lying in a manger."

We stop dead in our tracks when we reach the roughly carved-out cave on the hillside. A profound reverence grips our hearts as we enter. The love-filled eyes of Mary beckon us to come closely to the manger. With inexpressible delight she draws back the coarsely knit blanket. Can it be? The Son of God asleep in a feeding trough for cattle? Immanuel, God with us! Our hearts begin to sing; nothing is impossible now. God is down to earth!

A paraphrase of Luke 2:20 catches the triumphant transition: "The shepherds went back to work different people because of what they had seen and heard." They glorified and praised God. That was the difference. *Glory* means "manifestation"—praise and unfettered adoration. Now the shepherds manifested God in the way they lived, and all of life was freshly alive with gratitude for His presence in their world.

It's what happens after Christmas that makes all the difference. In a few hours we too will go back to work—back to old relationships and pressing responsibilities, back to our troubled world as it is, back to the frustration of all-too-familiar problems. But if we are daring enough to accept the gift that changes everything—Christ's love, joy, hope, and peace—we can go back to work different people because of what we have seen and heard, accepted and experienced.

Joyous Christmas to you!

The Heart of God

Luke 4:31-32; Mark 1:22

They were astonished at His teaching, for His word was with authority.
(LUKE 4:32).

Today let's claim what we know of God because of His own Word about Himself and Jesus Christ. Christ illuminated God...

- as a loving Father who is vitally interested in all His children's needs, and knows and cares for each individual soul.

- as a God who is in constant search for His children.

- as a God who forgives before people confess—not because they confess, but so they may.

- as a God who, because of His love, has allowed His children to be free and who stands with them even when they fail and cause themselves or others pain.

- as a God who exercises His sovereignty over the universe and shows His power in suffering love of the cross to heal hatred, sickness, and pain.

- as a God who is utterly available to His people through the creative conversation of prayer as a lifeline for guidance, power, and peace.

Thank God for God!
—JOYCE KILMER

Therefore!

Romans 5:1; 12:1; 1 Corinthians 15:58;
2 Corinthians 5:17; 1 Thessalonians 5:11;
Ephesians 5:1

I beseech you therefore, brethren, by the mercies of
God, that you present your bodies a living sacrifice, holy,
acceptable to God, which is your reasonable service.

(Romans 12:1)

We have just read a group of passages in which the word *therefore* appears. Notably, each time Paul uses this word *therefore,* it is after he has said something great about what God has done in Christ. He then goes on to spell out what that should mean for our character and daily life. A friend of mine said he never asked God for anything; his prayers were always of thanksgiving. I asked him, "Does your thanksgiving spur you on to live differently in grateful praise?" Hearing the gospel and being thankful is one thing; doing it in adoration is another.

Take time right now to review the difference Christ has made in your life. Draw a line down the middle of a page. List the things for which you are most grateful on one side. Across from each of these write what you have done in each area to express your gratitude. At the top of one side put "God's Grace and Mercy," and on the top of the other side put the word "Therefore."

How would your life be different today if your
"therefores" were responses to God's love?

Old Attitudes in a New Life

Romans 6:12-14

*Do not present your members as instruments of unrighteousness
to sin, but present yourselves to God as being alive from the dead,
and your members as instruments of righteousness to God.*

(ROMANS 6:13)

Why go on living with **old attitudes, behavior, and problems if God**
has truly forgiven, truly accepted, and truly empowered you for
a different kind of life?

In light of all we believe, why are we living the way we do, in
frustration, anxiety, and fear? How easy it is to acknowledge the
fantastic truth of the gospel and go on living the way we did before we believed it was true for us! We are like prisoners who find
it difficult to believe that we have been pardoned and are free to
live as released men and women.

We have the choice. We become what we concentrate on;
our picture of our life will be fulfilled in action and deed. What
if we accepted the true picture of our life as being under God's
control and an extension of His love? How would we act if we
truly believed our bodies were no longer instruments of sin but
instruments of God's righteousness? Hold that picture, and that's
exactly what you will find you are able to do.

*God can make you anything...but you have
to put everything in His hands.*

—MAHALIA JACKSON

Spread It Out Before the Lord

2 Kings 19:14-19

*Hezekiah took the letter from the hand of the
messengers and read it, and he went up to the house
of the LORD and spread it out before the LORD.*
(2 KINGS 19:14)

Note how Hezekiah spread his dilemma before the Lord. There
are three steps to discerning the will of God. First, tell Him your
need. Ask Him for wisdom to know what He wants and courage
to do it. Second, wait! Silence is crucial. Give God a chance to
impute insight and direction. Read the Bible quietly. He uses it to
instruct us in His will. Then third, act on what you've discovered,
knowing He can use even our mistakes for His glory.

"How can I be sure a direction is God's will for me?" Consider
some of the basic tests of any action or venture: By doing it, will
I grow closer to the Lord? Is it in keeping with the message of
Jesus Christ? Is it in keeping with the Ten Commandments?
Will God's reign and rule be extended? Will it bring the ultimate good of all involved? Is it an expression of love? Can I do
it feeling comfortable with the Lord's presence in it? Will it be
for the Lord's glory or just my own? I find that when I ask these
questions long in advance of a decision and give the Lord time
to work in my mind and feelings, the rightness or wrongness of
a direction becomes very clear.

The Lord can and will get through to you!

The Lord's Prescription

Isaiah 43:14-21

*Behold, I will do something new, now it will
spring forth; will you not be aware of it?*
(ISAIAH 43:19)

The Lord is up to magnificent things in all of us. We all need affirmation of the progress He has made with us, and a clear delineation of the next steps in being distinctly different people. We all bring an old nature into the Christian life. The new creation in Christ is both immediate and gradual. When we surrender our lives to Christ, accepting Him as our Savior and Lord, we are ushered into a dynamic relationship. The moment we say "Yes!" to Him, we are assured of eternal life, His presence, *and* a never-ending growth in His likeness.

The reason for this is that becoming a new creation in Christ is a thorough, ongoing character reorientation. We have been conditioned by the religious, cultural, and social values of our time. Attitudes, reactions, goals, and thought patterns have been inadvertently ingrained into the fiber of our natures. When we become Christians, everything is suddenly exposed to Christ's scrutinizing renovation.

*Focus on the areas where you need to grow in the new life in Christ.
If He were to diagnose your next steps, what would He prescribe?*

Remembrance and Resolve

Psalm 116:1-19

Return to your rest, O my soul, for the LORD
has dealt bountifully with you.
(PSALM 116:7)

The psalmist has given himself an admonition we all need on the last day of the year: rest and be thankful. Verse 7 is the fulcrum of the psalm. Before, it is the reason for thanksgiving; after, it is what the psalmist wants to do in praise to God. In the secret place with God he remembers what the Lord has done, and it changes his attitude about the future. That's how it works: Remembrance leads to new resolve. For what are you most thankful? What does that inspire you to do and be? The backward look, the inward look and outward look, and the forward look are all part of a vital encounter with the Lord. Reflection reminds us of what He has done; introspection exposes our need; awareness reveals what we are to do; and vision charts the future. Then we can say, "I love the LORD, because He hears my voice and my supplications."

What supplications has He heard and answered for you? Allow your mind to drift back over your life. Consider all the times you prayed and the Lord stepped in to give you what was best for your life. Remember? Now rest and be thankful. A New Year, a new beginning, is before us!

Blessed New Year to you!

Topical Index

Scripture Index

Harvest House Books by Lloyd John Ogilvie

Conversation with God

What if praying were like talking with a friend? Lloyd John Ogilvie shows you a fresh approach to prayer—one that is as much listening as speaking. He clearly and simply explains prayer's many dimensions and provides a 30-day guide so you can begin experiencing give-and-take conversation with God as part of your everyday life.

The Essence of His Presence

Longtime pastor Lloyd John Ogilvie comes alongside to strengthen you with five assurances of God's loving, always-loyal presence with you and within you. He affirms that God will *go before you to show you the way; go behind you to protect you; go beside you to befriend you; go above you to watch over you; go within you to give you all He knows you need.*

Praying Through the Tough Times

In this book of 100 prayers—blended with Scripture verses and encouraging thoughts—Lloyd John Ogilvie gently guides you to pray for God's desires: confidence in His nearness; His grace to love others; ability to see with His vision, grasping what the future can be when put in His hands.

When You Need a Miracle

Are your greatest needs—with family, work, relationships—going unmet? Are you limiting your life to only what is possible in your own strength and talents? Dr. Ogilvie points the way to the God who can meet your every need because He is Lord of the *im*possible—the One who can bring about miracles of healing, reconciliation, and growth.

To read sample chapters, go to www.harvesthousepublishers.com